WITHDRAWN
UTSA Libraries

D0709560

RENEWALS 458-4574

MAKING MARKETS

MAKING MARKETS

OPPORTUNISM AND RESTRAINT ON WALL STREET

—

MITCHEL Y. ABOLAFIA

Harvard University Press
Cambridge, Massachusetts
London, England
1996

Library of Congress Cataloging-in-Publication Data

Abolafia, Mitchel.
    Making markets : opportunism and restraint on Wall Street /
Mitchel Y. Abolafia.
        p.   cm.
    Includes bibliographical references (p.   ) and index.
    ISBN 0-674-54324-6 (cloth : alk. paper)
    1. Financial futures. 2. Bond market. 3. Stock exchanges.
I. Title.
HG6024.3.A26 1996
332.64—dc20   96-20665

To Amy

ACKNOWLEDGMENTS

—

This project has relied on the support of a long list of friends and colleagues. I begin by thanking the hundreds of anonymous informants whose participation made this study possible. Traders, for whom time is money, were often unsparing with the former. On hectic trading floors and before and after work, they shared their world with me. I have tried, as much as possible, to let their voices tell the story.

This book has had a long gestation. The earliest data derive from research for my doctoral thesis on futures markets. My debts reach back to two extraordinary teachers: Charles Perrow and Mark Granovetter. Many of the theoretical perspectives in this book are derived from Perrow's classes, his writings, and personal communications over many years. His perspective on power in social organizations is central to my thinking. Perrow's deep respect for good writing and disciplined thinking set the standard to which I have aspired. Mark Granovetter, who is leading the reemergence of economic sociology, showed me that markets are susceptible to sociological analysis. His development of the concept of embeddedness is also at the heart of this analysis. Both these teachers continued to encourage my ethnographic expeditions into financial markets. They have read endless drafts of this work for which I am grateful.

This study has been influenced by other teachers less directly. Karl Weick's work on enactment first helped me to see the cycles in my data. The work of Karl Polanyi helped explain the broader meaning of those cycles. Wayne Baker, Neil Fligstein, and Harrison White have done pioneering work in economic sociology. Their work inspired me to continue in what at first seemed dauntingly foreign and perhaps marginal to the concerns of my discipline.

My thinking about markets has evolved over the course of the three studies in this book. That evolution has been influenced by several wonderful colleagues. Gary Hamilton and Nicole Biggart helped me to survive exile from New York as they coaxed me to generalize my thinking about markets. Martin Kilduff offered insightful comments on a number of these chapters and is the co-author of an earlier version of Chapter 4. George Richardson patiently helped me design the figures in Chapter 8.

I have received helpful comments from a long list of colleagues and friends on the way to finishing this book. Alan Abbey, David Andersen, Wayne Baker, Carolyn Ban, Steve Barley, Ralph Brower, Jim Fossett, David Hart, David Krackhardt, Gideon Kunda, Richard Lachmann, David McCaffrey, Elaine Mitchell, Roger Noll, Paul Nugent, Ben Orlove, George Richardson, Bob Stern, Amy Svirsky, Todd Swanstrom, Frank Thompson, John Van Maanen, Brian Uzzi, and Walter Zenner provided many useful suggestions. Special thanks to Gary Hamilton and Nicole Biggart, who read the entire manuscript. Michael Aronson and Jeff Kehoe at Harvard University Press gave early and continuing advice, most of which I happily took.

Peter and Andrea Rothberg have supported this work from its beginning. Pete first exposed me to the social and political questions that are inherent in financial markets. Pete and Andrea provided encouragement, connections, and a place to crash after a hard day in the field. Truly, I would not have done it without them. Financial support came from faculty grants at the University of California at Davis and the State University of New York at Albany. I especially wish to thank Professor Tom Dyckman, who as Associate Dean at the Johnson Graduate School of Management, Cornell University, was unstinting in providing financial support for this research.

I am grateful to several publishers for permission to incorporate into this book materials that appeared in different form elsewhere. Portions of Chapter 2 are drawn from "Structured Anarchy: Formal Organization in the Commodity Futures Markets" in *The So-*

cial Dynamics of Financial Markets, ed. Peter Adler and Patricia Adler (Greenwich, Conn.: JAI Press, 1984). Portions of Chapter 3 are drawn from "Self-Regulation as Market Maintenance: An Organizational Perspective," in *Regulatory Policy and the Social Sciences*, ed. Roger Noll (Berkeley: University of California Press, 1985). Portions of Chapter 4 are drawn from "Enacting Market Crisis: The Social Construction of a Speculative Bubble," *Administrative Science Quarterly* 33:2 (1988).

As many authors acknowledge, it is their families to whom they owe the greatest debt. Jack and Sophia Abolafia, my parents, introduced me to Wall Street and to the tension between self-interest and restraint that motivates this analysis. Jacob Abolafia, my son, energized my efforts while restraining what must have always seemed to him as my self-interest. My daughter, Aliza, graciously waited to be born until I was almost finished. Amy Svirsky Abolafia, my partner in life, provided insight, perspective, meaning, and faith. To her I lovingly dedicate this book.

CONTENTS

—

MAKING MARKETS

INTRODUCTION: MARKET MAKERS
ON WALL STREET

—

On August 9, 1991, Salomon Brothers, the leading bond trading firm on Wall Street, admitted that its traders had systematically rigged the Treasury bond market, the largest securities market in the world. Several days later, on August 14, the chairman, the vice-chairman, and the president of the firm all resigned after disclosing that they had known about some of the violations since April but had neither reported them to authorities nor disciplined the members of the firm who had committed the violations. In fact, the most far-reaching manipulation occurred in May 1991, one month after senior management had been made aware of the problems in the government bond department. Shortly before he resigned, the chairman, John Gutfreund, told top executives at the firm, "I'm not apologizing for anything to anybody. Apologies don't mean [expletive]. What happened, happened."[1]

What did happen was that Salomon Brothers, the largest of the forty primary dealers, firms that hold an exclusive franchise to buy bonds directly from the U.S. Government, had repeatedly submitted bids in the names of customers who hadn't authorized them. It then bought the bonds for its own account. This scheme was used to buy 46 percent of the securities in the December 1990 auction and 57 percent in the February 1991 auction. It allowed Salomon to control as much as 94 percent of the securities offered in the May 1991 auction.[2] This not only exceeded the 35 percent limit permitted for any single firm, it allowed Salomon to "squeeze" other dealers who had promised the instruments to their customers.

In the end, the former top officers of Salomon all paid personal fines and the firm paid a fine of $290 million, second only to the fine levied on Drexel Burnham for its role in an earlier scandal.

There is a little known and rarely mentioned coda to this story. During its investigation of Salomon Brothers, the Securities and Exchange Commission (SEC) discovered that certain kinds of violations were common on the bond trading floors of investment firms. It revealed that 98 other banks and investment houses had engaged in phony bids in the debt markets of the governmental and quasi-governmental organizations that raise money for home-buyers, students, farmers, and banks. In announcing their fines, the chairman of the SEC, Richard Breeden, was frank about the extent of the corruption. "We uncovered a practice that was nearly universal in nature. Virtually 100 percent of the firms were involved in 'hyping' and in the creation of crib sheets so that when they lied, they lied consistently."[3] Breeden went on to explain that such practices had become part of the organizational routine in this segment of the bond market.

How is this possible? How does rule violation become a routine across diffuse firms in a market? Are these individual decisions or community norms? Where are the restraint systems? Does rule adherence and enforcement vary from market to market, and if so, why? These are some of the central questions motivating this book. Most accounts of this scandal and others on Wall Street in the 1980s have focused on the individuals involved; their personalities and their morals. Such accounts would suffice if each scandal were an isolated event. But they beg the question of what is happening on the trading floor. Why were these violations in the bond market apparently "universal"? Is there something "criminogenic" about this market? How is it organized? To answer these questions I will examine the social order of the trading floor: the culture and organization of the marketplace.

In this book I look at three related, interdependent, and complex market subcultures that co-exist on the southern tip of Manhattan Island. These subcultures organize their existence around trading in three commodities: stocks, bonds, and futures. I focus on "market makers": those traders at the center of each of these markets who trade for their own accounts while providing continuous bids and offers to a diffuse population of investors and speculators located throughout the world. In the 1980s, these once relatively obscure traders became both icons and villains as their salaries soared into the hundreds of thousands and even millions of dollars and scandals in futures, junk bonds, and Treasury bonds emanated from trading floors. Popular films and books like *Bonfire of the Vanities* and *Liar's Poker* introduced the public to the intensity and drama of this world, although the portrayal was necessarily a caricature.

To understand the behavior and environment of market makers I undertook extensive fieldwork on and near their trading floors. I began in 1979 by training as a futures trader for a study of trader self-governance. I continued to study futures markets for five more years. During the mid-1980s I studied traders in the bond market at four of the ten largest investment banks on the Street. Between 1990 and 1992 I gained access to the floor of the New York Stock Exchange. The common thread in my research was an interest in the relationship between the trader's pursuit of their own interest and the nature of restraint in the marketplace. To understand the differences in this relationship that exist among these markets, I will examine the strategies traders pursue, the norms they create, and the formal structures they establish for control.

Early in my fieldwork I felt the tension between individual self-interest and collective restraint that marks life on the trading floor. It was evident in trader's conversations, but even more so in the rules, norms, and procedures they took for granted. Trading floors are complex organizational phenomena that incorporate elements of gambling and combat with some of the aspects of an exclusive but legal cartel-like association that restrains its members. Put simply, traders want to make as much money as they can, but they don't want to chase away all the potential customers. They glory in their aggressive independence, but for the most part have organized collectively to maintain markets that are attractive to outsiders and stable enough to produce continuing profits for themselves. Traders know that restrained markets, free of the worst forms of fraud and manipulation, are in their long-term self-interest. This tension between short-term self-interest and long-term restraint suggests that neither the market nor its systems of restraint can be studied in isolation. They exist in relation to each other, each institution exerting pressure on the other. The market maker stands at the center of these pressures. I show the formal and informal means by which trading communities have adapted to the tension between individual self-interest and collective restraint in this highly individualistic community.

These studies also raise questions about the appropriate limits of self-interest. Wall Street culture extols the pursuit of individual self-interest and its ability to produce the greatest good for the greatest number. Both traders and academic economists praise the competitiveness and efficiency of these markets despite a seemingly unending stream of recent scandals that highlight the tendency of traders to break the bounds of their restraints. In each of these cases, individuals, often senior officials, took advantage of their situation to pursue their own interest, often employing deceitful methods, at the expense of customers, employees, and the general public. Such scandals reveal the point at which individuals and organizations transform self-interest into opportunism.[4] Going further, these scandals create cynicism about the markets and raise questions about the social benefits of this form of individual profit maximization. Does the provision of efficient financial markets require that extremes of self-interest are tolerated? Financial markets are a natural laboratory for exploring the limits of economic self-interest in a community.

Before discussing specific trading floors it may be useful to review some general information pertinent to all the studies in this book. In the first section I discuss the general trading environment during the 1980s on Wall Street. Second, I examine the traditional economic description of market making as a baseline from which to begin my analysis. In the third section I introduce the perspective on markets that will be used to develop the analysis. I conclude with an overview of the rest of the book.

The Trading Environment: Years of Volatility and Change

The fieldwork that underlies the studies in this book began in late 1979 and ended in 1992. These were the most turbulent years on Wall Street since the Great Depression. Both inflation and interest rates rose to dramatic heights and fell almost as dramatically. Many of the phenomena discussed in this book are a reflection of this turbulence: speculative manias, spectacular salaries, and the creation of many new financial instruments. Throughout this period, market makers' incentives and states of mind were shaped by the turbulence and its inherent unpredictability. This environment has its roots in the inflation of the 1970s.

The United States enjoyed very low inflation rates in the 1950s and 1960s. The average rates were around 2.7 percent. This rate rose to 7.1 percent in the 1970s. By 1981 it had risen as high as 13 percent. These levels of inflation elicited parallel interest rate plateaus. As a result of soaring inflation, the Federal Reserve Board shifted policy in 1979 toward stabilization of the money supply, letting interest rates float. This reinforced and increased the volatility of interest rates which, in turn, increased the risk of holding securities as assets in this environment. The major consequences of volatility were financial innovation and increased speculation.[5]

New financial instruments and new markets were created to deal with the increased risk. Derivative markets in options and futures were created to hedge the risk of owning the underlying assets, such as government bonds, foreign currencies, and stocks, which were susceptible to dramatic fluctuation. Market makers in the underlying asset suddenly became tied to market makers in a derivative marketplace. The creation and growth of these markets attracted young aggressive novices to the market, overwhelming the financial community's abilities to train and monitor them and changing the face of the marketplace.

At the same time as the innovation was increasing, firms and individuals were taking advantage of the rapid fluctuations in prices to speculate. Volatile markets may be frightening to the average investor, but they represent profit opportunities to the professionals. Firms increased their trading with their own capital and soon found their profits from trading exceeding their profits from customer service. At the same time, institutions such as pension funds and mutual funds responded to the volatility by increasing their trading and the size of their trades. This challenged market makers to also trade more frequently with more capital. At the same time, huge new markets in such instruments as mortgage-backed securities and junk bonds allowed investors to speculate on interest rate moves. More new faces flooded the trading floors. The world of the market maker was changing radically.

Market Makers

The traders in the three markets studied here have one thing in common: they are all market makers. "Market maker" is a native term. It expresses the trader's sense that he[6] creates the market by his own action. He stands at the center of the market mechanism. In continuous markets, such as stocks, bonds, and futures, there are specified trading hours. During trading hours the market maker is always available, offering to trade from his own inventory in response to market user's order flow. In a broader, collective sense, market makers have also been the market organizers.[7] They establish and maintain the trading floors. They do this by standardizing terms of trade, by enacting and enforcing rules of conduct, and by creating institutions to ensure that all traders' obligations are met.

In the stock market, the market maker is called a specialist. He stands at a "post" where he electronically displays his bids and offers for the stocks in which he has the franchise. He may process orders from the public by transacting for his own account or he may match buyers and sellers in return for a commission. In the futures market, the "floor trader" stands in a pit, really a three- or four-staired ring, where he noisily competes with other traders for the attention of brokers bringing orders from the public or the attention of other traders speculating for their own account. In the bond market, market makers sit at desks on the trading floor of a securities firm, trading with other traders on "the Street" by phone and computer network or with the firm's institutional customers through its sales force.

Hans Stoll, a financial economist, has identified three complementary views of the economic function of market makers: the market maker as a price stabilizer, the market maker as an information processor, and the market maker as a supplier of market continuity.[8]

Market makers react to the order flow coming into the market. They generally buy when there is excess supply and sell when there is excess demand. They are transacting against the market trend. Therefore, their behavior is price stabilizing. At the New York Stock Exchange the specialist has an "affirmative obligation" to reduce the price variation of his stock by intervening in the market. In the other markets studied here, the market maker trades when he thinks it will be profitable. Although some journalistic accounts have interpreted market makers' tendency to trade against the market trend as manipulative,[9] most research shows that it is a stabilizing influence. Buying on price declines and selling on price increases is generally a profitable strategy in itself.

Most market makers do not spend a lot of time learning about the affairs of the corporations whose securities they trade. Rather, their advantage comes from continuous surveillance of past, current, and pending transactions in the immediate market. As Stoll explains: "Being at the hub of the market, the market maker is in a position to collect and properly interpret market information. Market information includes knowledge of pending block transactions or other large orders in the process of being traded, knowledge of price quotes by other dealers in the same security or in closely related securities, and knowledge of limit orders."[10] Market makers set their bid and ask prices to reflect available information and thereby pass this information on to the public.

The market makers' continuous quoting of bids and offers makes it possible for the public to trade at any time. The cost of this continuous service is said to be reflected in the bid-ask spread; the difference between the bid price and the asked price. The market maker must be able to charge for his service or he will not stay in business.

The Social Construction Perspective: Markets as Institutions

The economic functions described above inform us that the market maker operates at the heart of financial markets. But knowing an actor's functions has never been adequate for explaining behavior. Economists assume that traders are rational maximizers and that they perform the functions described above because these functions maximize profits.[11] This book examines how these rational maximizers are bound together in a community that shapes their behavior. It develops the perspective that individual economic activities, such as market making, are socially constructed, i.e. individual behaviors are enacted in the context of the social relationships, cultural idioms, and institutions these actors continuously create. Economic actors, in the process of interaction, construct a world of norms, scripts, and strategies that shapes their future action. Market making differs in different subcultures because activities are embedded in their local context. Rational maximizing is not a fundamental human drive or instinct, but rather a socially and culturally defined *strategy* derived from a repertoire of strategies that is interpreted in each market subculture.[12]

Just as the process of social construction operates on individual economic actors to shape their behavior, it operates to produce the market as an institution. The focal institution of this study is the trading floor and its market arrangements. Such market arrangements, the set of rules and relationships that determine who trades with whom and under what conditions, are not created at the moment of transaction by parties to an exchange, nor are existing arrangements the only possible arrangements that could have developed in an efficient market. Rather, the fundamental premise developed here is that financial markets are socially constructed institutions, i.e. that stable and orderly market arrangements are produced and reproduced as a result of the purposeful action and interaction of interdependent powerful interests competing for control. Financial markets are receptacles of vested interest. These interests include such groups as the market makers, brokers, and institutional customers. Shifts in the balance of power among such groups determine who may design or redesign these arrangements to their own benefit. This perspective, then, examines the trading floor as an institution: a set of relatively stable arrangements for the repetition of exchange relations between buyers and sellers.

An individual's economic actions are embedded in a multi-levelled context. A market maker on the trading floor is an individual actor in an informal group of other market makers. That group acts within the context of a formal organization; either an exchange association like the New York Stock Exchange or an investment bank. Both the formal and informal levels are shaped by the political, economic, and regulatory environments of the market. Each level enables and restrains individual action. Individual and institutional processes mutually influence each other. It is the complex interplay between these levels that gives each market its unique institutional configuration.

The social constructionist perspective suggests that markets are not spontaneously generated by the exchange activity of buyers and sellers. Rather, skilled actors produce institutional arrangements: the rules, roles, and relationships that make market exchange possible. The institutions define the market, rather than the reverse.[13] The three markets studied here all involve the exchange of highly standardized financial instruments in an auction market, yet each will be shown to have somewhat unique institutional arrangements. These arrangements reflect social structural differences in the markets, including differences in the social cohesion of market makers' networks, distinctive jurisdictional conflicts among interest groups on the trading floor, and differences in the involvement of the government in the market. As these conditions vary from market to market, different patterns of institutional arrangements may be expected.

These institutional arrangements are neither frozen nor inflexible. They have responded to different historically determined pressures since their foundings in three different centuries: eighteenth (stock), nineteenth (futures), and twentieth (over-the-counter bonds).[14] Pressures for increased efficiency and profit as well as pressures for social legitimacy and restraint elicit strategies on the part of market participants that reshape the institutions. The studies in this book describe the range of pressures shaping these markets, but they also illustrate the range of strategies by which market makers respond to these pressures and actively shape their environment. There is a recursive relationship between the strategic actions of various groups in the market and their environment. Existing market arrangements reflect the efforts of powerful market actors to shape and control their environment even as it, in turn, is shaping and controlling them. Those groups with the most power will have the greatest influence in the reconfiguring of market arrangements.[15] This suggests that these arrangements are not the logical result of efficiency demands but rather historically specific strategic enactments. I will examine the strategies of individuals and groups as they create market arrangements that further their interests. Each chapter explores another aspect of this ongoing social construction of the market.

The Social Construction of Opportunism

The social construction perspective will be applied to one economic strategy in particular, the strategy of opportunism. The studies in this book are linked by the idea that the differences in levels of opportunism that are observed among financial markets are explained by social conditions on the trading floor, rather than by the psychological or moral inclinations of individual traders. Opportunism on the trading floor, like all other economic behaviors, is embedded in a specific social and cultural milieu.[16] This perspective on opportunism explicitly rejects the dominant economic notion that levels of opportunism are nothing more than the sum of individual actor's independent preferences.[17] Rather, it suggests that there ought to be discernible patterns of opportunistic behavior by market. This book will show that such patterns are systematic and that the conditions shaping these patterns can be identified.

Among the conditions shaping levels of opportunism are 1) the strength and efficacy of reputational networks among traders in the market, 2) the shifting distribution of power among stakeholder groups in the market, 3) the existence of institutionalized rules of exchange and means of enforcement in each marketplace, and 4) the threat and fact of regulatory intervention. In addition to the structural conditions in markets, each market has produced its own cultural interpretations of opportunism and restraint. Market makers, stock and futures exchange officials, and regulators, at all levels, are embedded in cultures that define tolerance levels for opportunism and for restraint. Recruits to investment banks receive very different socialization than do recruits to the New York Stock Exchange. As a result, social relationships and cultural definitions differ from trading floor to trading floor and the levels of opportunism differ in relationship to them.

In financial markets, social relations and cultural norms have been formalized into organizations and rule systems. Even as these institutions shape the patterns of opportunism, they cannot restrain them completely, nor do they try. The tension between individual self-interest and institutional restraint produces cycles of opportunism. When extreme acts of opportunism exceed the level of tolerance of various powerful stakeholders inside and outside the market, pressures rise to restrain the extremes. As restraint increases, opportunism declines. This often leads to a loosening of the restraint. Once vigilance declines, the testing of the tolerance for opportunism begins anew. The studies in the futures, bond, and stock markets will identify the formal structures, strategies, and conditions associated with the enactment of opportunism. I will show how restraints at both the informal and formal levels shape and reshape the dynamic cycles of opportunism observed among market makers.

Conclusion

The chapters in this book are organized to introduce readers to trading floors that are at different phases in their cycles of opportunism. Each market has its own historically specific cycle. I begin on the bond trading floor at investment banks in 1987. These markets are at a frenetic peak of opportunism. Descending from this peak, I move on to the hardly tame futures markets at the beginning of the 1980s. These are markets in which restraint is increasing as the futures exchanges attempt to expand into new financial futures instruments and at the same time inhibit the regulatory intensity of their new federal oversight agency, the Commodity Futures Trading Commission, established in 1975. My third case examines the trading floor at the New York Stock Exchange in the early 1990s. This trading floor has experienced thirty years of increasing restraint, effectively eliminating most of its notorious excesses. Its members believe it is poised for loosening of restraint.

In Chapter 1 I explore the proposition that the scandals of the 1980s, including the Salomon Brothers scandal, were not some bizarre aberration in this culture, but rather an exaggeration of behaviors that had come to be accepted on the over-the-counter bond trading floor. Chapter 2 shifts attention to futures markets and the structures their market makers created to organize and restrain themselves. Chapter 3 examines the strategies used to control cases of market manipulation by market makers on the futures trading floor. In Chapter 4 I examine how market makers mobilize to respond to threats from external opportunists. Chapters 5 and 6 offer a striking comparison with the preceding studies of the bond and futures markets. Having passed through their own periods of high opportunism and increasing surveillance, the market makers at the New York Stock Exchange (NYSE) have transformed themselves and their market arrangements into models of restraint. Chapters 7 and 8 interpret the findings in the previous empirical chapters in terms of their contribution to a broader understanding of opportunism and restraint in market exchange.

When taken together, these studies of three trading floors reorient our attention from economic explanation to social explanation, from the invisible hand of market efficiency to the visible hands of those who construct market arrangements. By closely observing those involved in "making the markets," a complex world of social organization is revealed. This is not a world that can be explained in terms of individual homines economici independently maximizing their utility. It is also not a world of unbridled competitive abandon, but rather a world in which powerful actors create systems to restrain themselves and others. Finally, and most importantly, these systems of restraint are not fixed and efficient responses to the environment, but rather contested terrains in which groups compete for control of market arrangements. These studies offer a new perspective on the conflict and complexity of socially constructed markets.

A recent spate of popular books about Wall Street has been marked by either ringing denunciation or unabashed boosterism. Financial markets inspire strong responses. I was not immune to the strong emotional responses elicited on the trading floor. Wall Street, like all social institutions, has both positive and negative aspects. I am impressed by the remarkable efficiency of these markets: their ability to match buyers and sellers from distant parts of the world in a matter of seconds. I was impressed by the intelligence and skill of the traders I got to know. Seeing the Street through their eyes deepened my appreciation, but at the same time made me wary. As the following studies reveal, there is a dark side to market makers' mastery. As Peter Bernstein has recently written, "Financial markets, like many other creations of the human imagination, mix dangerous tendencies with wholesome impulses."[18] In succeeding chapters I will examine how the financial community has organized itself to balance its dangerous tendencies and its wholesome impulses.

HOMO ECONOMICUS UNBOUND:
BOND TRADERS ON WALL STREET

1
—

Bond trader (looking out across the trading floor): Traders are dying to make money. That's all they care about. Most traders don't care about the diplomacy that you see in the corporate environment. They don't care about titles. They are here to make money. They live in a four-by-four foot space and put up with all the bullshit that goes on around them. They put up with a lot, but the money is worth it.

Mitch: What else is different from the corporate environment?

Bond trader: Wall Street salaries are so much higher that you are comparing apples and oranges. The typical guy that walks in the door on Wall Street is probably making what a senior V.P. is making in corporate America. And this guy is younger and cockier. A lot of guys under thirty making big bucks. You don't find that too much in corporate America . . . On Wall Street there is no "working your way up." You have a good year, make a million dollars. You're a hot shot.

Mitch: What happens to the guy who has a bad year?

Bond trader: There's always someone waiting to take your chair. Lose a few hundred thousand in a week or over six months and you're out. You see winners and you see losers. It's best not to get too excited for the winners and it's best not to get too close to the losers.

I began my fieldwork on bond markets in early October of 1987. I did not know then that I was observing the peak of a speculative mania in financial markets. Bond markets had experienced explosive growth since October 1979, when the Federal Reserve Board decided to let interest rates float. The mania came to an end on

October 19, 1987 when the Dow Jones Industrial Average crashed 508 points. Just four days before the crash a managing director in bond trading at a major investment bank explained the firm's strategy for growth: "The strategy is simple. You fill up one trading room, and you open a new one. You go out and hire the talent. A guy's making a million dollars a year . . . you can give him two million. He's making two you give him . . . [w]hatever the numbers are. Simple." After the crash, the heady optimism and bravado of the pre-crash era never totally evaporated, but the trading community was chastened. My fieldwork in the bond market continued for another year and a half after the crash. Market growth receded during this time, but salaries remained high and trading continued to be a profitable business for the firms.

My first day on a bond trading floor left a strong impression. My field notes recorded the youth, intensity, and pace: "There is almost no gray hair to be seen. Most traders are white men between twenty-five and thirty-five years old. They wear short hair and dark business suits with the suit jacket slung over the back of a chair. There are a few women, most of them clerks or analysts,[1] and a few older men . . . The people on the trading floor are highly focused. They stare intently at computer screens, hold several phones at once or shout information to nearby colleagues in staccato bursts. Their concentration on the immediate transaction is all-consuming. We are on the fortieth floor with windows all around offering spectacular views of New York harbor. No one is distracted . . . All of this activity is performed at a dizzying pace. Deals are begun and finished in less than a minute. Market fluctuations generate flurries of activity. Money, though invisible here, is in constant motion. The energy of the market infects everyone, myself included."

As the weeks went by the market slowed down and it became more difficult for traders to find profitable trades. Some of the energy began to dissipate. This gave the traders more time to talk with me. Behavior that had at first seemed like explosions of chaotic aggression began, instead, to look like a highly organized, even ritualized, game. Firms offered huge incentives to aggressive young people willing and able to play a game of deep concentration and discipline. The game required that they gather endless amounts of information to be applied in periodic bursts of risk-taking.

Based on their youth and incomes, bond traders looked like a fairly exotic group to study. But there was something familiar about them. This resemblance was not to any person or group but to an academic idea. Bond traders bore a striking resemblance to homo economicus: the highly rational and self-interested decision maker portrayed in economists' models. Bond traders' behavior appeared to come closer than I expected to the economists' assumptions of perfect rationality and unambiguous self-interest.

The Study

The subjects in this study are fifty-four bond traders employed at four of the ten largest investment banks on Wall Street. They perform the dual roles of broker and dealer. As brokers, they match buyers with sellers, thereby earning commissions for the firm. As dealers, they trade bonds for the firm's account, either buying or selling, to create profits for the firm. Traders are paid a salary plus a bonus that often exceeds their salaries. The work consists of a continuous stream of transactions each worth millions of dollars. The pace, which is often frantic, is dictated by the activity and volatility in the market.

The traders in this study work on large trading floors surrounded by one hundred to two hundred other traders, salespeople, and support staff. They work at desks that are typically four feet across and are piled with three or four quote screens, a personal computer, and two or three telephones. These desks are attached to other traders' desks on three sides. Traders can be seen standing by their desks, holding several phones at once on long extension cords, and simultaneously carrying on a conversation with a nearby salesperson or clerk. The air vibrates with the low roar of voices punctuated by an occasional effort to be heard above the tumult.

The data consist of formal interviews and extensive field notes based on observation. Interviews and observation were completed between October 1987 and March 1989. Formal interviews were conducted on the trading floor or in adjacent offices. All interviews were taped, transcribed, and coded. Less formal conversations took place through follow-up phone calls and meetings with informants.

Economic Man: A Grounded Model

Although the Wall Street bond traders interviewed differed in age, education, and personal style, certain common concerns predominated. The limits and variations of these concerns were explored in successive interviews. Taken together these concerns constitute a skeletal script for membership on the trading floor. The inductive model of economic man constructed from these interviews is based on the primary goals of traders, their strategies for attaining those goals, and the institutional rules that define both the actors and the action.

Economic behavior is pursued for more than one reason. The primary purpose of economic behavior in market societies is the accumulation of wealth. Extraordinary personal wealth is the dominant goal among bond traders. The trading floor of investment banks provides an organized and legitimate institutional context for turning undirected desires into viable strategies of action. It is a context in which a certain amount of specialized and focused self-interest is considered a very good thing. Self-interest is the raw material from which the local version of economic man is constructed and legitimated.

Even the drive for extraordinary personal wealth has a subsidiary meaning, a meaning given by the related but subordinate goals of the bond trader. Trading is construed as a source of both excitement and mastery among bond traders. Bond trading is a form of what anthropologist Clifford Geertz, writing of Balinese cockfighters, calls "deep play." In such games, successful play confers high prestige. As Geertz writes, "In deep (play), where the amounts of money are great, much more is at stake than material gain: namely, esteem, honor, dignity, respect—in a word . . . status."[2] Among bond traders, trading is often described as an ordeal that, if successfully mastered, confers status. A typical story told repeatedly on the trading floor involves the first time a trader goes home for the night having purchased a large block of bonds for the firm, especially when the market is particularly volatile. "Until you've taken your first position home and tried to go to sleep at night and woken up with a loss staring you in the face, you'll never know if you can make it." Like other games, the process of playing and winning is the reward. "It's not just the money. It's the excitement, the chance to test yourself every day," one trader commented.

The dominant metaphor on the trading floor is the game. Bond traders compare themselves to gunfighters, fighter pilots, and professional athletes. The comparison is not to team-based games but rather to one-on-one challenges. Traders also compare trading to such betting games as poker and shooting dice. Each transaction is a one time gamble in which there is no room for complacency or compromise. The trading floor is not understood as a place to foot-drag or merely survive, as are other organizational settings. It is a place to win. As one trader expressed it, "The sheer raw enjoyment of winning . . . you'll never find anything like it in any other business."

The money, the heightened materialism, is not the only goal in this game. For a significant share of veteran traders the ultimate goal is the excitement and status incumbent in winning. As one senior trader explained, "There is a tremendous feeling every day when you roll down here and you come onto the Manhattan Bridge and see the Wall Street skyline. This could be the day I win it all." "Testing" and the "raw joy of winning" are powerful seductions to professional athletes, fighter pilots, and professional crooks, as well as bond traders. Success in these forms of deep play results in immediate, visible status. Bond trading is the practical method available to these MBA graduates by their social position.[3]

If the trading floor is a context that attracts those with a pressing desire for extreme wealth, it is because it is constructed to do just that. Unlike most of corporate America, there is no career ladder for traders. There are only traders who make more and traders who make less in a continuous contest for wealth. Traders refer to themselves as entrepreneurs in the sense of being self-reliant. Ironically, it is a self-reliance framed by the organizational structure in which they operate. "You trade for your own account," one trader explained. "You have the ability to hang yourself here. They're giving you a framework in what you should do and that framework is pretty loose. Each individual is making his own market . . . Profit and loss is what the trader is all about."

The means for achieving entrepreneurial success are provided by the investment banks that employ the traders. These means must then combine with the individual characteristics ascribed to economic man: self-interest and rationality. They become visible as strategies that traders enact on Wall Street: opportunism and hyper-rationality. Bond traders construct their own version of entrepreneurial behavior, becoming local and somewhat stylized versions of economic man.

Strategies

The economist Oliver Williamson defines opportunism as "self-interest seeking with guile."[4] We will use the term to refer to those actions in which a trader uses his advantage to deceive his trading partner. Among opportunism's most significant forms is the selective or distorted disclosure of information in a transaction. Not surprisingly, none of the subjects in this study voluntarily described their own behavior as opportunistic. As J. Van Maanen notes, few informants in an ethnographic study are likely to reveal their hidden techniques,[5] but informants freely offered that deceptive practices were part of their business, that they had seen instances of deception, and that one had to be wary. In this sense, opportunism is part of the script in terms of what *other* people are likely to do to *you*. The trading floor is understood as a dog-eat-dog world, one in which individualism is a survival strategy. Thus, while traders would reject the label of "opportunist," they were quite comfortable describing incidents in which their own behavior had been particularly "aggressive" or "entrepreneurial." Such aggression often turned out to involve locally approved forms of opportunism.

Bond traders are at the center of the market-making process, yet they never deal directly with their transaction partner. They have two options. They may trade "in the Street" or with the investment bank's customers through its institutional salesforce. "In the Street" trading is based on bids or offers that are publicly available through computer screens or "broker's brokers" who cover specific sectors of the market. Trading through the salesforce involves dealing with a salesperson, usually on the same trading floor, who manages an average of four or five institutional customers that want to buy from the firm or sell to it. Trading through the salesforce is preferred in that it services the firm's customers and carries a higher return for the firm. It also affords most of the possibilities for opportunism.

Opportunism among bond traders takes the form of culturally scripted strategies. The first and simplest form of opportunism is "laying off" bonds. It involves offering incomplete information and taking advantage of a transaction partner's ignorance. Traders may communicate incomplete or misleading information to the salesperson when selling bonds out of the firm's inventory. As one trader admitted, "The trader will know the true story on a bond and sell it anyway, where they know they shouldn't sell it for as much." Although the trader knows that the bond is not worth that much, he also knows that such behavior is acceptable in this context. As Michael Lewis, a former salesman at Salomon Brothers explained, "The trader can pressure one of his salesmen to persuade insurance company Y that IBM bonds are worth more than pension fund X paid for them initially. Whether it is true is irrelevant. The trader buys the bonds from X and sells them to Y and takes out another eighth" (i.e. he charges Y a commission of an eighth of a point).[6] The belief that this happens frequently leads institutional customers, such as mutual funds and insurance companies, to resent and mistrust bond traders. This mistrust is reflected in the fact that institutional customers often seek information from four or five different firms before transacting. "There are a lot of accounts that feel that Wall Street is a conniving, calculating institution that would rip the eyes out of anyone they can," one trader commented.

A second, more deceptive form of opportunism is the use of false information. Traders not only conceal information, they may actively distort it by "showing a bid." This refers to posting a false, but highly visible bid on a computer network in order to support the price of bonds you already own. As a trader explained, "Frequently, if you own bonds you show a bid on the Street to support your position. If I own bonds and I think they are worth 65 I'm going to show a bid on the Street so that when an account comes in and wants to know what the market is, another trader in another shop will say, Well there's a bid on the Street for them . . .'" Traders may post a deceptively high bid on the Street and then strategically withdraw it. In the following instance my informant was lured into buying bonds cheap that he intended to sell to a high "bid in the Street." The high bidder withdrew his bid, leaving my informant stuck with the bonds he bought. He expects that he will still sell the bonds to that bidder, but at a considerably lower price, just as his adversary intended.

> I bought some bonds the other day based on a bid that was in the Street. The bid was very rich. When I turned around to sell those bonds to that bid in the Street the bid was no longer there. The guy who was bidding needed the bonds. He was probably short, but he wanted to smoke me out and make me panic. I think he needs the bonds but is just not showing his hand. So his bid is ridiculous now. Ten points below his bid before. It's just a waiting game. At first I thought I'd gotten raped and was going to get buried. Fortunately, it wasn't a large block.

The two strategies discussed above represent relatively mild forms of opportunism. They are considered a routine part of playing the game. As one trader put it, "You can be too honest and you'll go nowhere." The selective use of information is a taken-for-granted part of the local repertoire of strategies. At more extreme levels of deception are the third and fourth forms of opportunism: agent opportunism and insider opportunism. They involve the theft of proprietary information and are considered significant violations of the securities laws. The most common script for agent opportunism is front-running. In front-running a trader becomes aware that a customer is going to place an order. The trader then buys the bonds, marks them up, and sells them to the customer through one of the firm's salespeople. This form of opportunism is very hard to catch, although bond traders agree that it is fairly common. Insider trading is the use of information about the economic condition or intentions of a bond issuer that is not available to the public. It is sometimes referred to as "trading a leak" and is still considered a rare occurrence. Both of these are very clear violations, although traders believe that the former is more common and less egregious than the latter.

Much opportunism occurs in what traders themselves refer to as the gray areas: instances in which a particular formal market regulation is widely ignored. At such points traders bend the rules. "If an account [a pension fund, mutual fund, etc.] had given bonds to another broker/dealer for the bid and that broker/dealer goes to a broker's broker and you just happen to find out what account it is that has the bonds out for bid, now you're getting into one of the gray areas. You're not supposed to go direct (to the account), but more times than not you'll go direct and save the broker's commission."

Young traders acquire a working knowledge of these "gray areas," learning which forms of opportunism are part of the local script. Older informants suggest that the script in the bond markets became more opportunistic in the 1980s. "A lot of things that are OK now, we thought of and dismissed. Nice people wouldn't do such trashy things." In the eighties, following the floating of interest rates by the Federal Reserve Board, the bond markets grew in volume and volatility. There was much more trading and many new traders. The firms expanded their trading floor operations so rapidly that it became increasingly difficult to socialize trainees to the unwritten scripts and the institutional rules defining the limits of opportunism. In addition, the Reagan administration sent clear signals that regulatory oversight was being reduced. Noting the changes, one informant in his mid-forties explained, "It began to occur to me that I was playing some old game that is no longer. The rules have changed. To play ball, you really have to get in there and root around." Another said, "It used to be 'My word is my bond.' That was all you needed to know".

Opportunism, particularly in the first two forms discussed, was a common strategy among the subjects in this study. The strategies existed prior to the action—part of the tool kit available to every trader. Opportunism is one of the forms of rationality accessible to traders. In the next section I discuss the dominant mode of rationality on the trading floor: hyper-rationality.

Just as self-interest is constructed as opportunism on the trading floor, rationality appears as hyper-rationality. The question is not whether alternative forms of rationality exist, but rather the conditions under which they make their appearance and the resulting forms that they take. In recent years, economists have shown an increasing recognition that rationality is not a simple fact of nature. In the ideal type of economic man, the actor has fully ordered preferences, perfect information, and immaculate computing power. All of these assumptions have been called into question recently by economists[7] as well as non-economists.[8] The ideal type of rationality has been replaced by cognitive biases and heuristics,[9] rational foolishness,[10] and anomalies.[11] All are alternative forms of bounded rationality.

Bond traders exhibit a form of bounded rationality that might be called hyper-rationality. Hyper-rational decision makers are those who make the greatest use of analytic techniques, but still include elements of intuitive judgment in their decision process. Among bond traders, hyper-rationality is manifested in habits or ritualized customs that are tacitly but continuously invoked throughout the trading day. The most important elements in hyper-rationality involve context-dependent versions of vigilance and intuitive judgment.

Vigilance involves the ability to search and assimilate a broad range of information that one expects may be useful in decision making. Trading floors are continuously deluged by economic indicators and interpretations of those indicators. During their internships, novice traders learn which indicators and modes of analysis are most culturally valued on the Street and in the firm. Hyper-rationality involves dealing with continuous information overload using prescribed modes of vigilance. "Everybody is inundated with information," a trader noted. "Every machine in the world is spewing out technical information, fundamental information, news releases, everything. You have to be very agile, very focused."

Bond traders engage in a continuous and aggressive search using a variety of electronic, print, and interpersonal information sources. There is a sense that indicators must be assessed because they are available. Each represents a potential resource for reducing the uncertainty of highly consequential buy and sell decisions. Such indicators come in a wide variety of forms, from government statistics to experts' predictions and local rumors. Specific strategies of vigilance vary from market to market. Vigilance in corporate bond trading is slightly different than it is in government bond trading: the most valued specific indicators are different for each.

Vigilance consists of several related elements: sorting, checking, and establishing value. The first step in vigilance is sorting. The volume of information available is so overwhelming that a subsidiary

industry has grown up to supply information and analysis of market trends to traders. Most traders depend primarily on statistics
and the highly regarded interpreters of such statistics who publish
newsletters and have columns in the trade papers. These interpretations are important because all traders are presumably looking at
the same numbers. The interpretation of such numbers is somewhat equivocal. Every trading floor has an adjacent research department offering interpretations of the behavior of the Federal Reserve Board, as well as the latest government reports and statistics.
Every trader must sort through both the numbers and their multiple interpretations. Most develop a routinized sorting procedure to
cover their favored sources. This procedure is enacted daily prior
to the start of trading and continues throughout the day.

New information often interrupts the routinized sorting. The
trading community grabs at new pieces of information. Stories on
the newswire occasionally require immediate consideration. At the
moment when a key indicator is about to be released by a government agency, traders all over Wall Street stand poised at their
phones. When enough people with significant trading power share
the same belief about the meaning of this information, the collective effect may be a self-fulfilling prophecy. This is particularly evident when the government releases indicators like the Producer
Price Index or retail sales figures. If the news is surprising, it will
often move the market. If it fails to move the market, traders will
say that it has already been discounted.

Once information has been gathered and sorted, traders employ
a checking strategy to see how others are perceiving the same or
different information. They are in contact with an assortment of
brokers, salespeople, economists, and informants in government
agencies. Traders are generally aware that it is not the correctness
of the interpretation that counts, but rather the degree to which
others will read the same information the same way. As one trader
explained it: "A lot of smart people don't do very well at trading
because they know what information means. When you trade you
need to know what people *think* the information means. You don't
have to be smart, you just have to be perceptive. You have to have
a sense of what motivates people—to be a good listener to what
people think."

The same point is made by John Maynard Keynes. "[Professional investors] are concerned, not with what an investment is really worth . . . but with what the market will value it at . . ."[12] In keeping with this, most traders do little analysis themselves. Rather, they work hard, through sorting and checking, to stay appraised of what others are hearing and thinking. This is shown by their constant recharting of the yield curve, an indicator that reflects what others have most recently been willing to pay for bonds at a range of interest rates and maturities. Market rivals make buy and sell decisions by watching each other.[13]

Establishing value is the final step in the script for vigilance. It is the local term for making an estimate of where a bond "ought to be" in terms of price. It is at this point that traders focus on a particular bond. The most important rituals in establishing value are called "taking the runs," in which a trader finds out what's available in the Street from an intermediary known as a broker's broker and through the "inquiry" from the salesforce. These are ritualized morning activities that provide the trader with price information on past transactions and ongoing bids and offers. Both of these rituals allow the traders to begin to array their alternatives. In this kind of highly liquid market, recent transactions are among the most important sources of information for establishing value.[14] There are also norms about appropriate price movement over time and the influence of movement in one instrument on another that influence the process of establishing value. One trader explains his ritual: "Each morning I call my broker's broker to take what is called a run. This is a list of bonds I trade. These [pointing to long pages of handwritten price quotes] are the very active issues. On Friday I used five brokers. They gave me a whole run of issues and the size of those offerings or bids. Then the inquiry from the salesforce begins."

The post-modern trading floor is a setting that elicits vigilance. Every major investment bank reproduces this context for vigilance. All over the Street investment firms provide a nearly identical set of resources. They create the setting for vigilance activities in the form of daily strategy meetings, internal economic reports, and informal interaction that defines the meaning of various types of information. But in the end, a firm cannot make the individual, split second decisions required in bond trading. "The key thing is judgment," a trader explained. "It's the toughest thing about being here, not the mechanics (of trading). Those things are simple; very easy to follow and not a big deal. But that split second judgment that you have to make. (It) probably comes from some subliminal input you don't even recognize. That's what makes the difference. You can't be trained to do that. You just have to be exposed."

Traders often say that they did a trade because it felt right or felt good. Asked to explain this, one trader said, "It's a visceral thing. The brain to mouth reflex. Traders cannot put into words what they've done, even though they may be great moneymakers. They have a knack. They can't describe it." Intuitive judgment involves the use of tacit knowledge in an unconscious process to arrive at a decision. Jerome Bruner suggests, "Intuition implies the act of grasping the meaning or significance or structure of a problem without explicit reliance upon the analytic apparatus of one's craft. It is the intuitive mode that yields hypotheses quickly . . ."[15] Intuitive processes are built up through trial and error experience, independent of any conscious effort to learn. Intuitive judgment is most often contrasted with "analytic thinking" and is considered a critical decision tool by bond traders.

Although vigilance is a cultural capacity that may be developed through training and access to information resources, intuitive judgment about bond prices is a craft that is learned through practice. The bond trader develops an abstract sense of how the raw material, in this case the market, reacts under various conditions. These abstractions or images are developed through watching others trade, "paper" trading, and ultimately, the direct experience of trading for one's own account. The novice engages in a lengthy internship during which he is first exposed to the market and ultimately thrown in for a "baptism by fire."

Traders often say that successful trading is an art. "If you have to know how to trade you will never be any good. That's sort of a certainty here. It's not a science, it's an art. People who have to know never make money. You can't learn it. We don't teach it. We just sort of expose people." As Michael Polanyi explained, "An art which cannot be specified in detail cannot be transmitted by prescription, since no prescription for it exists. It can be passed on only by example from master to apprentice."[16] Recruits compete to apprentice themselves to the best traders. These traders do not reveal their "trading secrets," rather the recruits watch and listen as the trader connects disparate facts to arrive at successful choices.

The last steps in the trader's vigilance routine, "taking the runs" and "inquiry," are the precipitants to arriving at particular buy and sell decisions. Traders are faced with a series of immediate opportunities by their brokers and salespeople. They must assess this information in light of other information derived from sorting and checking. This assessment of disparate facts occurs instantaneously as the broker or salesperson waits for a response. It is the flow of bids and offers in the market that stops the vigilant search and precipitates choice. This "flow" forces decisions about whether to act or not.

At this point, the trader takes a leap, hoping that his interpretation is correct and that a particular bond will respond to the forces as expected. This is the point where most traders acknowledge such non-analytic tools as experience and "feel for the market." The technology of trading changes dramatically at this point. It is less like the continuous processing of information and more like custom craftsmanship. One trader explained, "Experience is the next step. You find over time that each issue trades a bit differently. You can only get it (experience) by being on the desk and trading. Just sitting on the desk and watching trades occur in your own positions. Seeing where they trade."

The uncertainty and ambiguity of the decisions described come from the nature of the information being gathered, the time constraints set by the rapid flow of bids and orders in the market, and the cognitive limits of humans as information processors. The flow of information about the market cannot be fully assimilated. As one trader explained, "The market is a nebulous type of animal that you can't get your arms around. It is always right. It is never wrong. It is something you spend countless hours trying to second guess, trying to interpret." Recruits learn that they must develop "the knack" or fail. Although judgment itself may not be easily taught, the belief in its efficacy has become an important cultural script in the decision process.

Institutional Rules

Recruits to the trading floor seeking extraordinary wealth do not arrive on Wall Street and create the world anew. They arrive to find an established institutional order. This order, most evident in its rules, is the result of traders' habituation to existing strategies, e.g. opportunism and hyper-rationality. These rules have come to have external force in the lives of traders. They are experienced as objective standards of behavior, even though they are derived from habituation to the most salient strategies. The recruit encounters an ordered social world that must be learned before he will be allowed to sit at a trading desk. "The institutions must and do claim authority over the individual, independently of the subjective meanings he may attach to any particular situation."[17] I begin this section with a discussion of the institutional rules on the bond trading floor and then turn to the socialization process through which these rules are learned.

The trading floor, as a social setting, is constituted by both general and specific institutional rules that define the identities of the traders and the patterns of appropriate action. There are historical rules legitimating the form of exchange (over-the-counter), the form of securities being traded (bonds), and the modes of rational calculation employed (yield curves, inflation rates). They reflect not only the local setting but more widely accepted strategies of finance capitalism. These rules are really accounts of how this part of the economic world works.

At deeper and more specific levels, institutional rules define both the identity of individuals and the patterns of appropriate action. They operate as vocabularies of motive, explaining to the trader and others the reasons for action. The institutional rules of the trading floor are, not surprisingly, caricatures of the "spirit of capitalism" identified by Weber.[18] Among the most significant are those relating to self-reliance, risk, and money—key elements in this version of the spirit of capitalism.

Self-reliance. Traders are very clear that they are expected to be self-reliant. "It's a very entrepreneurial business. No one is going to help you make money. They're too busy helping themselves." Traders sitting in a room full of other traders feel atomized and alone. In the words of another trader, "I don't really feel like I can rely on anybody here. *That's the way this business is.* You've got to rely on yourself." Such statements define both actors and action, revealing the rules of the game. They describe an impersonal environment in which trust and cooperation are nearly absent. One of the oldest informants stated, "There is an adversarial relationship in that the trader is not a fraternity type of brother. It is you against him. You would love to make money at his expense and that's all over the Street." In this context, trust is minimal, one's only obligation is to oneself, and opportunism is understood as an appropriate form of action.

Risk. Another institutional rule is that traders should excel at *calculated* risks. Money supplies the incentive, and rationality is the means linking money and risk. "Trading is taking calculated risks using the capital of the firm. We just went to an [Treasury] auction. I spent $200 million on seven year notes. They're ours. I have to do something with them. If I keep them and the market goes down, I've lost money." Traders are aware that the stakes are very high. "There is a high roller mentality ingrained in the job description. There are big dollars on the line." Although such commitments of capital are risky, "with risk comes reward." As another trader puts it, "You are rewarded for the risks you are incurring." Implicit is the understanding that the pursuit of extraordinary wealth requires some worthwhile risk.

At the same time that traders see themselves as risk- seeking, they also see the risk as highly calculated and rational. "You've got to keep your position balanced. You've got to be in a situation so that no one trade can take you out." A trader does not trade randomly; he tries to predict market direction. "You are trying to lower the odds against you. I mean, obviously it's a crap shoot. If we had all the answers we'd all trade our own accounts. You try to get a good feeling for the market." It is a game of chance with an extraordinary incentive to win attached. As one trader explained, "You have to make a rational game out of it." Many of the traders from high status MBA programs grudgingly admire the small but visible group of locally-bred risk-takers who seem to balance calculation with risk-taking intuitively: "You have to have a lot of street smarts to do trading, so some of the boys from Brooklyn have done very well for themselves."

Money Is Everything. It is nearly a cliche to say that the pursuit of money is at the heart of Wall Street culture. As one trader put it, "It's a money business. People are very focused on it and that's across the board." Like self-reliance and calculated risk, heightened materialism is one of the key elements in the contemporary spirit of capitalism. But on the bond trading floor that spirit is magnified and sanctified.

Money is more than just the medium of exchange; it is a measure of one's "winnings." It provides an identity that prevails over charisma, physical attractiveness, or sociability as the arbiter of success and power on the bond trading floor. The top-earning trader is king of the mountain. Consumption is often immediate and conspicuous. A young and aspiring trader explained, "It's about how much you made this year or what you bought with it. How many cars, where you go on vacation, where your apartment is or how big your house is. A lot of money goes into things that are just smoke: clothes, dinners. Nobody knows where it goes. There are a lot of status symbols in this business." This penchant for squandering reinforces the idea that it is not the accumulation of money that is important, but its symbolic ability to convey status. Money defines who you are and what you ought to be doing. Another trader put the rule more succinctly, "Money is everything in this business. Whatever money you make is what you're worth."

Self-reliance, risk-taking, and materialism are part of the culture of entrepreneurship that defines the contemporary spirit of capitalism. But the interpretation on the trading floor seems narrower and more extreme than that which is in general use. Self-reliance is enacted as aggressive opportunism, and calculated risk becomes hyper-rational gaming. These local interpretations or scripts are constructed in the process of interaction by traders and learned during the extended training programs with which every trader begins his career.

The initial socialization experiences of subjects in this study ran from six months to two years. These training programs included a short period of classroom work to learn the technicalities of bond trading, and a much longer period of internship on the floor. During this extended internship the recently graduated MBAs were rotated from desk to desk, mostly doing clerical tasks and trying to fit in. "You were supposed to go around from desk to desk in different departments. If they liked you they would offer you a job. If they didn't they'd send you on your merry way." During this time they are in an extended limbo, having low status, and are not yet guaranteed a space on the trading floor. Trainees are expected to ingratiate themselves with the traders. This "stripping down" of the self, common to a variety of socialization experiences such as boot camp, builds commitment to the role of trader and signals this commitment to others. The trainees are often left to fend for themselves on the trading floor, learning self-reliance. The training program ends when the recruit is awarded a trading desk and the opportunity to succeed or fail. As one recent graduate of such a program explained, the status degradation often continues until the trainee has made his first big win or behaved opportunistically with abandon.[19]

It is during this long internship that trainees become aware of the repertoire of strategies available. They observe senior traders, overhear conversations, and receive explicit communication about what it takes to survive. "You watch the guys around you . . . I got my post-doctorate degree in the bars, mostly after work, hanging around with the older guys, letting them beat me up and tell stories. Then you begin to see how things work." It is during this time that they acquire role-specific vocabularies and tacit knowledge about the rules of self-reliance and risk by which all traders live. Self-reliance and calculated risk are institutional rules that define the relationship of the trader to his actions. Traders can both draw their identity from these rules and define appropriate modes of action.

The significance of socialization in determining trader behavior was confirmed by the few traders in their late thirties and forties I was able to interview. The feeling among these senior traders was that the moral climate had changed. As one trader put it, "The kids coming in now are smarter . . . more educated really, but something's missing." The rapid growth in bond trading created pressure to bring in new recruits. Along with the increased competition among traders, this meant that each recruit received less

attention from a senior colleague and the attention he did receive
was focused on rapid return on the firm's growing investment.

Structure and Culture

Traders' construction of their culture does not occur in a vacuum.
There are important structural conditions that shape trader's strategies and are, in turn, shaped by the continued use of those strategies. These structural conditions are significant characteristics of
traders' environments. They are the variables most likely to cause
changes in the strategies and rules on the trading floor. In the absence of these conditions, or the presence of others, we should expect to find different strategies and, ultimately, different forms of
competitive capitalism.

The Structural Conditions of Opportunism

The key structural conditions underlying the probability of opportunistic action are extraordinary incentives, opportunity, and low
levels of informal and formal restraint.

Extraordinary Short-Term Incentives. The compensation system for bond traders is structured by the firm to inspire maximum
individual performance. Informants believed that average traders,
who were predominantly between 25 and 35 years old, made between $250,000 and $750,000 a year. The best traders were paid
into the millions of dollars. More important than the size of these
rewards is the fact that bonuses are known to fluctuate widely based
on individual contribution to the bottom line. Several older traders
pointed out that the association between contributions and rewards
was not linear. Some of it was based on what you were paid last
year and what it might take to keep you from jumping ship, as well
as on profits in the department and the firm. Regardless of the actual explanation for compensation calculations, traders believed that
the organization gave them strong incentive to maximize their individual performance through "aggressive" behavior.

Investment banking firms have given their traders unquestion-
able incentive to maximize personal income and firm profits as
quickly as possible. This is heightened by the fact that there is no

career ladder for a trader. There are few incentives for loyalty. Informants volunteered that they had no desire to move into management. Managers frequently earn less than their best traders. Traders move easily and frequently to other firms in search of higher rewards. In fact, there is considerable disincentive to delay proving one's financial worth to the firm given the competition for the best trading desk assignments. Failure to compete effectively leads to transfer off the floor or dismissal.

Opportunities for Information Impactedness. Opportunism requires a situation in which the opportunist has some potential advantage. Most opportunistic actions are based on the opportunity traders have to know more than their exchange partner or to offer incomplete or misleading information to a salesperson or customer. Traders' knowledge of the firm's inventory and of the placement of particular bonds gives them information not generally available in the Street. Like the used car dealer or antiques dealer who can hide the current market value of a commodity from the customer, traders are able to take advantage of their position in the marketplace.

Traders may also use knowledge of a customer's intentions to trade ahead of that customer without the customer knowing. The limited ability of customers to monitor traders' behavior enhances the impactedness of information, even when customers suspect that someone has traded ahead or taken advantage of them. Customers must choose their trading firms based on the firm's reputation and the alternatives available in the market. They are caught between the desire for aggressive agents who offer profit opportunities and the fear that this aggression will shade into opportunism against them. The resolution of this dilemma requires close monitoring of the trading process, which even the institutional investor is not in a position to design or enforce.

Limited Informal Restraint. Bond trading in this setting requires relatively little cooperative behavior or even interaction between the buyers and the sellers. Traders are anonymous to other professional traders, trading through brokers' brokers. They are buffered from customers by salespeople. There is little sense of obligation in this most fleeting of relationships. Traders talk about trading "for their own account" although it is the firm's money with which they trade. Under these conditions, there is very limited opportunity for restraint based on continuing relationships or trust. In contrast, market makers at the stock exchange and futures markets transact primarily with known participants in daily face-to-face interactive cliques, thereby developing bonds of trust and a reputational network. On the floors of these exchanges the participants constitute a trading community.[20]

Limited Formal Restraint. The de-regulation movement during the Reagan administration sent clear signals to the financial community about the level of formal restraint from government. Many of the older traders in this study remarked on the changed regulatory environment. Among Reagan's earliest actions was the appointment of John Shad, an executive from the brokerage firm E. F. Hutton rather than a securities lawyer, to head the Securities and Exchange Commission (SEC). Aggressive enforcement at the SEC was reined in.[21] This, in turn, took pressure off the National Association of Securities Dealers (NASD), the self-regulatory association in the bond market studied here. The self-regulatory system is most active in regulating the interface between retail brokers and the general public.[22] It is here that complaints from vulnerable retail clients, or what traders refer to as "widows and orphans," are most likely to attract intervention from Congress and the Securities and Exchange Commission.

The self-regulatory system is more passive and susceptible to politics when regulating the trading floor, an arena where traders trade only with other trading professionals.[23] The system seems to wink at the strategies of opportunism common to the trading floor. The rules of the NASD and the government oversight agencies seemed distant to my informants in the bond market between 1987 and 1989. When I mentioned them informants were mostly either ignorant or indifferent.[24] The manipulation of the Treasury bond market by traders at Salomon Brothers, discussed in the Introduction, is perhaps the most egregious example of the casual attitude toward self-regulation common on bond trading floors.

This, when combined with the bond trader data presented in this study, suggests a pattern of passive self-regulation and a culture of tolerance that is inadequate to inhibit opportunism on the trading floor. Self-regulation functions as a system of cooperation among firms to maintain a market that offers optimum benefits to the market makers. It has little impact on the day- to-day actions of traders whose opportunism is aimed at other traders and at large financial institutions such as insurance companies and mutual funds. The trading floor is thereby maintained as a stage on which economic man may play his part in a relatively unimpeded fashion and self-interest may be turned to aggressive opportunism.

The Structural Conditions of Hyper-rationality

A Rich and Continuous Flow of Information. Trading floors are designed to provide a steady flow of information to the trader in addition to the information he more actively searches out. There are also commercially available predictive models and interpretations by a network of associates. Another source of information for the trader is the continuous and immediate feedback on performance. Traders are provided with a daily profit and loss statement by which they assess their contribution. This feedback is an additional goad to hyper-rationality. The trader is reminded of his progress in the competition for high bonuses. He may also be reminded of specific bonds that are losing value. With computerization of the daily trading record of every trader, short-term profits and losses are closely tracked, visible, and salient.

High Outcome Uncertainty. The strategy of hyper-rationality is most likely to be employed under conditions of high market volatility. In highly volatile markets price is changing rapidly and in unpredictable directions, a common feature of the bond markets of the late 1980s. Volatility has several consequences. First, traders are uncertain of the appropriate market price for a bond thereby eliciting increased search. Second, bids and offers may disappear at any moment, forcing rapid action. Third, volatility enhances the potential for asymmetric information. Traders with better information, born of exhaustive search or better access, can take advantage of those with less information. The trader must increase his vigilance. Ultimately, the flow of information cannot be assimilated and the direction of the market remains uncertain. Predictive models and expert opinions are not definitive, and traders must make intuitive leaps.

High Stakes Outcomes. Hyper-rational decision making is most likely when the outcome is highly consequential. Like the fighter pilots and the surgeons to whom my informants compared themselves, bond traders perceive themselves as taking relatively large risks. Despite the fact that they are employees of large investment banks, the hazard is experienced as personal. "I commit my own capital, it's completely my own risk," remarked one trader. The result is exhaustive search behavior that is only interrupted by the unpredictable flow of transactional opportunities that force a rapid choice.

These structural conditions cannot stand alone as explanations of economic action. Actors must create a meaning system of personal strategies and rules. The strategies are themselves embedded in cultural idioms like "entrepreneurship" and "risk-taking" that interact with structural conditions to enable and constrain economic action. The structural conditions and cultural forms identified here are themselves social constructions. They are shaped and reshaped by the creative action of economic actors over time.

Discussion

The analysis of self-interest in this chapter and the scandals in financial markets in recent years suggest that there is a culture of opportunism in the bond market. It seems reasonable to wonder why customers tolerate such opportunism. Why doesn't a market for fair-dealing firms develop? In fact, reputation does operate in the bond market, but to a more limited degree than in the stock and futures markets discussed later in this book. First, in stock and futures markets trading is centralized on a single trading floor, like the New York Stock Exchange or the New York Mercantile Exchange, where market makers transact face to face, day in and day out. The bond market is "over-the-counter," meaning that trading, even among market makers, is over the phone and often buffered through intermediaries. The personal relations so important in reputation are mediated by distance, technology, and the rapid growth in the number of institutional investors.

Second, traders' relations with their firm's customers are mediated through the sales force. Traders feel little obligation to the customer or the salesperson. Institutional customers are faced with a dilemma in that it is the most "aggressive" firms, like Salomon Brothers and Drexel Burnham, that also provide the deepest markets and the greatest profit opportunities. In most bond markets, the number of primary dealers is limited and dominated by a few. While reputation is important, reputation for providing profit opportunities may take precedence over reputation for opportunism, especially if the uncertain cost of opportunism is less than the presumed or real profit opportunities afforded by a relationship with a top firm. Finally, traders and salespeople reported that institutional customers expect traders to use opportunistic strategies, but could not predict which of the many transactions conducted would involve opportunistic strategies. Even after Salomon Brothers admitted manipulating the Treasury securities market, most of their customers continued to trade government securities with them.

Bond traders in Wall Street investment banks in the 1980s produced their own version of homo economicus. He was hyper-rational, highly self-interested and relatively free of social control as he traded in the debt of corporations and governments. More specifically, he engaged in both opportunistic and hyper- rational strategies and was guided by rules of self-reliance, calculated risk, and extreme materialism. These characteristics are products of a unique environment in which new entrants to the labor force soon find themselves trading in millions of dollars of government or corporate debt. Tom Wolfe captured the ego inflation and cockiness inherent in this situation in his novel, *Bonfire of the Vanities,* referring to bond traders at investment banks as "masters of the universe."

But this version of homo economicus is not universal. While most economic actors exist in dense webs of trust, obligation, and reputation, investment banks in the 1980s constructed an environment with minimal interdependence, extraordinary incentives for self-interest and limited constraints on behavior: a poor prescription for a legitimate or stable economic system. Other financial markets that had high historic levels of opportunism responded by constructing systems of restraint. In successive chapters I will examine similarities and differences in how other parts of the financial community have dealt with extremes of self-interest on the trading floor.

STRUCTURED ANARCHY: FORMAL AND INFORMAL ORGANIZATION IN THE FUTURES MARKET

2

No one has died on the trading floor since a heart attack killed a clerical worker in 1978, but the (paramedic) team regularly treats chest pains, stomach problems, anxiety attacks, and accidental stabbings—a consequence of traders in the crowded pits bumping into each other with sharp pencils.

"To Keep Future," Wall Street Journal, *1982*

Of the three subcultures studied in this book, it is the institutional arrangements of the futures market which seem most anachronistic. Futures markets still look much as they did in the nineteenth century. Whereas bond traders sit at desks watching data-laden terminals, futures traders stand in pits, really three- or four-staired rings, shouting and signaling bids and offers to other traders in the pit. The history of financial markets is generally believed to exhibit a tendency toward increasing rationality and control. Even after more than a century of changes, the futures markets still reflect their origins in mercantile capitalism. At the center of these markets are open auctions where contracts for future delivery of such commodities as Japanese yen, coffee, heating oil, gold, and U.S. treasury bills are traded. The apparently anarchic behavior in the pit inspired novelist Frank Norris to describe the scene just as the opening bell is rung: "Instantly a tumult was unchained, arms were flung upward in strenuous gestures, and from above the crowding heads in the Wheat Pit a multitude of hands, eager, the fingers extended, leaped into the air. All articulate expression was lost in the single explosion of sound as the traders surged downward to the Centre of the Pit . . ."[1]

While this description may seem overly dramatic, it differs only in style from the economist's image of the futures market. To economists these gatherings of buyers and sellers are the representations of a perfectly competitive market. They are arenas where individual "articulate expression" is lost in the collective act of price determination. As such, futures markets are textbook examples for supply and demand. Paul Samuelson notes that "[o]ur curves of supply and demand strictly apply only to a perfectly competitive market where some kind of standardized commodity such as wheat is being auctioned by an organized exchange that registers transactions of numerous buyers and sellers. The Board of Trade in Chicago is one such example . . . [M]en from various brokerage houses are milling around on the trading floor while frantically giving hand and voice signals to the specialist who serves as auctioneer for each grain or company stock."[2]

The action in the pits does indeed fit the economist's model of the competitive market. But the conceptual lens of the economist focuses on the near-anarchy in the pit without noticing the layers of organization, formal and informal, which surround and buffer this market. With a different set of conceptual lenses, one which views the market as a social construction, the focus shifts to the context of all this dramatic action, a context which participants construct to pursue their own interests.

In this chapter I will analyze the systems of coordination and control in the futures markets. By exploring the complex social arrangements in and around the pit that organize the competitive action and looking at the larger system of organizational relations within which market exchange exists, I will show how these markets, like all others, are part of a market control system. In addition to the floor traders, this system includes the regulators of the domain, e.g., the suppliers of input and distributors of output, as well as public agents of control. Such systems consist of horizontal and vertical relations between competitors, suppliers, customers, public agencies, and other interested parties. As such, a market control system's components constitute a network of re-lationships which constrains and facilitates the operation of the markets.

I will look first at the formal and informal structure and second at the processes of control, concluding with the unexpected find-ing that futures exchanges exercise monopoly power in the midst of these otherwise classically competitive markets.

Structured Anarchy

In what sense can the futures pits be characterized as anarchic? A visitor to the floor of any futures market would see a lot of physi-cal chaos, as did Norris and Samuelson. But chaos can be mislead-ing. We may attribute chaos to a group's behavior because we do not understand the situation as the actors themselves understand it. Traders' behavior is not unintentional or without direction. It is highly ordered. But few traders in the pit would deny that every-day life in the pits feels anarchic and many admit that they wish to protect themselves against it.

The conditions in the pits are inherent in a risky and active mar-ket. The nature of transactions is not collective, but rather highly individual. In the market, traders are confronted with a continuous conflict of interest with all other traders for acquisition of a scarce resource, i.e., transactions, at the most advantageous price. It is these multiple, simultaneous conflicts which account for the im-pression of an absence of order. The traders' individuality is only intensified by the crowd of surrounding rivals, thus giving the ap-pearance of a lack of any sort of collective action.

Unlike the bond markets, where market makers can be anony-mous to one another, futures trading is done face to face. Whether trading for themselves or as an agent for a customer, futures traders accept each other's bids and offers. More importantly, as members of a futures exchange, such as the New York Mercantile Exchange or the Commodity Exchange of New York, they return day after day to trade with the same group of traders in the same pit. The predilection to recognize one trader's bid amidst many others is conditioned by prior experience with that trader in earlier transactions. As one futures trader at the New York Mercantile Exchange explained, "If you start reneging, it's going to hurt your image within the group, within the industry. If I don't like the way you trade, if you renege on me all the time, I'll leave you out. Go right around you every time." This is an environment in which reputation is a valued form of social capital.

At the same time that traders are engaged in a continuous competition with other traders in the pit, they are mutually dependent. They are dependent on their multiple exchange partners for completion of contract terms. They rely on each other to ensure that the market is maintained into the future and to see that it is not monopolized, that it remains competitive so that all sellers may easily find buyers and all buyers may easily find sellers. In general, they all desire a market in which strategies of opportunism, similar to those available in the bond market, are relatively restrained.

This paradox of dependence versus independence is a central feature in the social organization of financial markets. One trader, a member of the compliance committee at his exchange, explained this motivation: "We keep the market open. We keep it responsible. We keep it trading. We don't want problems during the day. We don't want to be constantly correcting situations." The result is the creation of social mechanisms which constrain and facilitate the operation of the market. These mechanisms include informal norms among traders, formal rules of trade, and organizational arrangements to coordinate collective action. In this chapter we will define the nature of these three types of control that members of the market have constructed to make their transactions more certain and predictable.

The study of control systems in a market does not lend itself to conventional analysis in terms of the familiar variables of bureaucratic structure. Rather, the technical language to be used here is derived from systems theory.[3] The usefulness of this language lies in the preeminence of lateral flows and feedback between the formal structures of control. Formal control in the futures market consists of several levels. The first of these will be referred to as the coordinating system.

The Coordinating System

This section will examine how the anarchy in the pit is structured into orderly business relations. Like formal organizations, markets have their own design or structure. This pit structure shapes the behavior of traders, and is, in turn, shaped by it. Traders have created a structure in which they may pursue their strategies effectively. This is not accomplished in the pit alone, but rather depends on the assistance of auxiliary organizations. The coordinating system consists of a core technology and the auxiliary organizational arrangements to move the transactions from input to output. The core technology in the futures market is the trading pit (see Figure 1). It is in the pit that transactions actually occur.

The technique used for the exchange of futures contracts is essentially identical from pit to pit across all eleven futures exchanges in the United States, although the analysis here is based on the exchanges in New York and Chicago. The technique of trading basically involves an open auction where buyers and sellers stand facing each other in a multi–tiered ring. At the opening bell traders begin making offers to buy or sell. They use hand signals and strong voices to offer and accept trades across the pit. These trades are recorded immediately on slips of paper or "cards" by each party to the trade. Trading does not stop after each transaction. It continues this way, more or less actively depending on the commodity, until the closing bell rings in the afternoon. The outlines of this process first emerged at central markets for commodities in pre–industrial Europe. These central markets were part of a mechanism which moved goods from their producers to the ultimate consumers. The development of futures markets represents an elaboration of that marketing mechanism. The role of broker, for instance, developed to serve as a middleman between producers and processors, one more part of a linear marketing channel.

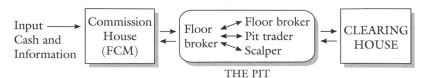

THE PIT

Figure 1. The coordinating system

The coordinating system in futures trading is a simple linear path. Cash, information, and later contracts are passed along this path in a determined fashion. In the case of a trade initiated by a non-member, such as one you or I might place, the input moves from our broker to a floor broker at the exchange. The floor broker buys or sells the contract(s). At the end of the day all trades are taken to the Clearing House where accounts are settled. Viewed in this manner, the futures market begins to look simple and its structural relations a bit overdetermined. By looking at each sub-unit in the coordinating system, however, we may bring back some of the chaos and complexity generally associated with the market.

The Commission House

When a customer approaches the market, his or her first contact is with a commission house. The customer is not part of the system, but only a bearer of inputs whose cash and information are transformed into contracts, commissions, and margin. The commission house acts as a gatekeeper who stands between the market and the resources flowing in. Commission houses that serve this function are members of one or more futures exchanges, and are officially referred to as Futures Commission Merchants (FCM). Customers usually refer to the person at the commission house whom they deal with as their broker or account executive. These are essentially salespeople for the FCM. The Chicago Board of Trade rules define an FCM as "A member who makes a trade, either for another member or for a non-member, but who makes the trade in his own name and becomes liable as principal between himself and the other party to the trade."[4]

So the market is never directly linked to the thousands of non–member speculators and hedgers that use it. Rather, the FCM requires its customers to deposit a specific cash amount for each contract purchased or sold as a sign of good faith that all obligations will be met. The sum is usually ten to twenty percent of the value of the contract, but may be as low as five percent. This sum, the margin, must not dip below some minimum level. If price fluctuation results in a loss, the customer is required to deposit more funds with the FCM. In extreme circumstances the FCM may demand the additional deposit within as little as an hour. Commission houses usually try to keep the margin on account well above the minimum, but this varies.

In this way the FCM stands as a buffer between customers and the market. Customers have been effectively defined as outside the system. It becomes the obligation of the FCM to strain out the financially unstable and to secure access to the assets of those deemed reliable.[5] Such precautions are essential given that the FCM is legally liable for the contracts traded and thereby runs the risk of insolvency in the face of large losses. Thus, uncertainty is considerably reduced by knowing that all traders can be held responsible for their losses through the liability of the FCM.

In the Pit

Before there can be losses or profits the order must be placed. Once the customer has deposited a margin and agreed to be responsible for any losses, the account executive at the commission house will accept orders. These orders are phoned to the exchange where they are passed to a floor broker. The floor broker may represent the FCM exclusively or may freelance, trading for other members and for his own account. He is paid a commission on each contract traded and therefore has an interest in cultivating business. He does this by developing a reputation for quick execution at the ordered price.

At this point in the coordinating system we have reached the pit, the technical core of futures trading. Here, in large open rings with descending steps, the chaotic outcry and gesturing of competing traders functions to determine the going price of a contract. A hundred or more traders may gather around an active pit in stock indexes, government bonds, foreign currency, or some other commodity, competing for their price.

The floor brokers are not the only participants in this scene, although their kind are usually the most numerous. Other members of the association, trading solely for their own accounts, add liquidity to the market. These traders, called scalpers and locals, often move in and out of the market, speculating on small price changes in the course of a few minutes, an hour, or a day. On the other hand, some floor traders, particularly those who are also involved with the cash commodity, may take large positions, occasionally influencing others to follow suit. Every trader in the pit may be considered a market maker. By standing in the pit, making bids and offers, they are providing a continuous market to the general trading public.

This then is the nearly perfect competitive market which economists study. Isolated from the buffers and strainers, it provides an arena for understanding price determination under competition. But the market does not and cannot work in isolation. The pit is but a component in an organizational system whose entire purpose is to maintain the integrity of the pricing mechanism in the pit and the stream of economic benefits that members derive from it.

The Clearing House

Although the anarchy in the pit may be an effective coordinating mechanism for price, it does not necessarily coordinate human behavior. The result of the tumult in the pit is that a price has been agreed upon by parties to an exchange. These promises of future obligation must be sorted and settled. These tasks are accomplished by the clearing house, which Mark Powers, despite the pit's centrality, calls "the heart of any commodity futures exchange."[6]

The clearing house may be a part of the exchange or a separate corporation, but whichever arrangement is chosen, it is directly linked to the pit. Membership in the clearing house consists of a subset of well-capitalized members of the exchange. These members hold stock in the clearing corporation and deposit a large sum in a guarantee fund. The clearing house is a not-for-profit corporation whose members oversee the financial integrity of the various contracts. The incentive for membership is that clearing members may profit from commissions paid them by floor traders, although the clearing corporation itself does not profit.

The work of the clearing house begins at the end of each trading day when floor traders submit the list of all their trades to a clearing member. The trader typically has an ongoing relationship with some clearing member and has deposited a clearing margin with that member. The clearing member hands cards representing each trade over to the clearing house staff where all trades are matched, recapitulating and verifying the buying and selling which occurred in the pit. At this point the clearing house becomes buyer to all sellers and seller to all buyers, thereby putting a buffer between the principals. Fulfilling of all contract obligations will be guaranteed by the clearing house from this point until expiration of the contract. No clearing house on an exchange in the United States has ever defaulted on this obligation. In most clearing houses one member's insolvency would cause an assessment on all other members until the obligation was met. This is informally referred to as the "good to the last drop" method of default recovery.

But the need for such measures rarely occurs. After the trades have been matched, the clearing house computes debit and credit amounts for all accounts. These are settled daily, just as in the customer margin. If payment is due the clearing house it must arrive before the opening bell rings the next morning. The opening of trading may be delayed if all accounts are not settled. In this way the clearing house functions in the manner of a homeostatic mechanism or system regulator.[7] Such a mechanism keeps the internal state of the system stable within fixed constraints. The constraints are the minimum margins which help guarantee the financial integrity of contracts against default. In this way, traders have designed a system that is buffered against fluctuations in the market. As Simon states in describing this sort of mechanism, ". . . the designer insulates the inner system from the environment, so that an invariant relation is maintained between inner system and goal, independent of variations over a wide range of parameters that characterize the outer environment."[8]

In addition to sorting and matching the pit's output, the clearing house collects debts, dispenses credits and guarantees payment and delivery. Despite a continuous flow of inputs, the system remains stable within certain constraints. These are formal constraints which market members have chosen to structure their behavior and to provide rules within which the anarchy of competition may be played out. The straining and sorting components of the coordinating system insure that it is played out within fixed dimensions of time and space. By mutual agreement, all obligations are met before trading resumes the next morning.

Of course, other possible sources of disturbance remain. Members may turn deviant, deciding that the incentive to violate the formal constraints exceeds the incentive to conform. Disputes between members may demand arbitration. Most likely of all, environmental conditions affecting supply and demand may change so much that system constraints must be reset to guarantee the financial integrity of the market. While the coordinating system was adequate to regulate the routine flow of resources, for all these non-routine disturbances there is a control system.

The Control System

If the coordinating system, described above, was a closed machine through which energy flowed and was transformed, our analysis might stop with the linear chart in Figure 1. Once the system's parameters had been established by its designers, the system's major vulnerability would be entropy, a natural running down of the system due to lack of input. But the coordinating system is not a closed machine where the flow of energy can be wired and its course made invariant. It is an open system constantly receiving new input, i.e., customers' orders; its constraints take the form of socially legitimized rules rather than calibrations; and its components consist of actors who make the rules and at the same time have an incentive to violate them. The constant flow of customers' orders keeps the system in negative entropy. As for the creation and maintenance of constraints, an elaboration is added to the open linear system: the exchange association. The new trajectories added by the control system reflect the various proactive and reactive strategies of the exchange association (see Figure 2).

Both stock and futures markets are organized by exchange associations: not–for–profit organizations owned and operated by the members. Members' shares in the association entitle them to act as floor traders, to pay reduced commissions, and to participate in governing the organization. The function of the exchange is to establish and maintain competitive markets for the use of the membership. The early history of these markets indicates that increasingly rigorous constraints were found necessary to keep these markets from being cornered.[9] The implication is that competitive markets do not emerge and maintain themselves "naturally." (If any tendency in markets exists, it is anti-competitive, as a result of the desire of successful competitors to reduce their uncertainty through

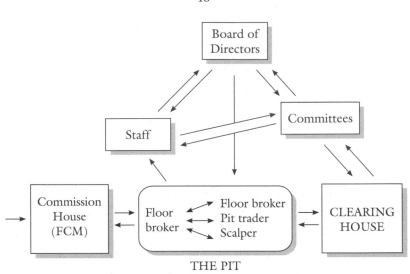

Figure 2. The Exchange Association

monopoly.) Rather, it is constraint which is "natural" in the midst of competition, a notion well developed by John R. Commons:

> Competition is not Nature's "struggle for existence" but is an artificial arrangement supported by the moral, economic, and physical sanctions of collective action. The theory of free competition developed by economists is not a natural tendency towards equilibrium of forces but is an ideal of public purpose adopted by the courts, to be attained by restraints upon the natural struggle for existence.[10]

In this view the competitive market and its restraint are equally artificial social arrangements. Members, who draw their income from commissions and trading profits, rely on the continuous operation of the market. They therefore have a vested interest in maintaining the market, which requires a limitation of the tendency toward monopoly. Of course, while the incentive of exclusive trading rights elicits conformity from the members, incentive systems are never perfect. As with any social system, someone is likely to test the system's limits. When the cost of such deviance is high, social systems resort to coercive control. The control system in futures markets includes a range of strategies and structures; we will examine the informal as well as the highly formalized.

Informal Control

At the most basic level, markets have everyday rules about business conduct. These rules may be as simple as the meaning of a word or gesture. "[If] you say 'sold,' you better mean it. If you have both hands up, you better mean what that means. Other pits are easier. You make a mistake, you have both hands up and you only wanted to do one. Well, they might laugh at you, but they won't hold you responsible. Here [in Treasury bill futures], you're in trouble."

Transactions valued at hundreds of thousands of dollars are signaled with little more than hand signs and eye contact between traders across a crowded pit. There are rules about mistaken or crossed signals, there are rules about the intentional and repeated reneging on agreed-upon transactions. Most such rules of conduct are enforced by group pressure and intimidation. Traders are not shy about letting another trader know that he is out of line. They may yell at him, or more significantly, freeze him out of transactions. "If there's a broker out there (in the pit) who's constantly having problems with other brokers, since it's an open outcry system, nobody has to deal with him. I don't have to trade with you if I don't want to. It's in your best interest to do the right thing out there."

In general, futures traders are both conscious of the rules of conduct and positively inclined toward them, as long as they don't grow more stringent. Rules reduce the anarchy in the pits. One trader compared it to driving a car. "You have to have rules. We all rail against the 55 mile an hour limit, but I don't know anybody that says that driving on the right side of the road isn't a good rule. You would have chaos." But at a deeper level, futures traders have internalized the need to inhibit opportunism. In the following quotation a floor broker, who trades for customers and for himself, explains why a customer's account always comes before the trader's own account. "An order comes in to buy something at a price. If I get it bought under that price, the profit goes to the customer. If it is worse than the order requested, I pay. The customer is always protected . . . Otherwise, you are liable to have all kinds of abuses. It keeps everybody sharp."

Ultimately, the trader understands that the rules are the key to continued profit opportunity. "We are happy that there is still such freedom of movement here, the freedom of the entrepreneurial spirit. We recognize the need for rules and generally everybody abides by them. It's rare that things ever have to get to the Business Conduct Committee."

Formal Control

Formal control strategies in the futures exchange consist of surveillance and corrective action. They are referred to by the members as "self-regulation." These functions are accomplished by committees made up of members of the exchange association. The members, in turn, have hired staff to perform administrative functions. It is the responsibility of the staff to oversee activity in the pit and to facilitate the operations in each pit by recording trades and posting prices. These administrators are for the most part managers of information. Figure 2 shows that information flows directly out of the pit and the clearing house to staff and committees. The flow of information to both staff and committees represents a redundancy in the system. Historically, the committees were the chief managerial unit. It was not until 1948 that the Chicago Board of Trade hired its first paid executive officer.[11] Together, the committees and staff monitor and regulate the exchange.

The surveillance function is common to all futures exchanges, although exchanges may differ on the names they use for committees. For the purpose of illustration I will look at the surveillance structure on the New York Mercantile Exchange.

The Business Conduct Committee is perhaps the most controversial committee on a commodity exchange. It has general supervision over the business conduct of the members. In the course of supervision it may investigate ". . . the dealings, transactions, and financial conditions of members and member firms, may examine their books and records upon request, and shall prescribe such capital requirements as it deems appropriate."[12] Among the conduct forbidden in the by-laws is the spreading of false rumor, noncompetitive trading, and fraudulent transactions with any member of the exchange.

The Floor Committee is responsible for maintaining good order on the floor. This is mostly a matter of decorum and first violations are treated as a minor offense. "We have a floor committee that makes sure no one bids through someone's offer, or no one offers through someone's bid, and no one approaches the market improperly. If someone asks for the market price for March sugar and its 80 bid at 82 and then they go at 79, then he's in violation of a floor trading rule and the floor committee can fine him right on the spot. I'm on the committee so I can fine him."

The Membership Committee oversees all applications and transfers of membership. It conducts investigations into the qualifications and financial stability of the applicant.

At the largest exchanges the committees and staffs have, to some extent, a parallel structure. The Office of Investigations and Audits (staff) supplements and supports the work of the Business Conduct and Membership Committees by gathering the investigative material needed for the committees' surveillance work. Guided by rules and by-laws, these and other committees assemble information on members' conduct in the market positions they hold, and on the progress toward liquidation and delivery in various contracts. Once this information on members has been gathered, it is then redirected back at the board and its committees in their role as correction agents, so that deviation from the association goals may be punished by suspension, expulsion, or a fine.

The ability of exchanges to take corrective action is the key to formal control. Many membership organizations have considerable surveillance capability but limited ability to take corrective action against members. Futures and stock markets are remarkable for their flexibility in this area. The board and its committees have a range of actions at their disposal to adjust the system in the context of events. In the next chapter I will discuss how and when these are used in practice.

In the short term the system reacts to rule violations and disputes between members. Rule violations are most often handled by the surveillance committees which are also part of the corrective feedback loop. In terms of internal disputes, the Pit Committee is the fire department of the exchange. It resolves any disputes arising from bids or offers in the pit. This is accomplished on the spot by the action of any two members of the committee. The Pit Committee may also levy fines up to $1000 for practices which are disruptive of orderly trading. The accused is entitled to a hearing, and the appeal is to the board of directors. Larger disputes over a transaction involving either members or nonmembers may be brought before the Arbitration Committee, where an informal hearing is held. Such disputes are typically over the identity of trades, over prices, and over quantities. The committee hears both sides and assigns awards, where fitting, which are binding on the parties. In this way, conflicts arising are resolved internally so that trading may continue.

At another level, corrective action resolves circumstances which threaten to interfere with the normal progress of a contract toward its final trading day. These circumstances include: "Events, conditions or positions which threaten a free, open and orderly market, the fair and orderly trading in any futures contracts, the orderly liquidation of or delivery pursuant to any futures contract, or a distortion of prices; a congestion, squeeze or corner or circumstances or positions which might result therein."[13] Most exchanges have a Control Committee or its equivalent which assigns several members to monitor trading in each contract, assemble information regarding open positions and to ascertain from clearing members their customer's intentions as to liquidation or delivery of specific contracts. If investigation fails to eliminate the threat to orderly trading, the board may invoke its emergency powers.

Emergency powers are used to disrupt the flow of cash and information into the system. Action in the pit is constrained within specific limits until conditions in the market are deemed to have stabilized. Among the corrective actions available are limiting trading to liquidation only, extending or shortening time for expiration of contracts, ordering contract liquidation and fixing a settlement price, ordering reduction of positions for any or all members, and suspending trading. Such action is rarely necessary. Informal means of persuasion, directed by the committees at specific members, are often sufficient. When such extreme actions are taken, however, it is often a source of conflict among traders. The exchange may at times take action to avoid the attention and intervention of federal regulators. These issues will be discussed in greater detail in the next chapter. This brings us to the second function of the control system, institutional control.

Institutional Control

A market control system, before anything else, is established to determine the operating policy in the market. This operating policy is the consensus by which the institution will be maintained. Since the founding of the first futures exchange in the United States in 1848, management of this consensus has been accomplished by the election of a Board of Directors, also known as the Board of Governors or Board of Managers on various other exchanges. These boards consist of between fifteen and twenty-five members and are elected by the exchange membership. As part of setting policy, the board is responsible for making and changing exchange rules and for the management of all exchange property and finances. The board is also responsible for maintaining the legitimacy of exchange function and policy to the wider financial and regulatory environment.

Most of the work of the boards is done through committees which are made up of board members and other exchange members appointed by the board, usually for a one year tenure. Typically, the board meets once a month and an administrative committee exercises its authority to manage the exchange on a day to day basis. The board and its committees are assisted by a small hired staff.[14] The board itself may be called into special session when issues of management or rule interpretation are considered by the Chair to warrant such action.

Such extraordinary circumstances are the exception. Most policy action involves incremental changes in contract terms, margin, and permitted daily price fluctuations. These things are likely to be handled at the committee level. Constituting the greatest part of the policy–making process, incremental changes are really a result of feedback from the technical core (see Figure 2). The policy–making process is represented by a loop running from the board through the committees to the coordinating system and back again. The committees' critical importance lies in their ability to receive information needed for policy making and to implement the board's will.

The board itself is most likely to respond to outside pressure from its political or economic environment. Under government pressure it may be required to amend a contract or change a procedure that the government feels is anti-competitive. On the other hand, the board is increasingly concerned with turning the tables on the regulatory environment. It is active in commenting on new federal regulations, testifying before Congressional committees, and lobbying the regulatory commission for approval of new contracts. As for rival exchanges, the board must assess competition from its rivals in various contracts and make the decision to develop new contracts. As competition and regulation have become more complex, this level of governance has created more of a buffer between the members and their environment. They may now leave internal control to the committees and external relations to the board.

Whereas most formal control is concerned with the maintenance or restoration of market efficiency, institutional control exists to ensure the long-term survival of the market and its market makers. In the short term, market order is maintained by the formal administrative functions of surveillance and conflict resolution. Institutional control, however, is dedicated to managing symbols more than people. Under the auspices of the board, by-laws are written and amended, and policies are defended in public appearances and through the dissemination of documents. These activities are more concerned with survival than efficiency. Markets, like other forms of social organization, do not continue to exist without reaffirmation of their goals and their legitimacy to the wider community. It is the incremental but continuous reconstruction of policy and the promotion of that policy in public forums that insures survival. In the next section I will examine the process by which futures markets act as institutions, attempting to control both internal and external affairs.

The Process Of Control

A well-articulated structure exists for coordinating and controlling the anarchy of futures trading. The competitive markets in the pit are only one component in the futures system. The pits are surrounded by buffers and sorters, surveillance agents and enforcers.

The combined structures of the coordinating system and the control system constitute a market control system, which includes the rules of conduct and formal structures constructed by market members to reduce the level of uncertainty in their markets. As such, market control systems are tools of collective action established for the benefit and protection of the membership. Having examined the structure of market control, I will now discuss the actual process of market control.

It is appropriate to begin by turning to the oldest and largest of the eleven commodity futures exchanges in the United States, the Chicago Board of Trade. The CBT accounts for approximately 50 percent of all futures trading in the United States. In specific contracts, such as soybeans and corn, it holds as much as 87 percent and 91 percent of the market, respectively.[15] Until recently there had been very little competition between exchanges over contracts in specific commodities.[16] Exchanges tend to specialize by commodity so that each has a dominant position in some group of commodities.

Indicators of the powers of exchanges are not limited to market share. Each exchange is the only means of access to trading in its particular commodities (futures contracts). They allow no trading outside the exchange floor or after the hours specified by the exchange. The members own the exchange. They are able to limit membership, establish rules, and change them at will.[17] Exchanges are, as such, legal monopolies which have retained their dominance not only through existing economies of scale but through active maintenance of the market to insure the survival of the institution for the long term.

Of course, the cartel-like behavior of commodity exchanges has not gone undetected. In a 1905 decision, the U.S. Supreme Court recognized that the CBT was restraining dissemination of its price quotes, but found that the exchange had a right to retain price quotes as its private property, even though this would eliminate competition from the prevalent off-exchange "bucket shops." In 1918 the court affirmed the right of the CBT to establish its own rules of trade, even when this restrained behavior in the market. In this decision Justice Brandeis found that in some cases market control is a reasonable restraint of trade in that its intention is the maintenance of market conditions.[18] The important precedent established is that firms may cooperate on a variety of rules of trade, as long as they continue to compete over price. More recently, efforts have been made to narrow the range of cooperative strategies permissible. In 1972 the Department of Justice brought suit against the CBT under antitrust law for price-fixing by setting minimum commission rates. These minimum rates inhibited competition between brokers, and, claimed the suit, kept commissions artificially high. By mutual agreement the exchanges have slowly phased out minimum commission rates. The effect has been an increase in competition and the appearance of "discount rates" from new as well as older brokerage houses. Since 1975, a new federal regulatory agency, the Commodity Futures Trading Commission, has been responsible for discovering the anti-competitive behavior of exchanges.[19]

Thus, there is a long history attached to exchanges' active control of market conditions, and the objections to this system have existed almost as long.[20] But the survival and success of such a system can not be taken for granted. Underlying any market control system are active efforts to define its boundaries and, at times, to defend them. An essential part of the process of control in a market system, especially one as formalized as a futures exchange, is boundary maintenance.

Boundary Maintenance Strategies

The boundaries in a market are defined by custom, precedent, rules, and assumptions. Boundaries define who may trade, what may be traded, and where and when trading may occur. They form the outline of what is deemed appropriate in the product and in the way it is exchanged. Participants recognize each other by these shared product and transactional definitions. Boundary maintenance refers to the process by which these "working rules" are tested and redefined. In the first futures market, at the Chicago Board of Trade, these rules were derived from mercantile custom. These customs established the norms of market control and reciprocity, which were then institutionalized by the exchange association.

How are such boundaries maintained? New actors come and old actors leave. Products, in this case the futures contracts, develop,

improve, and decline. Definitions of wl
This market metabolism would lead to a
ous change. Yet as a social entity, the mai
of behaviors which do not fluctuate very widely. This stability is the
result of three control processes: socialization, routine investigation,
and the resolution of boundary crises.

The limits of what one can "get away with" are constantly being tested in a competitive market. For this reason committees and
staff are continually monitoring behavior in the pits. In most cases
minor infractions are punished very lightly; often with a reprimand.
A commission house (FCM) which falls below the capital requirements or maintains under-margined accounts may be subject to
such punishment. More serious violations require stronger action.
In February 1979 the Chicago Board of Trade fined a member firm,
Clayton Brokerage, thirty thousand dollars.

> At a meeting yesterday, the exchange's directors found Clayton
> engaged in "reckless and un-businesslike dealings" and "acts detri-
> mental to the interests and welfare of the association." Specifi-
> cally, the directors held that Clayton "traded systematically against
> the orders and positions of its customers;" executed orders with-
> out obtaining margin, or security deposit, from its customers; did-
> n't adequately monitor an account to assure that trades were suited
> to the account's financial resources, and made misstatements upon
> material points to the Business Conduct Committee of the ex-
> change.[21]

Such incidents are infrequent: this was the only highly publicized
one to occur during my three-year period of research. A principal
actor in the Clayton affair was later expelled from the Chicago Board
of Trade; the first expulsion in six years. But the effects of such incidents are not lost on members. They are a topic for discussion
throughout the industry. Members become more conscious of the
self-regulatory machinery and the boundaries of acceptable behavior are reaffirmed.

On occasion these boundaries are sufficiently threatened to invoke a boundary crisis. Powerful actors inside or outside the market may call into question the working rules of the market. Such
action elicits a collective response by members of the market who

feel threatened. These crises appear as conflicts between the accused deviants and the defenders of the status quo. In futures markets these sides are often represented by venturesome speculators on one side and those who stand to lose on the other. It is in such crises that market members negotiate the acceptance or prohibition of products and behaviors. Two examples of boundary crises will be used to show how the market members maintain their most favorable positions. The first example will examine the details behind the 1905 Supreme Court case which had the effect of eliminating bucket shops. The second example examines a recent case of boundary maintenance in the 1980s.

Bucket shops first made their appearance around 1879, by which time futures trading was already thriving in Chicago.[22] They were an attempt to profit from futures speculation without playing by the working rules of the exchange. In the practice of bucketing one takes the opposite side of a customer's order without ever executing it on an exchange. Bucket shops were storefronts where people gathered to speculate by making bets on the direction a commodity's price might take on the exchange. Unlike exchange trading, one could bet any amount of money, had no worry about delivery, and needed no broker. For a commission the proprietor of the shop took the other side of all trades.

At first the exchanges paid little attention. It was not uncommon for members to bucket orders themselves. But as the shops grew and attracted more customers it became clear that they were objectionable on at least three counts: (1) they provided competition for exchange members who made their living from the commissions paid by customers; (2) they reduced liquidity in the pit and thereby affected market efficiency; and (3) they threatened the legitimacy of exchange trading by equating commodity speculation with gambling in the minds of the public and its officials. The issue of public perception was potentially the most threatening because it questioned the ability of the exchange to regulate the market and gave ammunition to populist groups, mostly farmers, calling for the abolition of futures trading.

The boundary crisis was really two crises: the exchanges had first to decide on the practice of bucketing within the exchange and then to face the challenge from the political environment. By 1882 the directors of the Chicago Board of Trade had noted the "demoralizing" effect of the shops and "their injurious effect on the business."[23] In 1883 the CBT finally approved a rule against those members who bucketed by the close vote of 281 to 251. Although this rule proved difficult to enforce, the construction of new boundaries to limit members' behavior set the stage for a protracted struggle to eliminate the external threat.

Efforts to control information by denying telegraphic price quotes outside the exchange proved worthless. Bucket shops contrived ways to get the quotes, even using wire taps. Telegraph quotes were soon resumed. In 1894 the Directors finally decided to put an end to bucketing within the exchange by suspending and expelling bucketers. After this the CBT was able to fight the bucket shops in court, raising their illegality according to Illinois law as an issue. This legal struggle culminated in a 1905 Supreme Court decision in the case of Chicago Board of Trade vs. Christie Grain and Stock Company (a bucket shop). Oliver Wendell Holmes, Jr. writing for the majority, found that quotations are the property of the exchange and that the exchange's activities were clothed with a legitimate public purpose.

The decision signaled the demise of the bucket shops and thus the elimination of serious external competition. More important, it established the legitimacy of the exchange as a self-regulating body with a public function. As the next example shows, legitimacy is an increasingly critical part of a market's boundary maintenance.

Perhaps the single most important tool that exchanges have for maintaining the financial integrity of the market is their ability to set and change the margins paid by brokers and customers. Margins are the cornerstone of self-regulation. A challenge to the appropriateness of exchange-based margins might be felt as a challenge to the competence of the market control system in general.

Just such a challenge occurred in the spring of 1980. As in the example of the bucket shops, the threat was external, but this time it was from the federal government. In the interim between these two crises the boundaries of the market changed little, except perhaps in that custom and precedent made them more solid. But starting in the 1920s these boundaries were codified in federal law, so that their violation might be made a public matter. By 1975 the codification had been strengthened to include an independent federal regulatory agency, the Commodity Futures Trading Commission (CFTC), which oversees the market control system described above. At this point the conditions for a new boundary crisis between the exchange and the government were set.

The precipitant to the boundary crisis was a threat to the integrity of the silver market. A monumental struggle between buyers and sellers of silver was being played out. This threat not only questioned the self-regulatory ability of an exchange, but played havoc with a commodity of great importance to the U.S. Treasury and Federal Reserve Board. As such, both Congress and the CFTC began to raise questions about appropriate self-regulatory behavior on the New York Commodities Exchange (Comex). The Board of Governors of the Exchange had raised margins, set limits on speculative positions, and finally ordered trading for liquidation only.

The issue was whether Comex had acted with sufficient alacrity. It was claimed that while Comex members were making money on the high volume trading, the Board was reluctant to take action to cool off the market. Rumors began to circulate in the industry that the power to set margins might be transferred to the Federal Reserve Board, where margin setting for the securities industry is determined. During a Senate hearing on the adequacy of regulatory action during the "silver situation," Comex representatives took great care to forcefully defend their competence and thereby their boundaries.

> In reviewing the history of the Federal Reserve Board in establishing securities margins it is interesting to note that there has not been any change in the 50 percent stock margin requirement for over five years. During the seven months in question, Comex changed original margin requirements regularly to keep pace with a dramatically moving and volatile silver market. To establish futures margins, regular review of futures markets and a constant awareness of economic factors within the markets is essential. No entity is more appropriate to discharge that responsibility than futures exchanges. As evidence of the effectiveness of futures exchanges in establishing margins, it should be noted that there has never been an incident of brokerage firm failure resulting from commodity defaults.[24]

Comex was not going to depend on the success of this presentation to defend its boundaries. One month later it was reported that "the CBT, CME, and Comex have joined forces to retain a high-powered Washington lobbying firm, Charles Walker Associates, in an effort to head off Senator William Proxmire's efforts . . . to shift margin setting authority to the Federal Reserve Board."[25] When the dust finally settled and the silver market had recovered, the exchanges had lost none of their self-regulatory powers.

The two cases discussed indicate several notable aspects of boundary maintenance. Both were set off by activity which was part of the market's operation. Both were the product of deep conflicts between traditional actors in the market. What separated this activity from all others was that it threatened the continued autonomy and legitimacy of the market control system. In both cases the communities rallied their resources and fought to defend their boundaries.

Both the bucket shops and the collapse of the silver market were in themselves damaging to the exchanges. Both caused a reduction in customers, the key resource input of the market. The exchanges took action to eliminate the problem, but found opposition from outside public or private agents. When this opposition threatened the legitimacy of market custom and behavior, a boundary crisis was created. At this point the exchanges responded by quickly resolving their own affairs, i.e., the market conflicts, and defending the issue of their actions in a public forum. In maintaining their boundaries the futures markets have aggressively sought and acquired legitimation. As the public interest in particular markets increases, the process of boundary maintenance may be forced into public arenas more frequently.

Finally, it is important to note that both of these efforts restored competition to the market. Futures exchanges can never afford to stray too far from conditions of free and open markets. By eliminating the practices which were most costly to market members they sustained competitive conditions. That those practices eliminated were also those which society found least legitimate has helped these institutions of market control to survive despite opposition from Populism, Progressivism, and more recent reform movements.

Conclusions

In this chapter I have used the social construction perspective and systems theory to study formal structure in the futures markets. The analysis presented here has shown that behavior in these markets is highly structured. Futures trading is a competition carried on within strict rules. These rules are created and enforced within a well-articulated set of organizational arrangements. Players are closely observed and even punished on occasion. By stepping back from the pit, one begins to see the construction of the competitive arena and the institutional arrangements for insuring the reproduction of that competition. The analysis in this chapter reinforces J. R. Commons' notion that competition is not a natural process, but rather an artificial or social arrangement.

It can also be concluded that the shape these arrangements take is not arbitrary. Organizational arrangements are isomorphic with the market structure. Futures markets are organized as exchange associations. In these associations, control is formally democratic, access is formally open, and members share equally in the decision making. This, of course, mirrors the perfectly competitive market where all are equal and all have equal access to the process of price determination. But in the context of organizational arrangements, the free market ideals of unfettered trade are selectively displaced by considerations of maintaining the market and protecting the personal advantages of membership. The maintenance of competitive conditions, from which traders earn their living, requires the ability to control that competition, to routinize it, and to exclude those forms of behavior which threaten it.

These organizational arrangements constitute the market control system. As Figure 2 indicated, the various parts of the coordinating and control systems are linked by flows and feedbacks of cash and information. It is the system as a whole that maintains the market mechanism. Judging from the survival of exchange associations since the second half of the nineteenth century, the system is highly effective and robust.

The market control system really has three interrelated tasks. In the pit, where financial contracts are exchanged, efficient transaction is the central task. In fact, futures markets are most familiar to economists as exemplars of efficient transaction. In the coordinating system and formal control committees the task is discovering problems in the pit and taking whatever corrective action is necessary to protect market efficiency. The task of the Board of Directors is the management of the material and symbolic assets of the system as a whole. This includes the management of exchange property, the production of new and innovative contracts to keep the exchange attractive to customers, and the maintenance of organizational autonomy in the face of potential government regulation. Each of these tasks contributes to the overall effectiveness of the market control system.

Finally, it is important to reiterate that the structures discussed are not the product of either economic or historic necessity. The market control system described here, copied at futures exchanges throughout the world, is the product of traders' efforts to enact a structure that would serve their interests and maintain the market. Organizational structures reflect the strategies of their creators. At the same time these structures are critical determinants in the process of reproducing the culture of the trading floor. Each new generation takes for granted the structures and strategies it receives.

TAMING THE MARKET: CONFLICT RESOLUTION AMONG MARKET MAKERS

3

Suppose someone has a percentage of the marketplace that is larger than we are comfortable with. Our staff would contact the firm. If it gets to the point where they are not going to move, the Business Conduct Committee will get involved and possibly we will send out a letter to them saying that "We think your position is large. We know it's large. We are watching you closely. You, as a member, have a responsibility. You may be called in later if this market functions in a disorderly way. You may be called in for manipulation . . ." So everybody has a responsibility and it is passed on down and it's monitored to see that it happens.

A trader serving on the Business Conduct Committee

The futures pit is an arena for intense competition. Nevertheless, even in the highly competitive futures markets opportunists may attempt to disrupt the competition for the aggressive pursuit of their own self-interest. When a trader attempts to manipulate the price of a commodity by acquiring a "high percentage of the marketplace" it is known as a "squeeze." This opportunistic strategy involves crossing a subjective line from competition over into conflict. The opportunists push their exchange partners into financial positions which they, and perhaps others, consider "distorted." Parties no longer compete over price in the open market. Rather, the opportunist confronts his victims and the victims either succumb to his power or demand the protection of the market control system.

This chapter and the next examine market control under conditions of market conflict. I will argue that the practice of market control, which traders call "self-regulation," is not simply a neutral arbiter of market relations. It is a powerful tool for both the pursuit and restraint of self-interest. I observed the practice of self-regulation through the analysis of three cases of market conflict that occurred during my fieldwork in these markets. These cases illustrate how opportunistic action may serve as the catalyst to escalate normal levels of competition into market-rending conflicts. Informal control breaks down, coalitions of rival market actors emerge, and status quo power relations are called into question. In these three cases, the market control system is used in practice to resolve conflicts.

Historical Context

Futures markets were first formed in the United States in the middle of the nineteenth century. Since that time a complex body of rules and regulations has been elaborated by generations of traders. The Chicago Board of Trade (CBT), the first and largest futures market, was established in 1848 and inaugurated its self-regulatory structure in 1865. I will use the development of self-regulation at the CBT as my model because its history is well documented, although the development of the New York Mercantile Exchange (1875) appears to be quite similar.[1]

The CBT was established with a heritage of rules of trade that had been developed by merchants at trade fairs since the eleventh century. The trading instruments and by-laws established in 1865 were extensions of regulations in the areas of contract terms, payment, inspection, and sampling developed at such fairs. What were really new were the formal hierarchical arrangements discussed in the last chapter, developed to enforce order in the market.

In 1848 the CBT was a loose association of local merchants created for the general advancement of commerce. Among its first acts in that year were efforts to get the State of Illinois to improve the canal system and to pass legislation for a general system of banking.[2] As the volume of trade increased in Chicago with the extension of the railroad, the association added the functions of

standardization of contracts, establishment and enforcement of rules, and arbitration of disputes. By 1865 a structure of committees accompanied by a system of rules and by-laws was in place. The most important rules to be developed and enforced were those defining the conditions of rule violation and specifying the consequences of such a violation, including fines, suspension, and expulsion.

This organizational rationalization complemented the rationalization of commodities trading accomplished by the formal adoption of the futures contract itself as the instrument of commerce on the CBT. The futures contract evolved out of conditions developing in Chicago in the 1850s. As Chicago became a central Midwestern market, farmers and merchants began to arrange for delivery of specified amounts of grain on particular dates. The first record of "forward" contracting in Chicago appeared in March 1851.[3] Such contracts were informal. Quality was not standardized, terms of payment varied, and contracts were not interchangeable. By 1854 the CBT had standardized weights and in 1856 it had fixed grades.[4] These new terms were quickly incorporated into forward contracts. It was not long before people with capital recognized the potential for profit in simply buying and selling these contracts for speculation. By the early 1860s standardized futures contracts were being bought and sold by farmers and merchants as well as by a growing pool of speculators at the Chicago Board of Trade. The unique character of these contracts is that they are for later consummation. There is no exchange of title and only one or two percent of contracts ever result in delivery. Most are simply closed out before the consummation date by an equal and opposite transaction on the part of the trader. A trader who had bought 5,000 bushels of wheat for delivery by November fifteenth would sell them before that date rather than take delivery.

At almost the same time that the futures contract was developed, the CBT adopted its first rules to restrain behavior. In 1863, it adopted a rule providing for suspension of any member not complying with contract terms. By 1865 procedures for recovery from default, arbitration of disputes, and provision of a security deposit on all contracts (known as margin) had been developed. Since that

time the Board of Trade and all other exchanges established thereafter have added to the mechanisms of restraint at their command. While use of these mechanisms has not been consistent, causing scandals and protests in the Populist and Progressive eras, it has always been sufficient to insure the survival of the institution. As noted in the previous chapter, futures exchanges have been clothed with a legitimate right of restraint by Supreme Court decisions.[5] This right has been questioned and curtailed, the de-regulation of fixed commissions in the 1970s being the outstanding example. But it has never been overruled. Those restraints which apply equally to all traders have remained relatively uncontroversial. It is those applied to single traders or small groups that are most frequently disputed.

Strategies

Market control systems perform a number of functions such as public relations, government relations, collection of statistics, development of uniform standards, and arbitration of conflicts. These functions reflect the strategic goals of a broad cross-section of members of the associations. By coordinating their efforts, traders are rewarded with the provision of expensive services and avoidance of some aspects of competition (standard sizes and contract design, knowledge of other traders' purchases and sales). Among the most important services provided to members is conflict resolution. Strategies of conflict resolution are put into effect when a trader or group of traders uses their dominant position in the market to affect the price of a commodity. The application of strategies to resolve conflict is less universally supported by Exchange members than those mentioned earlier. The point at which free competition becomes unfair competition is ambiguous, making intervention often unwelcome. The point at which reasonable restraint becomes damaging depends on who is benefiting and who is being hurt by the application of restraint in the market.

Students of government regulation know that strategies for the restraint of market-threatening competition in such areas as electricity production and railroads have often been delegated to the government's economic regulatory agencies.[6] The futures industry had no regulatory agencies on which they could rely back in 1865, so it created its own hierarchical arrangements based on the mutual dependency of its members. Like the Interstate Commerce Commission and the Civil Aeronautics Board, the self-regulatory associations (exchanges) maintain the conditions that will support continued profits and the survival of firms already in the market.

For the majority of members, the most desirable condition in the futures market is competition.[7] Ongoing competition attracts the commission-paying speculators from whom most members draw their income. Participants rarely want the market to be dominated by one or a few traders, for this creates an instability in which small traders are easily wiped out. Futures markets, therefore, act in the interests of the majority of their members when they prevent anti-competitive behavior. Even before the era of federal regulation, exchanges had acted to adjust their rules and contract specifications so that the extreme power plays or "corners" of the nineteenth and early twentieth centuries were much less likely.

Once an imbalance of market power exists on either the buy or sell side, the resolution will disproportionately favor one side or the other. Each actor uses the power at his or her command to get a favorable price. Large traders with extensive market positions can have a greater effect on price than can small traders. This is particularly true as the delivery date for contracts approaches and traders with large positions are able to withhold contracts from those seeking an offsetting trade. At this point the competition reaches its peak as aggressive traders push their advantage.

It is also at this point that market manipulations occur. Holders of contracts to buy may demand delivery on a short supply and exact an artificially high price. Holders of contracts to sell may aggressively flood the market with the commodity and bring the price down by delivering. In either case liquidation of outstanding contracts is not orderly, in that prices may rise or fall very sharply a few days before the contract closes. To a certain extent such competition occurs frequently as traders press their advantage based on the available supply of the underlying commodity. But, as the delivery date approaches and there are very few traders left, the competitors begin to address each other. The action shifts from competition over an abstraction (price) to conflict between opponents over the limited number of contracts left to buy or sell. On occasions when price fluctuates widely in the closing days of the contract the conflict results in accusations that the market has been squeezed or manipulated.

The implication is that at some point, to be determined retroactively in each situation by regulatory or self-regulatory authorities, aggressive trading becomes market-tampering. This involves a reaction to practices deemed unacceptable in terms of the interests of the members (or certain members). The free market is then really only free within the limits prescribed by members of the market. Although manipulations were fairly common in the early days of the exchanges, exchange rules and laws have since been established to inhibit them. The notion of "free and open markets," used with frequency by my informants, has been redefined as the system developed. But what are these restraints, when are they applied, and by whom are they initiated?

The answers to these questions are complex. Despite considerable effort by legal scholars, no formal definition of manipulation has been established. Neither the Commodities Exchange Act, the Commodity Futures Trading Commission regulations, nor any exchange by-laws contain a definition. There are, however, several characteristics that the courts have associated with manipulation.[8] Manipulations are usually alleged to include: (1) a dominant or controlling position in either futures or deliverable supplies; (2) a distorted price; and (3) manipulative intent. Each of these characteristics is difficult to define. Their definitions are situation-specific, constructed by those who have been harmed or who feel threatened. Their application has been inconsistent and enforcement somewhat random.

It is my position that manipulation is not a recognizable act, but reflects a reactive decision about the degree of conflict that should be tolerated in the market. Whether manipulation has taken place cannot be predetermined: there is no fixed point beyond which all actions are manipulative.[9] Rather, the definition is situationally determined according to whose interests are at stake and the amount of influence they can muster. It is for this reason that most accusations of manipulation are made after the fact, once the consequences of the struggle can be assessed by the interested parties.

Strategies for Conflict Resolution: A Typology

The line between competition and manipulation is clearly a matter of selective definition. Market members are reluctant to label any activity as manipulation. Self-regulatory officials prefer the term congestion, which actually describes the situation when traders on one side of the market are unable to find traders on the other side to liquidate their contracts. This bypasses the critical issue of manipulative intent. It simply describes a conflict between the two sides of the market. In the free market culture of the futures pit, most traders favor a hands-off approach in which contracts would be allowed to "trade out" to the advantage of those with the stronger market position. But in their role as regulators of the market, members have an interest in resolving this conflict, because it may create short-term instability in trading. Thus market congestion receives attention from member committees and staff offices assigned to monitor and resolve such conflicts. There exist several strategies at hand for this purpose: containment, formal restraint, and cessation. In the following typology these strategies are classified from least to most severe, and examples of each are given.

By far the most common strategy of conflict resolution is containment. This refers to the situation in which an expiring contract, such as May Treasury bills or the December stock index, is allowed to trade out under the watchful eye of exchange officials. Holders of dominant positions are cautioned to avoid any action that might be interpreted as manipulative, such as standing for delivery of more of a commodity than is available.

Should containment fail, the exchanges have recourse to strategies that more specifically limit the behavior of traders. The strategy of formal restraint involves the board of directors invoking emergency powers to establish temporary trading rules. Like the strategy of containment, the purpose is to induce orderly liquidation. This is to be accomplished by limiting activity in the market in several ways. These include: (1) limiting the size of permissible positions in a specific commodity; (2) reducing the number of available contracts in that commodity; and (3) increasing margin requirements. Each represents a different method for restraining the conflict between buyers and sellers.

The third and final type of conflict resolution strategy involves the total cessation of trading. Participants in the market shut it down—for their own good. Such action is extreme and rare. It usually sets off a string of lawsuits by those who feel they could have done better by playing it out, and it causes a major loss of income to members who would have profited from commissions. Needless to say, an exchange must feel extremely threatened before it will take such a move.

The two cases below introduce two market conflicts and the self-regulatory strategies elicited by them. The first, March wheat, is at the lenient end of the enforcement spectrum. The second, March potatoes, reflects the most draconian response available in self-regulatory practice. In the next chapter I discuss a variety of strategies that lie between these two extremes and come under the intermediate category of formal restraint.

Containment: The March Wheat Case

Under normal circumstances the market continuously resolves the question of how much will be bought and sold, by whom, and at what price. Under containment, the Board of Directors or a committee summons those holding dominant positions and tells them to maintain an orderly market. Traders will not be told exactly what they can and cannot do; rather, they will be encouraged to contain their activities to their present position. The chairman of the Business Conduct Committee of the CBT recounted one such encouragement: "The law allows you, and you have permission, to have 3 million bushels. This Exchange will not permit you to allow artificial prices to exist, in *our* best judgment . . . I want your pledge that if people get nervous on one side of the market (being the opposite side), you are therefore, for orderly liquidation, to make sure these prices will never get out of control."[10]

The exact nature of the expected containment is a negotiation between the traders serving as regulators and the traders acting as competitors. It assumes a shared understanding of the local connotation of such terms as "out of control." The subjectivity of the standard for artificial prices is signaled by the basis for evaluation: "if people get nervous." In such a case the trader still has considerable discretion. He knows there are now limits, but the limits are loosely defined and it is up to the trader to estimate how much aggressive behavior will be tolerated. There is always the implied threat that more severe strategies of resolution can be invoked or that the individual's behavior might later be judged manipulative, resulting in the imposition of fines, suspension, or expulsion. Thus, containment is to some degree equivalent to the warnings given by regulatory agencies, but containment reveals the informal and clannish nature of self-regulation. Containment is accomplished by the application of informal pressure tactics. Its meaning is communicated by the native terms for the process of containment, "jaw-boning" and "moral suasion," referring to a subtle but persistent influence process.

Case No. 1: March Wheat

The March 1979 wheat contract at the Chicago Board of Trade (CBT) presents a classic confrontation between buyers (longs) and sellers (shorts) in which the exchange made strategic use of its powers of containment. The basis of the conflict can be traced back to the small harvest of soft red winter wheat in the summer of 1978. This is the class of wheat that is most frequently and easily tendered for delivery through CBT contracts. Adding to the wheat shortage was a shortage of transportation facilities to move the wheat and of warehouse space in which to store it. Together, these factors represent the typical conditions for a squeeze: longs demand delivery on a large number of contracts when the deliverable supply is limited.

By September 1978, the CBT's Business Conduct Committee was aware of the shortage of deliverable wheat and ordered staff members in the Office of Investigations and Audits to watch the progress of the September contract. The following synopsis, adapted from the minutes of the Chicago Board of Trade's Business Conduct Meetings (6 September 1978–15 March 1979), shows the continuous surveillance that accompanies self-regulatory action at some futures markets. By September 15 the committee was already concerned enough about congestion in the expiring September contract to call in for discussion all traders with dominant long positions. The process of jaw-boning had begun. By September 18 concern had centered on Leslie Rosenthal, who would be a major player in the conflict over the next seven months.

9/6/78. Committee reviewed September complex; requested Office of Investigations and Audits (OIA) to watch September wheat. Requested OIA to obtain cash and stock information on wheat and determined the makeup of plywood positions of houses discussed.

9/14/78. Committee directed that letters be sent to participants holding one million or more bushels in September wheat futures.

9/15/78. Participants in September wheat appeared.

9/18/78. Donald Bidgood, Administrator of the OIA, advised committee of conversation with Leslie Rosenthal covering his futures position in September wheat. Committee requested OIA to monitor wheat.

10/2/78. Committee request OIA to obtain additional information and monitor December wheat.

10/16/78. Committee reviewed information concerning December wheat; requested OIA continue to monitor December wheat.

10/23/78. December wheat was discussed. Closer review of November contracts requested.

10/30/78. Reviewed December wheat situation; decision to continue to monitor.

11/20/78. Discussed December wheat contract; decision to continue to monitor.

11/27/78. Discussed December wheat; decision to monitor closely.

12/4/78. Requested letters be sent to participants holding one million contracts or more in December wheat. Also, decision to monitor closely. (Attached report detailing wheat supplies.)

12/7/78. Discussed December wheat; determined phone calls should be made to participants holding one million contracts or more in December wheat to inquire as to intentions.

12/11/78. Discussed December wheat; decision to continue to monitor. Meeting scheduled for 15 December 1978 to discuss the expiring contracts in wheat.

12/15/78. Leslie Rosenthal appeared and discussed the intentions of Rosenthal as it related to their December wheat house positions. Committee requested OIA to review and develop certain information covering December, March, and May wheat positions.

12/18/78. Noting material changes in wheat today, the committee directed OIA to continue monitoring the December wheat contract closely.

1/3/79. Decision to continue to monitor January contracts.

1/15/79. Committee discussed information concerning the monitoring of expiring wheat contracts as initiated in September 1978.

Committee requested that OIA continue monitoring the expiring wheat contracts.

1/22/79. Committee discussed certain information involving the March and May 1979 wheat contracts; decided to continue monitoring, paying particular attention to wheat contracts.

2/5/79. Committee reviewed information concerning the expiration of the March and May wheat contracts; decided to continue monitoring March/May wheat.

2/20/79. Reviewed March wheat.

2/26/79. Discussed March wheat.

3/2/79. Committee requested that letters be sent to participants in March wheat contract with 700,000 bushels or greater.

3/5/79. Discussed March wheat.

3/8/79. Committee reviewed March wheat contract. Directed OIA to call major participants, both longs and shorts, to determine intentions.

3/12/79. Committee reviewed March wheat; determined to call in major participants, both longs and shorts, for meeting later in the day to determine intentions. Discussed letter from CFTC regarding March wheat.

3/12/79. Major participants of the March wheat complex appeared individually to discuss intentions. Decision to continue to monitor.

3/15/79. Business Conduct Committee met with Board of Directors. (See minutes for Board of Directors meeting.)

3/15/79. Discussed day's activity in March wheat and determined that market continued to trade in orderly manner. Requested Wilmouth to so inform CFTC. Decision to continue monitoring March wheat on daily basis.[11]

In the December contract, the next expiring contract after September, the deliverable supply was even smaller. As the contract moved toward expiration the threat of manipulation increased. The committee again contacted the dominant longs. Rosenthal was once again summoned. After warnings from both the exchange and the Commodity Futures Trading Commission (CFTC), Rosenthal and a partner, Alan Freeman, continued to increase their positions until they held 75 percent of the remaining long contracts with only two trading days left. One trader finally did liquidate his entire position on the last day. The other stood for delivery of 2.2 million bushels of wheat. During the last three days of trading the price of wheat rose more than 25 cents a bushel. The CFTC judged this to be uncommonly high in relation to wheat at other markets.

After the experience in December the March contract was watched closely. Letters of warning were sent to major participants early in the delivery month. Several days later these traders were phoned to ascertain their intentions in terms of liquidation or delivery. On March 12, those holding major positions, both longs and shorts, were called before the Business Conduct Committee. At this point Rosenthal, Freeman, and two others held the vast majority of long positions. In later testimony the chairman of the committee described the meeting:

> These individuals gave me their verbal assurance that there would be an orderly liquidation . . . They agree(d) to keep it an orderly situation, because of the basic cosmetics, *that it looked bad,* that three individuals or four individuals or a small number of individuals can create a lot of bad-looking things, so that they must have utmost responsibility to the marketplace and to the people on the other side of the market. Those people cannot be allowed to pay outrageous prices.[12]

It is clear that the self-regulators had an ongoing concern for the integrity of the market. From this point until expiration, members of the Business Conduct Committee were in the pit monitoring the liquidation and jaw-boning with Rosenthal and his colleagues. The contract closed out on March 21 without any extreme fluctuation in price, but containment alone cannot be credited with the resolution. On March 17, Alan Freeman had sued the CBT to prevent it from forcing him to offset instead of taking delivery. The CFTC saw this as a threat of manipulation and ordered a suspension of trading. The CBT fought the suspension in court and won, but its containment was aided by the CFTC's threat.

The application of group pressure, which characterizes containment, belies the reluctance of exchange members to interfere with market integrity. The president of the CBT expressed this reluctance in a letter to a CFTC official. "Free markets like the Chicago Board of Trade must perform the passive function of recording all prices honestly arrived at, no matter how rational or historically correct they may or may not be. All of our efforts to maintain vigorous, competitive trading would be for naught if we felt entitled to intervene whenever the collective judgment of the market place deviated from that of our Business Conduct Committee or our board of directors."[13] In specific circumstances this comes down to a reluctance to tell an aggressive trader to limit his or her profits. It goes back to the notion of drawing the line between aggressive trading and manipulation. How much profit is too much?

Most traders resented the CFTC and CBT intervention. One informant put it this way: "Suppose they had let March wheat trade out and it went up a dollar. Even if the whole damn 8.8 million bushels had been liquidated at a whole dollar higher, that's 8.8 million dollars. Yeah, but how much is 8.8 million dollars? There's 160 million bushels of wheat in Chicago and more in Minneapolis and Kansas City. Now that's a lot of money. Well 8.8 million is a pittance to pay for the integrity of the market."

Despite this criticism, self-regulators are unlikely to let a conflict between the longs and the shorts go that far. There are too many powerful groups inside and outside the market, including farmers, several federal agencies, and Congress, demanding tighter control of opportunistic behavior. The next section examines a far more severe strategy, one in which self-regulators overcome their reluctance to use more formal powers.

Cessation: Case No. 2: March Potatoes

The New York Mercantile Exchange (NYME), the third largest of America's commodity exchanges, is more than a hundred years old. Its most active contracts are in potatoes, heating oil, and gasoline products. Our interest is in its March 1979 potato contract, which is based on the delivery of U.S. No. 1 round white potatoes from Maine.

To understand the action taken in March 1979, I will go back to May 1976. In that month the largest default in futures trading history occurred in the potato contract at NYME. Dominant longs had pushed the price sky high. Two Western potato growers decided that the price was inflated, since the new crop was coming in. They drove the price down in its closing months by high volume selling and by moving large quantities of potatoes to market. As the contract expired the longs were unwilling to offset. They demanded delivery of 50 million pounds of potatoes. The CFTC prosecuted the traders involved but also publicly blamed NYME for its inadequate self-regulation.

When the NYME Board of Governors suspended trading in its spring contracts on March 9, 1979, it came as a total surprise to most traders. On Monday, March 5, the administrative staff alerted the board that when shorts had begun delivery on the expired March 1979 contract it was found that 90 percent of the potatoes for delivery did not meet contract specifications. They had been damaged by bad weather during the growing season, but the pressure bruises did not show up until shipment. The board realized that if these early deliveries were bad, the whole crop might be undeliverable; the result could be a squeeze by the longs that would distort prices or, worse, precipitate another default.

On Thursday, March 8, the board met. In their haste to offset their positions, shorts had already driven up the price. There was no corresponding rise in the cash market, and the board felt that the proper relationship between the futures and cash price, which underlies futures trading, was in jeopardy. Some believe that the price could have been pushed from approximately six dollars per hundredweight to over twenty dollars per hundredweight.

Based on this potential manipulation, NYME ordered a cessation of trading in the April and May contracts and their liquidation at respective settlement prices of $7.16 and $8.14, which were their closing prices on Thursday. No one was forced to make delivery for March. At the end of the month a settlement price would be set by a special committee for any remaining contracts.

The major issue of contention was the speed with which NYME acted. Industry analysts wondered why the board did not wait to see whether the whole crop was undeliverable (it was not). Several informants claimed that the shorts were protected while the longs were denied a chance for profit. Nevertheless, the CFTC heartily approved NYME's radical strategy. One commissioner even called it "in the best tradition of self-regulation."

Yet the strategy of cessation is hardly traditional.[14] It is occasioned only by threatened or real defaults, which are the most serious conflict a self- regulatory body can face. A default is a refusal or inability to fulfill the legal obligations of a contract. Since contract performance is the premise upon which the entire competition is laid out, default would call into question the basic legitimacy of the system and its rules. By stopping the competition and setting a price the game is maintained, even if both sides are unhappy with the settlement. Of course, resolutions, especially such expensive ones, are hardly ever unbiased.

The Social Construction of Manipulation

The tension between opportunism and restraint, referred to in the introduction to this book, can be seen in microcosm in the social construction of manipulation. The attribution of manipulation arises out of a conflict between buyers and sellers where one side is pressing its advantage. The opportunist quietly, even surreptitiously, acquires a dominant share in the market. There is nothing illegal per se in pressing one's advantage in a market. Exchange officials are reluctant to restrain such behavior. In fact some degree of opportunism is deemed culturally appropriate. There is no fixed point at which aggressive trading becomes manipulation. The decision to intervene is subjective based on such local assessments of disruption as whether people "get nervous." The market control system is itself caught between members' interests in short-term profits and longer term legitimacy. The point at which manipulative action will no longer be tolerated is a variable rather than a constant.

In the wheat futures case the CBT saw no manipulation and allowed the market to trade out. In the potato futures case, the NYME saw the potential for manipulation and halted trading. These determinations were not made because of any difference in the real or potential strategies of opportunism employed. In both cases, the opportunists were responding to supply and demand factors in the market and applying a classic "squeeze" under conditions of short supply. The inclination to take advantage of such conditions is a constant. What varies are the conditions themselves and the threat of self-regulatory response.

Congestion in the balance of supply and demand conditions is, in fact, a relatively common occurrence in futures markets as contracts reach their expiration date. Exchange staff routinely monitor the closing days of contracts to see if either side of the market (buy or sell) is concentrated in the hands of a person or group. Some concentration is considered normal. One side or the other may press its advantage without much consequence. But there is an understanding that price variation must be limited. This is known as "orderly liquidation."

The process of jaw-boning and its goal of orderly liquidation is in itself manipulative, if manipulation refers to interference with the conventional market process by which price is determined with the intent of affecting price. In the midst of a culture based on the aggressive pursuit of self-interest and the integrity of market price determined at open auction, traders are told how far they may press their advantage and the ordinary forces of supply and demand are stifled. Jaw-boning and directed settlements reduce the strength of one side of the market. The attribution of manipulation is not an objective social fact, but rather a label for a social institution in which the winner in a competitive struggle is restrained and the loser is protected.

This argument suggests several questions. First, how deep is this culture's commitment to the free market? Second, why and when is the charge of manipulation applied? Third, and most important, what structural conditions are associated with who will be allowed to trade out and who will be restrained? These questions are explored in the next chapter.

RESPONDING TO EXTERNAL THREATS

4

In a congressional hearing room in May 1980, the Hunt brothers, oil billionaires from Dallas, Texas gave testimony about their role in the creation of a speculative bubble in the silver market and the self-regulatory response by exchanges in New York and Chicago.

Mr. W. Herbert Hunt: As I testified before, I did meet with the CBOT [sic] and Comex and they asked what my intentions were about futures positions and this sort of thing, and I basically told them that I was going to roll them forward, et cetera, as I had done in the past; that was my intention . . .

Congressman Deckard: Do you think that the decisions of these exchanges to take these emergency actions were disinterested?

Mr. W. Herbert Hunt: I think the parties taking those decisions were not disinterested parties.

Mr. N. Bunker Hunt: I would be interested in knowing, you know, just how much money the people who write the rules and change the rules in the middle of the stream made . . .

Congressman Jeffries: As a result of these events, in your opinion, who has been hurt? Who has been hurt the worst?

Mr. W. Herbert Hunt: At the moment I think you are looking at him.[1]

On October 26, 1979, the Chicago Board of Trade decreed that those traders holding in excess of 600 contracts for speculation in the silver futures market had to reduce their positions.[2] "You can't do it," was Nelson Bunker Hunt's incredulous reaction. "You wouldn't dare. You're the last bastion of free enterprise in the world."[3] Hunt found himself confronted by an organization with the power to redefine the rules of transaction and the temerity to violate the sacrosanct principles of a free market. Over the next six months the Hunt brothers of Dallas were to receive more lessons on the organizational context of free markets, as self-regulators sought to control what they regarded as a disruptive inflation in the price of silver.

The control systems in futures markets are reasonably effective at inhibiting extremes of competitive behavior among their members. Social control is provided by the informal mechanisms of containment discussed in the previous chapter, the formal restraints available to the exchange's self-regulatory associations, and perhaps most important, the reinforcement of internalized rules of behavior during the long apprenticeship period for market makers. But the market control system has little influence over outsiders. Opportunists with great wealth may gain access to these markets, trading through insiders who act as their well-paid agents. The outsiders are likely to be unaware of informal norms and beyond the reach of informal controls. Such an outsider could disrupt the market and challenge the insider elite. The result may be an externally generated market crisis.

This chapter demonstrates how market crises, such as the speculative bubble in silver in 1980, are managed by the market makers and their self-regulatory mechanisms. The traditional phase structure of speculative bubbles, typically described as mania, distress, and panic, is used to examine the repertoire of strategies employed by speculators, brokers, bankers, media, and regulators. These actors, who are members of overlapping and interdependent subcultures, engage in a conflict over the norms and rules of transaction. The crisis is the outcome of a struggle between these competing subcultures, each seeking to promote its own parochial interest. The crisis is resolved by the carefully orchestrated actions of government and market regulators concerned with preventing further damage to specific participants in this market and related markets. The resolution described here reflects economic behavior that is strategic, political, and highly self-interested.

The Social Construction of a Speculative Bubble

The economic definition of a speculative bubble as a deviation from the intrinsic value of a commodity has tended to remove the phenomenon from its social and cultural context. In contrast, this chapter emphasizes that a speculative bubble is a process of conflict between various coalitions trying to influence the rise and fall of an asset's price. This conflict is carried on in the context of rules, roles, and routinized control structures. During the critical period of the speculative bubble in silver, the rules, roles, and relationships that organize futures trading were severely tested by the actions of market participants.

My emphasis on the social construction of speculative bubbles differs from the economic view of bubbles, which stresses the irrationality of crowd behavior. In his *Manias, Panics, and Crashes,* economist Charles Kindleberger emphasized how price movements influence people, whereas I focus on how market participants strategically organize price movements. He assumed an atomized and disorganized crowd of market actors, but a social construction perspective concentrates on the purposeful actions of powerful actors and groups of actors. According to Kindleberger, speculative bubbles pass through three phases: mania, distress, and panic. These terms describe a cycle of emotions among the crowd.[4] In this chapter I emphasize that these phases result from and in turn influence three related processes: the actions, attributions, and regulatory efforts of powerful market participants. I will call the action-attribution-regulation process "enactment" in order to focus attention on how market participants create the environment that then impinges on their activity.

Kindleberger has argued that speculative bubbles are triggered by market shocks such as "the outbreak or end of war, a bumper harvest or crop failure, the widespread adoption of an invention with pervasive effects, . . . some political event or surprising financial success, or a debt conversion that precipitously lowers interest rates." Following Kindleberger, I will also call the first phase of crisis the "mania," but focus on how market traders take advantage of such shocks to realize profit opportunities rather than on how shocks influence crowd behavior.

The "distress" phase of market crisis is dominated by the attribution of blame for the disruption of normal trading activity. Those who have lost money, or are threatened with losses, begin to seek institutional changes to salvage their positions. In the "panic" phase, speculators rush to liquidate assets. At this point, the label "market crisis" is used to justify regulatory intervention that eventually alters the distribution of gains and losses from competitive trading. Economists generally agree that the actual declaration of crisis is preceded by a shortfall in the supply of credit to market participants trying to cover their losses.[5] From the social construction perspective, the declaration of crisis is a political act in an ongoing competitive game.

The speculative bubble is a process governed by the strategic actions, attributions, and regulatory interventions of various conflicting coalitions. Figure 3 summarizes the relationship between the enactment process and the environmental conditions. The figure captures the fundamental recursive linkage between the strategies of market participants and the environments they create. According to this model, for example, panic can be initiated by the adoption or threatened adoption of new regulation. The announcement of anti-takeover legislation apparently contributed to Black Monday, the October 19, 1987 stock market crash, for instance, by precipitating an early sell-off that provided the signal for other investors, including program traders, to sell.[6] In the case of Black Monday, the recursive link between panic and regulation is clear.

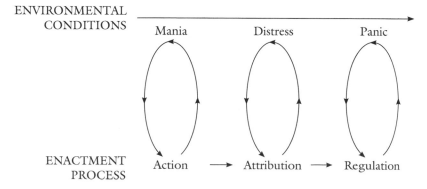

Figure 3. Cycles of organizing

Not only did regulation induce panic, but panic led to regulation: immediately following the crash the New York Stock Exchange tried to reduce volatility by limiting program trading.

The Silver Crisis of 1980

A speculative bubble is generally preceded by an exogenous shock (an event or circumstance outside the market). In the case of the silver crisis, the shock came from a spike in the inflation rate during 1979 from 12 to 20 percent. Although inflation had been climbing through the mid-1970s, 1979 was unusual. "Throughout 1979 the rate of inflation was near, and for a period of time exceeded, the cost of borrowing. This situation made investments in real assets such as precious metals particularly attractive, especially when leveraged by loans."[7] Inflation was a necessary condition for the silver crisis, but it is not sufficient to explain why the crisis occurred.

Strategic Action: Enacting a Mania

To analyze the fluctuations in the price of silver in the winter of 1979–1980, we must examine the behavior of the Hunt brothers of Dallas, who played a major role in determining the supply and demand conditions for silver in this period. The actions of the Hunts and their collaborators provide a textbook lesson on the entrepreneurial stage management of a speculative mania.

Nelson Bunker Hunt began buying silver, at least $20 million worth, as early as 1973.[8] Together with his brother Herbert, he switched to purchasing silver futures in 1973–1974, which required payment of only 10 percent of the value of contracts. The Hunt brothers found they could considerably increase their involvement in silver by using futures markets. By early 1974, the Hunts had contracts for the delivery of 35 million ounces of silver. Normally, speculators do not insist on the physical delivery of the products that they have contracted to purchase. Instead, they sell the contracts before the delivery date at a profit or loss. The Hunts, however, held on to the contracts and watched the price of silver futures rise as the March delivery date drew closer. The price climbed from $2.90 an ounce in December to $4 in January and $6.70 on

February 26. Current warehouse supplies were insufficient to meet the imminent demand for delivery. But the Hunts apparently underestimated the resourcefulness of their strategic opponents on the other side of the market, the sellers of futures contracts, or "shorts."[9] One short in particular, Dr. Henry Jarecki, the head of a major silver bullion firm, successfully deflated the Hunts' speculative bubble by convincing the Mexican government to flood the market with 50 million ounces of silver. The bullion dealers, who were members of Comex, the largest silver futures market, represented a subculture internal to the market. This group would not easily relinquish control over its domain.

The Hunts, however, continued to accumulate silver bullion and, by the summer of 1979, had accumulated at least 100 million ounces, worth approximately $500 million. They arranged to trade not only through their own accounts but also through a Bermuda corporation (IMIC) in partnership with two Saudi merchants. The Hunts also appear to have coordinated their trading strategy with a group of immensely wealthy foreign investors (including members of the Saudi royal family) represented through an omnibus account by a broker employed by ContiCommodity Services (CCS). IMIC began buying silver futures on behalf of the Hunts in July of 1979, and in August 1979 the CCS broker started purchasing on behalf of the omnibus investors. Together these traders represented tremendous wealth and shared remarkably similar trading strategies. They constituted a coalition of powerful outsiders largely immune to the informal controls of the market.

Between August and October 1979, the price of silver futures soared from $8.97 to $15.92 per ounce. In September, the mania was heightened when the omnibus investors took delivery of 5,920,000 ounces of silver and paid $1 million to have it flown to Switzerland. By removing the silver from New York warehouses, these investors intensified the atmosphere of uncertainty and fear, reducing the deliverable supply and thus feeding the mania.[10] This highly unusual strategy of insisting upon physical delivery of the silver was continued in December 1979 when the Hunts took possession of 6 million ounces and the omnibus account had 16.82 million ounces delivered. By January 1980, the Hunts and the omnibus account together held claims on 50 percent of the deliverable silver inventory at the Commodities Exchange of New York (Comex) and 70 percent of the Chicago Board of Trade's. During this period the rapid price increase had attracted a large crowd of smaller speculators hoping to ride the Hunts' coattails.

During a mania, attribution and regulation are latent but significant processes. My informants in the silver market began talking about the Hunts' involvement as early as August 1979. The Hunts' strategy soon became an open speculative activity. The attribution of responsibility for this speculative activity to the Hunts was further validated by their unusual demands for actual deliveries on their contracts. While these attributions were fanning the flames of mania, an appreciation of the latent force of regulation was shaping the strategic actions of the Hunts. The complexity and caution of the Hunts' strategy reflected their understanding that manipulation was illegal and that both the exchanges and the Commodity Futures Trading Commission (CFTC) were monitoring the orderly fulfillment of contracts. The Hunts traded through dummy corporations, like IMIC, and spread their trading among many brokerage houses. In the early months, they allowed contracts to trade out in an orderly fashion at delivery. At this point, regulation existed as a passive constraint on their discretionary actions.

Attributing the Blame: The Strategic Control of Distress

The distress phase of market crisis is controlled by powerful traders who form coalitions to question the orthodox definition of the situation in order to salvage their potential losses. In the distress phase, the attribution of blame for the market manipulation is the chief strategic weapon employed by the market participants. The success of an attribution depends on the discovery of a readily identifiable scapegoat, whose market behavior can be portrayed as inimical to the best interests of market integrity. The Hunts, as traders pursuing a highly distinctive and consistent strategy that offended the prevailing market consensus, became visible targets for blame. The attribution of blame justifies the call for increased regulatory control to reaffirm the rules of transaction and the pre-existing social order.

In the case of the silver crisis, the speculative mania threatened to cause losses in the millions of dollars to representatives of the commercial silver trade. These actors were owners or managers of silver bullion trading firms who had been selling futures contracts to hedge their inventories of physical silver. They took the short positions opposite the speculative long positions of the Hunts. As the price continued to climb and margin calls required borrowing at very high rates of interest, many of these firms felt threatened.[11] By September 1979 a member of one of the largest firms reported that he was looking for ways to get out of silver futures. Although these firms were habitual rivals in the market, their common distress at the activities of the Hunts united them.

Among the traders threatened by the mania were several elite members of Comex and the Chicago Board of Trade, the two exchanges on which silver futures were traded. These elite members, insiders in the social hierarchy of the market, sat on exchange committees and on the Comex board of directors. Usually the bias of exchange members is to explain price changes in terms of the abstract forces of supply and demand. In this case the insiders needed to create doubts about the openness of the market. They needed to attribute the blame for the mania to a target more tangible than the "Invisible Hand." The damaged insiders cried foul and pointed to the Hunts and their partners. Rather than passively suffering through the distress of impending losses, the shorts acted together to manage the strategic attribution of blame.

By September 1979 exchange members at both the Chicago Board of Trade and Comex were aware that something unusual was happening in silver. Major floor traders began to avoid silver speculation because of its uncertainty. One member of the silver pit declared he would stay out of silver "'til those cowboys decide they're done." Bullion dealers who held short positions began pressuring Comex to take action against the longs. Comex formed the Special Silver Committee on October 3, 1979 to monitor the trading in silver. The committee, which was designed to avoid any appearance of conflict of interest, included no silver traders and was chaired by an economist who was one of the outside members of the board of directors.

The insiders' attributions were tied to their regulatory agenda. Behind the scenes, through informal talks between members and their elected board members, the shorts continued to press for direct action against the longs. In early September, the president of Comex responded to the pressure of the shorts by instructing exchange officials to request the holders of large positions to "monitor their situation." By September 17, the longs, in order to defend themselves against the imputation of market manipulation, had been persuaded to promise that no squeeze on the market was intended. The Special Silver Committee, in hearings from October through December, forced the Hunts and other large volume traders to explain their intentions in formal depositions. These procedures focused attention away from the unpredictable fluctuations of market prices and on to the trading strategies of a group of wealthy outsiders (the nonmember Hunts and their associates). The mania could be explained as the result of the deliberate actions by outside speculators, not as a hiccup in the supply and demand equilibrium. The Hunts and their partners, as highly visible outsiders, were perfect targets upon whom blame for the speculative bubble could be pinned.

Regulating The Panic

On October 26, 1979 the Chicago Board of Trade decided to limit to 600 the number of contracts that individual speculators could hold. As the quotation at the beginning of this chapter indicates, Nelson Bunker Hunt was completely unprepared. The Hunts had apparently accepted at face value the exchange members' fervent rhetoric in favor of unregulated trading, a rhetoric on which many observers have commented.[12] Ideologically, the Hunts and their opponents on the exchange were fully agreed about the virtues of free enterprise, but this ideology of freedom was more a self-justifying belief than a description of the degree of discretion allowed by the rules of transaction on the exchange. In practice, trading behavior was subject to the set of formal and informal rules that had been built up over the 120–year history of the market and usually operated invisibly to regulate the behavior of members. The Hunts had violated the norms by standing for delivery, trading in concert with allies, and going beyond the limits of accepted speculative practice. These violations triggered a response designed to reaffirm these limits in a visible way, as well as protecting the interests of the established members at the expense of outsiders.

The chronology of the application of constraints reveals a gradual escalation in the exchanges' struggle to manage the price volatility of silver in favor of the insiders. The October 26, 1979 imposition of position limits by the CBT was followed with a similar action by Comex on January 7, 1980. As the price of silver continued to rise, reaching 50 dollars per ounce on January 20, 1980, the Comex board realized that the containment efforts of its Special Silver Committee had failed to convince the longs to reduce their positions. On January 21, the Comex decided to go beyond containment to strategies of formal restraint. They declared a "liquidation only" order. The longs could no longer buy, they could only sell to bullion dealers and other commercial investors (i.e., the shorts). Not coincidentally, nine members of the Comex board held a total of 75 million ounces of silver in short positions and stood to benefit tremendously from the new regulation. This strategic manipulation of the rules of transaction reaffirmed the control of the self-regulatory system and reversed the speculative mania.[13] The price of silver immediately began to decline, bottoming out at $10.80 per ounce on March 28, 1980.

The pressure to regulate events in the silver futures markets came not only from members who faced massive losses but also from outside groups affected by the speculative bubble, such as the Federal Reserve Board and the Commodity Futures Trading Commission. These regulators were responsible for controlling inflation and interest rates and maintaining integrity in financial markets. During meetings in October, the four CFTC commissioners were equally divided between those who favored strong intervention and those who favored a free-market approach. On January 4, the chairman of the CFTC, James Stone, stated that it might be "embarrassing to the commission" later if they took no action. The same day, in a meeting with Comex officials, CFTC officials suggested the possibility of emergency government intervention. Position limits were ordered by Comex on January 7.

The Federal Reserve Board (FRB) was less ambivalent than the CFTC. Speculative activity had clearly inflated the price of silver, contributing to the nation's overall inflation rate. In addition, the Hunts' borrowings for speculative losses during February and March accounted for 12.9 percent of all business loans in the United States at a time when interest rates were reaching a historic high. Ultimately, it was the scenario of a domino-like collapse of major lending institutions involved in loaning money to the Hunts for speculation that most disturbed the officials at the FRB. Paul Volcker, chairman of the FRB, had warned American banks in October 1979 not to supply loans for speculation. He strengthened his warning on March 14, 1980, with specific restrictions on the financing of speculation in commodities and precious metals.[14]

As a direct result of this tightening of credit, the Hunts failed on March 28, 1980 to meet a margin call of $100 million from one of their brokers, Bache and Company. Several other brokerage houses, including Merrill Lynch and ContiCommodity Services were also severely strained. Similarly at risk was the solvency of banks that had loaned the Hunts money for margin as the price of silver declined. Among the most extended were First National of Chicago and Swiss Bank Corporation. Trading in Bache and Company was suspended on the New York Stock Exchange. There were calls for closure of the silver markets, and the New York Stock Exchange Index began a rapid decline as stocks held as security for the Hunts were sold off.

The panic phase of the silver crisis was short-lived. The possibility of a default in futures and the specter of amplified consequences in other markets brought forth a swift response from the government's financial disaster prevention unit. On March 21, a week before the Hunts' failure, Paul Volcker called a meeting of all the agencies that would be involved if a major brokerage house, such as Bache, defaulted. The meeting included the Comptroller of the Currency, the Deputy Secretary of the Treasury, and the chairs of the SEC and CFTC. They decided to keep the market open to avoid a panic at the banks and brokerage firms tied up with silver speculation. A week later, Volcker organized a consortium of ten banks to float a $1.1 billion loan to the Hunts.

An explanation based on the interplay of free-market forces would have suggested letting events run their course in the silver market. An explanation based on the social construction of market crisis suggested a much different scenario. The exchange officials took actions to reverse the fortunes of the Hunts and other longs, and the federal officials oversaw these actions, concerned with their timing and the impact they might have on other markets and the economy. Galvanized by the possibility of widespread bankruptcies among major lending institutions, federal officials had monitored the situation almost from its beginning, taking a series of increasingly strong actions themselves to ensure that the price decline was orderly and a spiral of bankruptcies was avoided. This direct government intervention ensured the survival of the interlocked system of banks, brokerage houses, and exchanges. The intervention prevented extended repercussions, even as it signaled a decreasing tolerance for manipulation and the increasing control over market behavior by outside regulators.

Market Crisis: A Social Constructionist View

From the social construction perspective, the speculative bubble in the silver futures market was caused by those who took advantage of opportunities created by market forces. The classic phases of mania, distress, and panic were dominated by the processes of action, attribution, and regulation. The speculative bubble was less a social contagion in a crowd than a social construction of self-interested actors. Although the crisis depended on an exogenous shock, only the speculative actions of these actors produced the cycle of mania, distress, and panic.

The silver crisis of 1980 can be understood as a struggle between three coalitions: insiders, outsiders, and government regulators. These coalitions struggled to create new environments, to impose their own interpretations on unfolding events, and to control the flow of regulatory action. The resolution of the silver crisis reflected the reassertion of control by the exchange and the government. The Hunts were skillful strategists, but their free-market ideology bore scant relation to the regulated reality. Regulatory power rather than the free market forced down the price of silver. Throughout the crisis, the market environment was an arena in which actors from interdependent domains competed for control.

The silver futures market, then, can be viewed as an arena in which dormant agents of market control were awakened and opportunists were punished. The Hunts tested the limits of the silver market's normative system and thereby revealed the boundaries of acceptable strategic action. The market community acted to prevent damage to the silver market, related markets, and regulatory institutions. The fundamental uncertainty of the silver market was not whether these agents of control would intervene, but rather when and with what severity. Timing and scope of intervention were critical in determining the velocity of the enactment cycle.

According to traditional economic analysis of speculative bubbles,[15] the silver crisis was caused by rising inflation and an increasing demand from both industrial users and market speculators. The surge in the price of silver was "needed to signal both holders of silver to give up their positions quickly and buyers of silver to cut back their demands."[16] Prices were high because the system needed high prices to be in equilibrium. In this view, the price escalation is defined as a servant of market equilibrium, rather than a symptom of market crisis.[17] The strategic action of both the speculators and the regulators, and the relationship between them, is replaced by abstract forces moving toward equilibrium. This perspective obscures the conflictual nature of crisis. The perspective developed here clarifies the role of strategy and restraint in market crises.

The strategic actions of the Hunts and the restraining actions of the exchanges and government officials represented the fundamental recursive cycle of the market crisis. The Hunts' actions influenced the regulatory responses of the oversight agencies, and these responses shaped the subsequent strategies of the market participants. Only by focusing on the strategic actions of key institutional and individual players can the shifts in supply and demand be explained.

In this chapter and the last I have examined three cases of market conflict. Knowledgeable human agents took advantage of opportunities created by market forces. But their pursuit of self-interest did not go unchallenged. In each case the self-regulatory system of the market responded to the conflict, employing strategies of restraint which favored one side or the other. In the next section I will use these three cases to examine the structural conditions shaping which strategy is chosen over another, and who and what determines "the integrity of the market" in any given situation.

Structural Conditions Influencing Choice of Strategy

Self-regulators are reluctant to stop competition. Market members believe that the exchange is an instrument for assuring competition. Longs and shorts are competing to see whose convictions about the direction of price are correct. Price registers the state of the competition at any given moment. Considering traders' deep commitment to and engagement in the competition, it is not surprising that in most situations they prefer to "let em fight it out." Glick quotes an egg trader on the Chicago Mercantile Exchange: "As long as we're set up with the economic system we have, we either have free enterprise—which means you can have squeezes and corners—or we have to control the thing altogether and not even have a futures market. My own opinion about squeezes and corners is that I don't think women and children belong on the markets. The person who gets caught in a squeeze should be made to pay. They know what's going on and shouldn't get caught."[18]

The law of supply and demand lies at the heart of the trader's belief system. For futures traders the law of supply and demand is more than economic theory. It is an institutional logic by which they attribute meaning and significance to their own behavior as well as to the behavior of commodity prices. It is the link between behavior in the pits and supply and demand in the world market that is critical. As long as traders believe that what happens in the pit is a reasonable facsimile of reality in the cash market, they are able to attribute their fortunes to economic forces rather than to the behavior of their aggressive peers. Thus, when traders express reluctance to allow intervention in the market, it is often accompanied by the statement that the market (supply and demand) will assert itself.

Reluctance to intervene is also a matter of costs. Any containment, restraint, or cessation of trading will deny members possible commissions. Also it is likely to hurt at least one side of the market more than the other; usually, traders who are winning the competition will be denied further winnings. Finally, the reputation of the market will be damaged and its liquidity reduced for some time. With all these costs it is reasonable to ask what factors can overcome this rational reluctance and why one strategy is chosen over another. The following four conditions shaped the choice of strategy in the silver, wheat, and potato cases discussed.

Degree of Government Involvement

Although the self-regulatory structure preceded the era of regulatory agencies, in the three cases discussed here government agencies were involved. These agencies are now part of the larger market control network. In recent years their involvement in these situations has become a major factor in the adoption of a self-regulatory strategy. In the wheat case at the Chicago Board of Trade, the CFTC sent warnings to the traders and the exchange. In the silver case at Comex, the Federal Reserve Board voiced concern seven months before the emergency, and the CFTC held meetings with the traders and exchange officials. In the potato case at NYME, rapid and dramatic action was taken with an eye to the regulatory consequences if another default occurred. But this does not mean that conflict resolution is only a response to federal prodding. In fact, several Congressional hearings were held to examine the slowness of federal response in the wheat and silver cases. In these cases the CFTC was a late entrant to the proceedings.

The influence of government involvement is also affected by the size and strength of the exchange. The CBT, by far the largest of the exchanges, resisted government intervention when it came and managed to limit its self-regulatory activity to containment, which it had begun before the government was even aware of the situation. When the CFTC ordered a cessation of trading the CBT took them to court and won the right to trade out the contract.[19] Comex was clearly aware of government pressure and kept the CFTC informed of its actions. Its strong but perhaps somewhat belated actions always received CFTC approval. Expressions of concern from Congress and the Federal Reserve Board were indirect and seem to have had little effect on the independent and deliberate action at Comex, which was actively protecting its members from the Hunts.

It is at NYME, at the time one of the smaller exchanges, that the hand of government is most evident. NYME had been blamed and fined for the 1976 default. Its audit and surveillance systems had been heavily criticized by the CFTC in a 1978 review. By 1979 NYME was extremely sensitive, if not vulnerable. The CFTC was not even aware of the delivery problem, but its potential response influenced what appears to have been hasty action in the potato futures market.

Not only are larger exchanges more capable of resisting federal pressure, they are better prepared to resolve conflicts. At both the Chicago Board of Trade and the Chicago Mercantile Exchange, the directors have a reputation for informal shows of strength. Committee and board members appear to act as elder statesmen. Several informants told stories of board members acting against their own interests on important self-regulatory matters. This respect for the authority of the board enables the CBT to control its members through containment and the threat of restraints.

Status of Dominant Competitors

The strategy chosen by an exchange to resolve a conflict is very much influenced by the identity of the dominant competitors. Status on an exchange varies on a continuum from elite insiders (members of the board of directors) to unknown outsiders. Less prominent members of the exchange are simply insiders. There are also prominent outsiders, the well-known, high-roller speculators. Dominant positions in the market require large investments, so they are held only by elite insiders and prominent outsiders.

This sort of status differentiation seems to undermine the formal equality required for perfectly competitive markets. But as sociologists have found in most other situations, the formal equality of an institution is often undermined when it comes to a conflict between insiders and outsiders.[20] Harold Demsetz made a similar observation about the stock market: "There is little doubt that self-regulators are motivated by a concern for society that extends beyond a narrowly conceived notion of self-interest. But there is even less doubt that their own interests and the interests of those with whom they associate most closely, their peers, will have an impact on their regulatory decisions."[21] The insider/outsider distinction has two major implications. The first is that treatment is not even-handed: insiders fare better at the hands of their peers. The second is that it is easier to get peers to put limits on their acquisitive tendencies than it is to control outsiders. The two implications operate together in the cases reviewed.

In the case of the Hunt brothers' dominant position in the silver market, the resolution reflects the strategic use of restraint by insiders against a prominent but troublesome outsider. While some in the industry claimed that the dramatic reversal of the silver market in January 1980 was a case of the market reasserting itself, other observers—among them the Hunts—identified a culprit more tangible than market forces.

They claimed the purposive restraining action taken by the Comex Board was a disguise for manipulative action intended to bring down the price of silver. The Hunts maintained that nine silver traders represented on the Comex Board held a total of 75 million ounces in short positions, a statement that was later confirmed by Senator William Proxmire, Chairman of the Committee on Banking. These traders stood to lose millions for themselves or their firms as the price rose through autumn. Thus, the Comex Board members can be viewed as having simply switched hats from traders to rule-makers in furtherance of their self-interest. While the Special Silver Committee, formed in October, included no one with silver interest, skeptics point out that the Comex Board acts much like a private club, where personal and collective interests easily mingle. Insider interests required that the speculative bubble be broken. It was fortunate for Comex that government and public interests agreed.

In the wheat case at the Chicago Board of Trade, the dominant positions were held by insiders. The two largest positions were held by Leslie Rosenthal, vice-chairman of the CBT, and his partner Alan Freeman. The board seemed justified in accepting Rosenthal's assurance that he would liquidate in an orderly fashion. Rosenthal had already made a very tidy profit on his 2.5 million bushels. Containment, then, is the strategy of preference when dealing with cooperative insiders. Not only can the board rely on the traders' continuing cooperation, those in a winning position need not be denied some degree of profit.

In the potato case at NYME, the shorts stood to take a beating if the price continued to rise. The longs who would have benefited appear to have been scattered unknowns. The shorts were large potato processors hedging their risk as well as traders from major brokerage and trade firms. It is not surprising that NYME's decision to set a settlement price at the current market price largely favored the shorts. In general, the maintenance of the market requires that hedgers and trade firms, who are the basis of and justification for the market, be protected.

Extent of the Conflict and Destructiveness of the Strategy

These two remaining factors are treated together because of their strong interactive effects on choice of strategy. Whether an exchange chooses to invoke containment, formal restraint, or cessation is influenced by the severity of the conflict and by the effect conflict resolution will have on the integrity of the market. To use a cliche, one does not use a hammer to kill an ant. In the market, overkill can be very costly.

If an insider, such as Rosenthal in the wheat case, is pushing a bit too hard, containment should be sufficient. In such a case the trader is simply behaving in a manner that is likely to have negative consequences for other members. When Rosenthal and his colleagues' actions raised the threat of manipulation, the CBT sent out a message to the traders which one informant summed up as, "Get the hell out of here—quietly." The CBT fought to avoid stronger action because of the destructive impact it would have on the profitable and widely used wheat futures market.

In the Hunts' silver case the conflict was at fever pitch when the exchange began its formal restraint. Silver prices had soared from nine dollars per ounce to fifty dollars per ounce in six months. Such volatility is profitable in terms of commissions, but it was clearly a distortion. The Hunts, with their hoard of silver and desire for delivery on expiring futures contracts, were firmly in position to squeeze the silver market. The jump in price had affected worldwide spot silver prices, as well as the value of the dollar and government securities. While Rosenthal's activities had barely affected the spot market, the Hunts' activities were damaging to the silver industry represented at Comex, silver-using industries, and other financial markets. The effects of the conflict were thus widespread. The restraining action taken was deemed necessary despite the destructive consequence it eventually had on trading volume at Comex. In this situation the industry was willing to take severe action.

In the potato case the relationship among the variables is clear. The board believed that if it did not take extreme action, the situation might result in a default. The consequence of a default may well have been the banning of futures trading in potatoes, which had already been proposed in Congress several times; any self-regulatory action was preferable. NYME had to demonstrate its willingness and ability to control the market. While the action was initially very destructive for potato-trading at NYME, it led to a revised contract in which traders had greater confidence and, eventually, to an increase in trading volume.

All the conditions influencing choice of strategy are closely related and may combine in a variety of ways. For example, an exchange may take strong action before a conflict has reached major dimensions because it is aware that outside pressure on the CFTC might force it to intervene at an early stage. On the other hand, the exchange may resist a destructive strategy even in a severe conflict, because of the profits being made on high-volume trading. But there is no single influence pattern, except that the most severe conflicts appear to result in the harshest remedies.

Limits and Advantages of Self-Regulation

I have discussed three cases in which the strategies for self-regulation restore competition to the markets through a purposive restraint of trade. Not all self-regulatory strategies involve such dramatic opposition of actors' interests; actors are often restrained by rules, procedures, or persuasion, before competition turns into conflict. Most regulatory actions are routine and have a negative impact only on a small group of traders or an individual. In general, market members have agreed to occasional temporary restrictions of their freedom so that market integrity may be maintained and their businesses may prosper in the long run. Firms come to accept controls as an occasional annoyance, sometimes favoring them and sometimes not. On those occasions where the limits of unfettered competition are tested, it pays to be an insider.

The markets discussed in this chapter are among the most free and competitive in the modern economy; indeed, economists often study these markets for their competitive nature and price-determining functions. In theory, futures markets ought to respond effectively to the laws of supply and demand: if one charts futures prices, they do look like a textbook reflection of price theory. Some, including commissioners of the CFTC, thought that the rise and fall of silver prices at Comex reflected the kind of automatic self-regulation of price first described by Adam Smith. Though market forces certainly exist, the behavioral realities of power, trust, and legitimacy are also present. A complex system of formal and informal restraints is invoked to inhibit the use of power, to maintain trust, and to restore legitimacy, when necessary, to exchange relations. These sorts of intramarket arrangements appear not just in oligopolies but even, and perhaps especially, under conditions of competition. Financial markets have found self-regulation a practical mechanism for the pursuit of common interests.[22]

There is probably an ineluctable limit to the efficacy of self-regulation. Financial markets will never be made up of members of equal power. Interests will always be aggressively pursued despite collective agreement, and the method of market restraint chosen may not always be in the public interest. For these reasons the futures markets are monitored by the CFTC. The government cannot tolerate manipulation or price distortion in the futures markets. When such manipulation threatens to have an unfavorable impact on an important or powerful industry, the balance of trade, the national debt, or the inflation rate, Congress and the executive departments feel compelled, or are compelled by interest groups, to exert control. It was issues such as fraud in the commodity options market, the explosive growth of futures trading in the 1970s and, in particular, the inflationary effects of the Russian wheat deal that led to the establishment of the CFTC in 1975, just as the Great Crash of 1929 led to the creation of the Securities and Exchange Commission in 1934.

But futures markets are too complex and change too quickly to be directly regulated by outside bureaucrats. Although regulators are capable of broad economic oversight and enforcement actions, there are regular adjustments in the parameters of the control system that require the kind of intimate knowledge of a complex and changing system that resides only in its operators. It is the market participants themselves who are most sensitive to changes in such system control parameters as margins and daily price limits. It is also market members who have the direct access and continuous contact with the players needed to monitor the subtle emergence of opportunistic strategies in the pit. And it is the social relationships and reputation networks of market members that make containment strategies effective.

A Modest Restraint

Markets makers have created elaborate control mechanisms, yet there remains room for opportunism in futures markets. Although I have focused on manipulation, simpler strategies of opportunism also exist. As in my discussions with bond traders, my futures market informants mentioned that they had seen others trade ahead of their customers, known as "cuffing orders" in futures markets. Despite Exchange rules and surveillance efforts to monitor the sequence in which transactions are completed, some traders cannot resist the seduction of taking a well-priced transaction for their own account, instead of assigning it to the account of a waiting customer. But in the futures pit such action is obvious to ones' competitors who are standing all around and it is less tolerated. "They make money initially. You will see them make a quick profit. And then they get greedy, feed on it themselves and they become more flagrant. And then, all of a sudden the pit realizes what they are doing . . . We might let him off a couple of times. But if he does it often the guys notice. When they know he's been in front of an order they are going to sell him the first part and then absolutely lay on the market. Crush him. Intimidate his trading."

Futures trading differs from bond trading in several ways that facilitate such restraint. First, trades are done through open outcry and are thus highly visible. Second, market makers trade with the same group of people every day, allowing reputations to develop and decline. Third, market makers are able to enforce norms through direct and immediate action. Traders in the pit clearly constitute a trading community. They know each others' business and have a shared sense of membership not visible in the atomized bond market. Traders know that a high level of cuffing on the trading floor may precipitate greater regulation. Their freedom is something they value very highly. Futures traders in the pit engage in informal control to maintain both their market and their freedom.

Despite the general acceptance of some degree of restraint by futures traders, certainly more than I saw in the bond market, there are clearly differences from pit to pit in the degree of restraint. Older agricultural markets tended to be more restrained, new financial futures pits less so. These differences were associated with different levels of tolerance for opportunism in each pit.

How is tolerance for opportunism established? There is a dynamic relationship between the actions of traders and the response of the market control system. When financial futures markets were first being created in the 1970s and 1980s, there was a rapid influx of novice traders into the markets. These young traders were often poorly capitalized. As their early efforts at trading failed, some became increasingly desperate, using opportunistic strategies, including reneging on trades, with increasing frequency. These pits became known for their higher levels of opportunism. The informal control system in these pits never became as strong as those in the older pits just described. A greater degree of opportunism is tolerated both by the pit community and the exchange. Yet, it should be noted that even these new financial markets are tame and highly rationalized compared with their nineteenth-century ancestors.[23] What Nelson Bunker Hunt referred to as "the last bastion of free enterprise" has attained a measure of restraint.

The last two chapters offer a picture of the strategies employed by market makers to "tame the market," i.e. keep the competition from overheating and maintain the flow of benefits derived from providing a marketplace attractive to outsiders. Self-regulators are, in fact, engaged in a delicate balancing act between profits and prudence. Although the seductions of supercompetitive profits may beckon to major insiders, they know that the market's legitimacy is essential to their long-term viability. In futures, where outside attention has been relatively minor and government regulation relatively weak, self-regulators have retained considerable freedom in their own domain.

HOMO ECONOMICUS RESTRAINED: IDENTITY AND CONTROL AT THE NEW YORK STOCK EXCHANGE

5

If you look at the rule book, and I've studied it, you'll see that the majority of those rules are concerned with conflict of interest and fairness and equity to the customer, and I'm telling you, it's a culture these guys believe. They venerate the rules. They think there is a rule for every circumstance. And they value that protection. They complain about the regulations, but they venerate those rules . . . What we've done here, because of this veneration for rules, this great concern for equity, is that we keep layering the rules. Something new comes up, someone says, "Well, that's not exactly what the rule says." O.K., add a new layer. Fine. You wind up with silly stuff . . . I'm a guy who loves the rules, studies them. But I know most of them are no longer applicable to what's going on.

Member of the New York Stock Exchange

My fieldwork at the New York Stock Exchange (NYSE) began in early 1990 and ended in late 1992. After the first several weeks I found myself reflecting on the differences between the trading floor of the NYSE and the trading floors in the bond and futures markets I had studied. It was striking that the market makers at NYSE were, on average, a generation older than the bond traders I had recently studied. Rather than holding MBAs, most of these traders had risen from the position of clerk, and many had inherited the business from their fathers. There were also architectural and technological differences, as well as differences in the structure of social relationships on the floor. But the most significant and telling difference was the strength of formal control compared with those other markets. The futures markets now seemed like the Wild West compared with the relative civility and order on the NYSE. Although the stock prices at NYSE were still volatile and capable of dramatic swings, the market control system dwarfed the one I had observed in the futures markets in both size and complexity. The floor of the NYSE was still far from a bureaucracy, but it seemed that Exchange rules and "obligations" played a comparatively intrusive role in the world of its market makers.

Exchange officials were far more visible on the floor than they had been in the futures market. There seemed to be a higher concentration of floor governors (members acting as self-regulatory officials). Market makers, called specialists at NYSE, frequently consulted with floor officials for a ruling or a variance based on special circumstances. Most of all, the rules were part of their everyday conversation. Among themselves members would present ambiguous situations for comment and interpretation. When talking with me they would explain trading by citing rule numbers: 104, 106, 390. Surprisingly, traders were relatively unconcerned about the layers of rules. In general, members exhibited a boastful pride in the rules and in the rules' consequences for a fair and equitable marketplace: "We have a clear, transparent, proficient, regulated, and pretty damn terrific marketplace. Better than anything they have in Australia, better than anything they have in London. I've visited Amsterdam. I've visited London. We're the top . . . We're a national asset." Other traders are more ambivalent about the continual updating of the rules: "The people that designed this place did a phenomenal job as far as rules and regulations. I get very upset every time I see a minor rule change because I think it weakens the place. Some of the rules may have been changed for the better. Some were certainly worse. The jury is still out on it." Frequently, NYSE members expressed pride in their market in comparison to others: "This is a public place and what goes on in a public place has to be different. In an over-the-counter market you can do a lot of things that people would say are unacceptable in a public place. I stood in the commodity pit. If you wear a beard and I think its barbaric to have hair on your face, I will never trade with you. I can avoid your bid . . . But once you make a marketplace public, you can be held to a higher standard."

My first reaction to the pride and rule veneration displayed by members was skepticism. Were these market makers exaggerating the importance of the rules and their own adherence to them for my benefit? If so, why? Certainly, the bond and futures traders hadn't bothered to impress me with their veneration of the rules. My earlier research in those markets had exposed vast gray areas in the rules and how these rules are used to an insider's advantage. But none of my informants had ever talked about rules with the frequency and reverence these specialists did. In fact, most other market makers had been unguarded about revealing opportunistic strategies and rule violation in their markets. I was familiar with accounts of the 1920s at NYSE when specialists aided and abetted "bear raids" and manipulated their stocks.[1] Had something happened at NYSE in the intervening years to make today's specialists into rule venerators? Was the veneration sincere?[2]

This chapter examines the relationship between the market control system at NYSE and the identity of its market makers. I will explore the proposition that identity and control are linked.[3] Changing contingencies in the environment of the market makers trigger efforts to control market makers' behavior. These control efforts by the self-regulatory association, in turn, re-shape the market makers' identities. Identity and control have varied together among market makers on the floor of NYSE. I will use historical accounts, as well as my own data gathered at the New York Stock Exchange between 1990 and 1992, to understand the nature of restraint on the floor and the contradictions reflected in the identity of NYSE specialists.

The Setting

Walking in at 11 Wall Street is like entering any other downtown office building, except for the guards that stop you just past the second set of doors. If you don't have a NYSE I.D. badge hanging on your suit they expect you to state your business. At a second checkpoint you use your badge to pass through the sensor or await a member who will come out and sign for you. Even after I received my own ID badge, the security ritual often reminded me that I was entering America's temple of capitalism.

After passing these checkpoints, you are immediately surrounded by the din and bustle of "the floor," actually four connected trading rooms. Raised high above the floor is the podium from which a bell is rung to begin and halt trading. All the area above your head is dominated by electronic displays carrying a continuous flow of information of all kinds. This includes trading volume, the Dow Jones and other averages, newswires, and, of course, "the tape," a consolidated and continuous accounting of transactions in NYSE-listed stocks on the floor and at stock exchanges around the country. Along the walls, below these electronic displays, are endless batteries of phones, staffed by floor brokers and their clerks and connected to securities firms.

The rest of the floor is taken up by the "posts" at which actual trading is done. Each specialist stands at his post, a six- or seven-foot space along the perimeter of an oval counter. The oval itself houses a dozen or more specialists, each handling his own group of stocks. Each NYSE-listed stock is currently allocated only to one specialist. Each handles anywhere from one to nine or ten stocks. (Most specialists are part of a specialist firm and are surrounded by partners trading in their own assigned stocks.) This is where the action happens, where markets are made. Some specialists, those with the most active stocks, are surrounded by a crowd of brokers buying and selling or just seeking information in a stock. Other specialists may be interacting with orders that come to the floor through an automated system called SuperDot, the Designated Order Turnaround System. Still others stand at the post waiting for business, responding to price inquiries, and bantering with others in the floor community.

Above the heads of the specialists are display monitors that face out to the floor. They list each of the stocks assigned by the Exchange to the particular specialist. Next to the name of each stock is the last price at which it traded and the price at which the specialist stands ready to buy or sell stock from his own account. Inside the post are the clerks who work for the specialist. They handle paperwork from the SuperDot system and keep the "book," an accounting of customer's orders that are above or below the current market price and therefore waiting to be executed.

The floor is noisy and crowded. It is full of members of the messenger squad and exchange officials, as well as specialists, brokers, and clerks. The noise level is a good indicator of trading volume: they rise and fall together. In this sense, "the floor" of NYSE is a classic marketplace in that it brings buyers and sellers together in a central location to determine price. But it is also quickly becoming an anachronism. In an age when bids and offers can be communicated electronically and matched by computer, the NYSE maintains its floor community. From the bell and the messenger squad to the consolidated tape and SuperDot, the floor encompasses both person-to-person and electronic communication. At its best, the Exchange assimilates technological change. But such change is not without its contradictions for market participants.

The Functions of the Specialist

The specialist has two major functions, agent and dealer. As agents, specialists execute orders for other members of the exchange. These orders either arrive at the post through SuperDot or are entrusted to the specialist by brokers on the floor. If the price of the order is other than the current market price the order is put in the specialist's "book" to be executed when the order price becomes the market price. The book offers the specialist a rough picture of supply and demand conditions in his stock. But large block trades (10,000 shares or more) from pension funds and mutual funds and more recently, computerized program trading, have added an increased element of uncertainty as they may instantly alter supply and demand conditions.

As dealers, specialists trade for their own accounts as principals. The specialist is expected to smooth disparities in the flow of market orders by buying or selling for his own account to narrow price changes between transactions and give depth to the market. If the best bid is 62 and the best offer is $62\frac{3}{4}$, the specialist may bid at $62\frac{1}{4}$ and offer at $62\frac{1}{2}$ to narrow the spread. Specialists' activity as dealers accounts for 10 to 12 percent of trading activity at the NYSE.[4]

As the reader may have noted, there is an inherent conflict of interest between the agent and dealer functions. As agent, the specialist is the guardian of his customer's interests in the market. As dealer, the public expects the specialist to put his own interest first. Observers of this conflict of interest have long suspected that the specialist traded ahead of his customer's orders, taking the best bids and offers for himself. Proposals to segregate these functions appeared regularly between the 1930s and 1960s. They play a significant role in shaping specialist identity.

The specialist has at least two other less important functions. He serves as a bystander in a large number of transactions between institutions (e.g., pension funds, insurance companies, and mutual funds). An increasing share of NYSE trading volume occurs in large blocks of stock where the price of the transaction has been arranged by "upstairs" traders. Once the parties to the transaction have agreed on price, the block is traded at the specialist post. The specialist is, in effect, a bystander. The specialist also, at times, serves as auctioneer, setting what he thinks is a fair price in his stock. This occurs most frequently at the opening and after trading halts, when he must look at the buy and sell orders since the last transaction and find a price that he thinks will clear the market.

A Legacy of Control: Internal Control

The two-hundred-year history of the New York Stock Exchange reveals a legacy of successful internal control efforts by market makers. As in the futures markets, control here does not refer to control over price. That must be allowed to fluctuate freely to keep the market attractive to customers and maintain market legitimacy. Rather, control refers to such self-regulatory restraints as who may trade, under what conditions, and how much it will cost to trade. As described in earlier chapters, market makers create informal and formal rules to preserve and enhance the advantages derived from the markets they have created. NYSE members trace their history back to their earliest control effort, a historic pact signed on May 17, 1792 by a small group of brokers at 68 Wall Street:

> We, the Subscribers, Brokers for the Purchase and Sale of Public Stock, do hereby solemnly promise and pledge ourselves to each

other that we will not buy or sell from this date, for any person whatsoever, any kind of Public Stock, at less rate than one-quarter of one percent Commission on the Specie value, and that we will give preference to each other in our Negotiations.[5]

This pact among the traders, called the Buttonwood Tree Agreement, focused on two strategies for the advancement of members' own self-interest. The first was that commissions charged to customers were to be fixed by the group, thereby avoiding competition among themselves. The second was that members would deal preferentially with each other, thereby excluding others from the collective goods created by participation. These rules were venerated for 183 years until pressure from several agencies of the federal government and a change in the securities laws forced negotiated commissions and the beginning of a national market system. The pact reminds us that the Exchange was, from its founding, a club with rules that benefited the financial interests of its members. The members had strong incentive to maintain tight control over commission rates and limit access to their market.

The role of "specialist" did not emerge on the Exchange until the 1870s. The advent of continuous trading, as opposed to the previous intermittent auctions, prompted busy members to leave orders with other members who would specialize in particular stocks.[6] Exchange lore has it that the first specialist was a member who broke his leg and was therefore forced to stay in one spot, handling his favorite stocks. The number of specialists grew rapidly. By World War I every stock on the exchange was assigned to a specialist who would be responsible for making a market in that stock.[7] In the 1920s specialists became central players in the manipulative pools of the era. These pools played a significant part in the demand for and establishment of federal securities regulation in the 1930s.[8]

Unlike bankers and brokers, New Deal securities regulation had little effect on specialists. Despite the perceived conflict of interest between the agent and dealer functions, specialists retained complete control over their domain until well into the 1960s. Specialists successfully defended themselves against the efforts of the regulators. The House version of the progenitor of the Securities and

Exchange Act of 1934 contemplated the elimination of the specialist function. The Act itself only called for a report to consider
segregation of the agent and dealer functions. The Segregation Report (1936), written at the new Securities and Exchange Commission, failed to recommend segregation, but echoed the 1934 Act
by directing that "the specialist's transactions should be limited to
those *reasonably necessary* to permit the specialist to maintain a fair
and orderly market." In 1937 the Securities and Exchange Commission (SEC) issued an interpretation of the report, examining in
particular the phrase "reasonably necessary." In 1970, Wolfson and
Russo wrote that the Saperstein Interpretation was the last formal
Commission announcement on permissible dealer activities of specialists until the 1960s and "evidently had little effect."[9]

The Commission was apparently so ineffectual toward specialists
in this era that it became part of the lore relayed to me by several
specialists in the 1990s. The first two chairmen of the SEC, Joseph
Kennedy and James Landis, put little pressure on the Exchange.
When William O. Douglas became chair in 1938 he told NYSE
leaders, "The job of regulation's got to be done. It isn't being done
now and, damn it, you are going to do it or we are."[10] Douglas
eventually accepted a deal in which the NYSE agreed to implement
a program of self-regulation and reform of the Exchange governance structure. NYSE leaders would compromise with Douglas on
every point except on the issue of the specialists. As one specialist
explained it: "The president of the Exchange went down to Washington to negotiate with the SEC. The SEC said, 'We're going to
separate out the broker and dealer function.' There was some nod-
ding and agreement in the room and then the president of the Exchange said, 'That's fine. We're not opening Monday.'" The threat
of a "capital strike" was too much even for Douglas in 1938. He
backed down on specialists.

Specialists' control efforts were rewarded. They enjoyed nearly
unquestioned power from the 1930s through the 1950s. Specialists became the dominant force on the Exchange floor, replacing
the investment bankers and their floor representatives who had
dominated in the early part of the century, but were decimated by
the Depression and securities regulation.[11] Robert Sobel, a close
observer of Exchange politics, believes that the specialists' rise is

largely explained by the SEC's decision not to segregate broker and dealer functions. It left the specialists unscathed to fill a power vacuum.[12] Joel Seligman, in his history of the SEC, explains how the floor leaders, primarily specialists, took control:

> Soon after Douglas's departure from the SEC, the reforms in the New York Stock Exchange's governance structure negotiated in 1938 began to erode. The Exchange's floor leaders, led by Robert Stott and John Coleman, first secured a formal expansion of their power in 1941 with the creation of an Advisory Committee, to which the Board of Governors delegated certain disciplinary questions and the power to recommend the allocation of securities to specialists. The Advisory Committee generally followed the recommendations of the floor leaders.[13]

The Douglas reforms were further undone in 1950 when NYSE amended its constitution to increase the power of floor members, including a provision that increased the number of floor members on the Board of Governors. During these years the specialists dominated the exchange leadership positions. They also increased their aggregate trading for their own accounts. Between 1952 and 1959, their trading increased by approximately 50 percent.[14] During this time specialists were among the most powerful traders in the markets they made.

A Legacy of Control: External Control

By the 1960s the era of internal control was coming to an end. The dominance of the specialists on the floor was challenged and replaced by the "member firms," the securities firms that used their seats on the Exchange to act as brokers. It was the member firms' institutional customers that increasingly accounted for the pick-up in volume. At the same time it became clear that specialists were ill-equipped to accommodate the large block trades of the institutions. In thinly traded markets, the specialist was unlikely to have adequate capital to trade with an institution. The result was that large gaps in price would develop. Specialists were increasingly unable to maintain "fair and orderly markets."[15] It was only a matter of time until regulation caught up with them.

The critical test of the specialist system came in May 1962. A dramatic bear market (a predominance of falling stock prices) had developed in response to President Kennedy's firm response to a U.S. Steel price hike.[16] The market went into a tailspin and did not recover until July. When the SEC investigated, it found that during the crisis a number of specialists had failed to perform their market stabilizing function by not buying enough stock in a falling market, although others had performed well. It also found that the specialists held undue power on the Board of Governors, the Advisory Committee, and the Nominating Committee in relation to the member firms (brokerage houses). As a result of the Special Study, as the investigation became known, and subsequent negotiations with NYSE, the SEC implemented Rule 11b-1. It required, for the first time, that the rules of the New York Stock Exchange must include five basic provisions regarding specialists.

1. Adequate minimum capital requirements.

2. An "Affirmative Obligation" requiring that a specialist engage in dealings for his own account to assist in the maintenance, insofar as practicable, of a fair and orderly market . . . Substantial or continued failure by a specialist to engage in such a course of dealings should result in suspension or cancellation by the exchange of the specialist's registration in one or more of his specialty stocks.[17]

3. A "Negative Obligation" limiting specialist's dealings to those reasonably necessary to maintain a fair and orderly market. It is a warning not to distort the market through excessive trading. The terms "reasonably necessary" and "excessive" continue to be ill-defined but generally agreed upon.

4. Provisions defining the responsibilities of specialists as agents.

5. Procedures to provide for effective and systematic surveillance of specialists.[18]

These rules were adopted by the Exchange and revised through the 1970s and 1980s. They continued the shift in control away from the specialists and into the hands of their customers, the member securities firms. External control efforts were also enhanced as the SEC became more active.[19] The Exchange became increasingly responsive to its political environment. Power migrated to an increasingly large, professionalized, and independent Exchange hierarchy that was concerned with multiple constituencies, especially the member firms and the federal government. In 1972 the specialists' political dominance of the Exchange was ended when SEC-inspired reform created an equal number of public and industry directors on the Board, leaving specialists with only token representation. In 1975 nearly two centuries of fixed commissions ended after pressure from Congress and the SEC. In 1976 control of the allocation system for stocks was taken out of the hands of the Board and a system of performance evaluation for specialists, based on a survey of their customers, the floor brokers, was instituted. Most significantly, the trading environment was rapidly changing. The increase in block trades and program trading reduced specialists' ability to interact with, let alone influence, the market.

The specialist has endured a massive erosion of power and control. Much of the behavior of the abusive and swaggering old market maker, described in greater detail in the next section, is no longer possible. The growth of large institutional trades, program trading, and order flow with which they cannot interact has reduced their centrality in the market mechanism. At the same time, their domination of Exchange governance has been undermined. The affirmative and negative obligations and the stock allocation system are powerful restraints in their work life, altering their trading identities.

Trading Identities

What was it like before the era of external control? Many of my informants, who came into the business at the end of the old era, remembered the "characters" of that time. They spoke of a time thirty years prior, when specialists were the dominant traders on the floor. They could use their privileged access to customer information to trade for their own accounts. "I was shocked when I first came into the business by the incredible power of the specialist. Talk about thieves and gonifs![20] It just blew me away. He might trade in front of you and call you something ethnic and you'd have no recourse because you would have to trade with him. I was staggered by it. I didn't think they had any concept of what a customer was. None whatsoever. Absolutely none."

They often got away with it because others had little recourse and were dependent on the specialist for future transactions in that stock. "They were so used to being bigger than everybody and bullying everybody and bluffing . . . If you felt ripped off by the specialist you could go and complain to somebody, but unless there was a blatant violation of the rules or some discernible thing with a witness, the specialist would just say, 'I don't remember Mitch telling me exactly that way. I thought he might have an interest in buying.' And you would say, 'But I told you I'd buy 50,000' . . . So the specialist would just say, 'Gee Mitch, I guess I misunderstood you' . . . A lot of that, almost all of it, is cleaned up now."

So specialists at times were known to use their market position to trade ahead of their customers. These same characters were not particularly concerned about external control agents. The legendary specialist Jeff Marcus was often mentioned by NYSE members. I heard this story in several forms with varying details that characterized both specialists' power and their attitude toward government regulators.

> Jeff Marcus was brought down to the SEC. I guess this was in the 1930s when they were first building the SEC. They interviewed Marcus. He was a little guy. Built like a bull. He was a Golden Gloves prize fighter. All of these SEC attorneys were interviewing him. They asked him what he did. They asked him what he made a year. He said, "A million dollars." They asked him what university he went to. He never graduated from high school. And these guys had all these marvelous degrees from fancy places. And Marcus said, "If you guys had any balls you'd come down and trade." And they had a hatred with a vengeance for the not-so-well educated tough guys that controlled a game that was so tremendously lucrative . . . I gotta tell you, in the old days a lot of this stuff happened. Whether it was John Coleman saying, "Find yourself a new place, we're not going to open tomorrow" or a Jeff Marcus–type story where he put them in short pants . . .

Today's specialists think of their predecessors as powerful actors who had much greater control over their environment than they themselves have. Perhaps not all were like Jeff Marcus and John Coleman, but they were sharp and tough traders who could use their market position to bully and bluff. Today's specialists have learned to cater to their customers, the member securities firms, who are now the real powers on the floor. The specialists of the

1930s through the mid-1960s dominated their market control system. The specialists of today are dominated by market controls. The rule veneration described at the beginning of the chapter is one reflection of this. This is not to say that specialists are wholly unlike their predecessors or their market-making cousins in bonds and futures. Today's specialists exhibit the classic "trader's mentality" seen in earlier chapters, i.e. a risk-taking, hyper-rational, seat-of-the-pants cognitive style. But this cognitive style is coupled with a unique overlay of rule veneration. The following examples of traders' mentality could just as easily be found in the bond and futures markets.

> The specialist has to be of a mentality that risk is something he measures every day of his life. You can be highly educated, or highly trained, but when you're dumped into this system you still can't live with it. Very few people in the world are really good risk takers . . . What makes them good is knowing when to take losses. Any jerk can take a profit. That's easy to do. It's difficult to accept that you were wrong and you have to deal with that . . . A good trader knows when he's wrong. His ego does not get in the way. He turns around and sells off and comes back again. This is the hardest thing to do. You have to be very agile.

> We are not analyst-type traders. We are more seat-of-the-pants traders . . . The floor is not conducive to reflective thought. That is not to say that the people down here are not bright. It doesn't mean that they're dumb. They are just looking for what they really need to get done.

> Floor culture is direct and dynamic. You need to be as quick and as certain as you can be. They tell a joke about a guy from the floor who goes to buy a car. Most people when they go in, the salesman likes to walk them around. The floor guy is the type who walks in and says, "Do you have that in green with a radio?" The salesman says, "Yeah, but let me show you . . ." "Do you have it in green with a radio? Can I pick it up this afternoon?" That guy is used to buying a piece of XYZ corporation right now. Instantly.

> Being a specialist is not something very cerebral. It's something that is more of an art. Some people have a knack. Not too long

ago you had guys that never finished high school working next to guys that graduated from Harvard.

The trading mentality reflects the rather distinctive set of uncertainties faced by market makers in volatile financial markets. On the other hand, the rule veneration at NYSE gives specialists an occupational identity decidedly different, especially from bond traders in the over-the-counter market. This identity is based in an articulate, comprehensive, and moralizing ideology consisting of the institutional rules of the trading floor.[21] Among the most important rules are 1) the rule of agency and 2) price integrity.

The rule of agency, despite its legalistic sound, has been taken over as a native term on the floor. It refers to the understanding that the customer's order always gets executed before the specialist's at any given price. This rule reflects the clear recognition that market power has shifted to the customer, the member security firm, which evaluates the specialist quarterly to determine future stock allocations, pays a "negotiated" commission, and increasingly shifts its business away from NYSE and toward other competitive marketplaces. Usage of the term on the floor was remarkably consistent.

> The rule is pretty simple: agency orders come first, period. So the specialist can't have much conflict, really none. There really isn't conflict because the rule is so simple: At any given price, the agency order goes first.

> You remember also that on our floor the agent order at the price comes before the specialist's own purchase. That is a very important thing for keeping the game on the up and up . . . I don't think you want front-running and I don't think we do front-run.

> I don't even think about the rule of agency. There is a sort of rule of agency that transcends what the Exchange rules might be. But if you are an agent, whoever you are an agent for has to come before you.

> Because we earn a commission we have this agency obligation to the customer. You know, we act as their agent. Their orders come first. And in liquid stocks, where the customers have a big interest on both sides, you're kind of frozen out of the game because the customer comes first.

It should be emphasized that for the specialist, the "customer" is actually a relatively small set of floor brokers who represent the major securities firms. These are people with whom specialists trade continuously. Often, they have been in ongoing exchange relationships for years, sometimes decades. The sense of obligation is emphatic. Of course, it is now backed up by computerized surveillance at the Exchange, but one senses a deeper, internalized commitment. The following story, told by a floor broker about an incident that occurred when he was acting as a floor governor, expresses this native sense of the rule of agency.

> [A certain stock] was frenetic at best. There were thirty to forty people all screaming and bidding and I was the governor. I got up on the jump seat right in front of them. The specialist was gonna make the market, but I was the traffic cop. The worst thing that can happen is for a stock to be trading 95 on this side of the crowd and somebody else trading 96 over there. That's not what a centralized agency auction market is. So I was going, "It's his bid over here. You trade with him. This is still offered here." That kind of thing. A lot of screaming. After an hour it had calmed down somewhat. I told the specialist I'm gonna go down and get myself a Diet Coke. I got up and walked around the crowd. There were some earnest-looking young people in business suits standing with somebody from the Exchange. As I walked by, one of the gentleman said to one of the other gentleman watching this seething, pounding crowd, "Isn't it a shame what greed will do." I stopped dead in my tracks, and I said, "Excuse me. I don't mean to offend you, but you are looking at a crowd. If they were putting money in their own pockets, it would be greed. But you're watching fifty-year-old men risk heart attacks and friendships to get an eighth better for a person they never met. That's a rather miraculous thing. That's the rule of agency." The guy looked at me as if I had two heads. I found out later, they were trainees from the SEC.

The rule of agency is deeply embedded in the floor culture. I saw it being reinforced with specialist trainees and clerks. "You cannot go in front of one of your customers," they are often told. When adhered to, it was a means of reproducing an attractive and therefore profitable market. Its violation might endanger both the material and social rewards of membership in the floor community. One other rule shared this significance and salience for specialists, the rule of price integrity. This rule defines the kind of market mechanism specialists are trying to create. It encompasses notions of fairness, equity, and open competition, all of which are required for price integrity to exist. To the specialist, it is what makes "the floor" uniquely attractive.

> Fair pricing is exposing all bids and offers to the market. The method of price discovery, which is what we do for a living, has probably created a price that has more integrity than those prices created anywhere else in the world.

> It comes right back to the auction market being the fairest pricing mechanism that there is. Face-to-face contact, I don't know how you would put a price on it, but if a Salomon broker comes in, he is going to get a better picture, a better view, a better idea of what is going on over the last three or four or five days than he is going to get from a CRT screen . . . You have an actual two-legged buyer meeting an actual two-legged legitimate seller. And that has to be fair by the nature of the beast.

Price integrity is, of course, a subjective judgment. Specialists are fully confident of their ability to make this judgment. They have a strong sense of "where a stock ought to be trading." Much of this comes from their privileged access to the "book" which gives them a clear picture of supply and demand for the stock at an array of prices. But it also comes from intimate familiarity with a stock's historical patterns of movement. These patterns give the specialists a sense of how the stock "ought to move." Price integrity is said to exist when the market price best reflects these current and historical patterns. "When someone comes in and wants to sell fifty thousand shares of the stock, he should be getting the same bid no matter who he is because *that is where the stock should be selling* on fifty thousand shares. When you lose sight of that, you are lost . . . Merrill Lynch has an obligation to that customer. I have an obligation to the stock. That is the first thing you learn as a specialist. That is where it is at."

The notion of price integrity often came up when specialists compared their markets with dealer markets, such as the OTC (over-the-counter), with which they increasingly compete. Combining the rules of agency here with price integrity, specialists complained that in the OTC the dealer trades ahead of the customer, giving himself the best price. "The value that the Stock Exchange brings is to have all the fairness of execution, where all the orders are competing with each other. The best price. The specialist doesn't intervene unless there are no other bids or offers. In other systems, it is always dealer's order first, customer's order second. By definition." They also complained about an Exchange plan to allow after-hours trading without the specialist. In after-hours trading, large institutional trades could be matched without the intervention of specialists or any other customer. "The Exchange is now looking at after-hours trading where you could match up orders but not interact with the market. Institutions, brokerage firms could come in and put on prints [on the tape]. But these prints are only going to go on if no one interacts with them. *That is not integrity to a price.*"

The righteous tone of these statements reflects more than just the specialists' offended sense of propriety. It reflects a continuing threat to specialist power and ultimately, their existence as market makers.[22] While price integrity is an institutional rule, a guide to reproducing the market mechanism, it is also a legitimation of the specialist's function. At this point in the decline of specialist power, the two processes, reproduction and legitimation, are closely related. Having lost much of their power, specialists cling to the characteristic rules that define them and their markets. It is the latest phase of their continuing efforts to control their environment. They have woven internal identity and external controls into a complex culture of restraint.

A Culture of Restraint: The Prime Directives

Although the rule of agency says that a specialist may not trade ahead of his customer, it doesn't say anything about how the specialist should behave once he gets to trade for his own account. The affirmative and negative obligations, referred to above, are the basic rules of trading for specialists. The use of the term "obligation" denotes that specialists have been given a franchise to act as agent in their stocks. This franchise brings with it special benefits, among them commissions and privileged access to the orders on the "book." In return, specialists are obligated to perform their market-making function in a prescribed manner. This is an obligation that specialists have internalized.

> Well, let's face it. The specialist has a knowledge of what he's got in terms of the agency orders he has. So does he have an edge? Yeah, I guess he has an edge, if you want to define it as such. He has to balance that. He has to act responsibly in his agent role as well as his principal role and one of the things that does this is our own negative and affirmative obligation rules. These basically state that you can't over-trade and yet you had better be there when you are needed. That is probably not all bad.

The affirmative obligation is understood as the responsibility to make orderly markets. The NYSE Floor Officials' Manual asserts the formal expectation on this. "In performing as a principal a specialist should buy and sell securities . . . when such transactions are necessary to minimize an actual or reasonably anticipated short-term imbalance between supply and demand in the auction market and do not upset the natural longer term forces of supply and demand, and effect such transactions when their absence could result in an unreasonable lack of continuity and/or depth."[23]

The specialist is required to make bids and offers that will maintain the continuity of the price movement. To insure that specialists' transactions perform this function, the exchange has specified guidelines for every stock that it monitors closely through market surveillance. The guidelines define how much a stock should move on a transaction, e.g. $\frac{3}{8}$ for 3,000 shares. This tells the specialist when he is obligated to intervene. The specialist is obligated to buy or sell stock even though he may lose money on the transaction. By doing this, specialists provide liquidity in thin markets and reduce price volatility. This creates additional risk exposure for the specialists. Many specialists, used to the fixed commissions that provided a cushion of profits, find the risks created by the guidelines too high.

> Specialists are constantly providing liquidity when there aren't any real sellers or any real buyers. But the rules are that you have to maximize your exposure all the time . . . You can take hits. You

can't take $100,000 hits and make $25,000 profits. You can't make just eighths and quarters. If you are going to take that kind of risk, you have to have commensurate rewards. So, the rules of trading are changing a little bit. And how do I look at it? I find it difficult to change from years ago. My time has come to turn it over to more aggressive traders.

The negative obligation requires that the specialist not over-trade his stock. It defines what the specialist cannot do when he is trading. Basically, he cannot get in the way of orders coming to the floor and he cannot trade aggressively in the same direction as the market trend. The specialist is expected to "lean against the wind," i.e. sell when the market has moved up (an "up tick") and buy when the market has moved down (a "down tick"). Studies have found that specialists perform this function in as much as 90 percent of all their transactions and that it is a profitable strategy for them.[24]

> Our purchases and sales, by and large, have to be on stabilizing ticks. When we buy stock it has to be a minus tick or a zero minus tick and vice versa. That keeps us from . . . manipulating the market. When we want to do something on a de-stabilizing tick we have to get some sort of an O.K. from a floor governor or whatever. It is more of what we do to make the market the way it should be. The rules and regulations are there and we follow them.

Specialists seem to experience this as the most significant constraint on their trading, despite the fact that this contrarian strategy is generally profitable. As one trader explained, it keeps him from being as "aggressive" as he'd like to be.

> The market is a quarter [bid] and a half [offered] and there is fifty thousand offered at a half and the market is screaming and you would love to buy the half stock but it is a plus in our stabilization measures. That is not something you can do. You can't just take the offer or half the offer . . . You couldn't take it if stock hadn't sold there yet, any of it, without permission. You might be able to get a floor official to O.K. it, particularly if you were short and the market was screaming, to cover, reliquify your position. If it has already traded there, you can take half of it. You can't take all of it.

Specialists are conscious of being watched closely for "destabilizing" trades. This function is performed by the market surveillance department of the Exchange. As one specialist explained it, "You have to do a lot of stabilizing and a little destabilizing. If you are constantly doing destabilizing then your franchise is going to be at risk." There is, of course, a limit to how much stabilizing the specialist can be expected to do. The specialist is not expected to exhaust his capital in an effort to counter a long-term price decline. The specialist cannot support a stock that is in free-fall, yet the specialist has always been an easy target to blame. Specialist culpability for major market breaks is one of the myths about the market that most offend specialists. It is also the one that gets them in the most trouble. In the wake of major market collapses, like those in 1962 and 1987, specialists were targets of attention. Much of this attention has reflected both a misunderstanding of the specialist function and a contradiction between specialists' obligations and abilities and the need to find a scapegoat. As one specialist explained with rising anger:

> We had instances in 1987 where the specialists did *everything they were to supposed to do* and six months later the stocks were taken away from them because "they should have, they could have . . ." The guidelines were exceeded because of the situation. On a normal day you will not have the occurrences that took place on October 19th of 1987. But don't judge me by November 1990 standards. That is not fair. Judge me by October of 1987. I followed all the rules. I stepped out of the guidelines because the market was down five hundred points, not because it was down thirty points. The seller said, "Sold." You want to stop trading, fine, *but don't tell me that I should be doing something that really shouldn't be asked for.*

The situation described here suggests how fully specialists have accepted and resigned themselves to the culture of restraint. The affirmative and negative obligations are part of the economic relationship between the specialist and his customer prescribed in the rules. To the specialist they constitute legitimate restraints on his pursuit of self-interest. The specialist is willing to do "everything that he is supposed to do." He accepts his obligation to intervene in the market "on a normal day" as part of the responsibilities that come with the franchise. The specialist's moral indignation comes from his belief that financial suicide was not part of the bargain.

Bases of Control

The reforms of the early 1970s at the Exchange made the governance structure less like a private club and more like a public corporation. The thirty-three–member Board of Governors was replaced by a Board of Directors consisting of ten public directors, ten securities industry directors, and a full-time salaried chairperson. They created an administrative hierarchy that was largely autonomous of the floor community. Members who were used to receiving gracious service from the Exchange staff found themselves resentful of the power of the new administrative/regulatory professionals who represented an obdurate and consequential new structure. The growth of the administrative hierarchy at the Exchange, one that was increasingly capable and eager to oversee specialist activities, was a critical contingency in the changing identity of specialists. The dictum that administrative hierarchy, once established, takes on a life of its own, operated here.

A second critical contingency was the adoption of new technologies for the communication, storage, and retrieval of transactions. Specialists frequently credited NYSE Chairman John Phelan, who served from 1984 to 1990, with bringing the Exchange's technology into the twentieth century. This technology not only made transactions more efficient, it made them more available for surveillance. It provided the Exchange administration with the ability to monitor more broadly than it ever had. Both of these relatively recent changes enhanced market surveillance capabilities and reduced specialist autonomy.

Specialists believe that these changes created a significant deterrent to rule violation. Like so many others in the information economy, they find themselves closely though unobtrusively watched.

> They monitor us constantly. The Exchange sees every trade we make on a not-quite-real-time basis. It is sent electronically. They have files on everything we have done. They can see "the book" because it's all electronic. They have a whole surveillance system that is constantly looking over what we do. They may not look

at all that information or compare it every day, but there are eight surprise audits a year where they literally go through all the orders and compare them to the book, rebuild the average day that week. They take all the paper orders and see how they were executed and just reconstruct the whole thing. So if you are going to play games, you are pretty foolish.

The specialist feels he is going to get caught. Everything is in the machine. You can say "I made a mistake" once but after a while there are records . . . The consequences are fines, loss of stock, etc., depending on how far you've gone. You do it once, fine. It can happen. You are only human. The clerk can make a mistake and you sell short because you felt you would pair off and you had ten thousand to buy on balance . . . As I said you can't do it too often. If you do it too often there is something wrong with you.

The bullying and opportunism of an earlier era no longer made sense to the specialists. In the old days, monitoring was lax and informal. Today the risks are much higher.

If you were a little shady in your dealings, the margin of error was there. You had a cushion. You couldn't tell if a guy was a bad guy or just a sloppy record keeper . . . Originally, under the old system, it took several months to reconstruct the day's trading activity. So then they introduced the audit trail, which gives you the contra broker's badge number and the exact time the trade takes place. It gets compared the next day. So through the process of making a more efficient clearing system and locked-in trades, being able to recreate a day's activity in any stock in a matter of hours instead of a couple of months, the instilling of a greater sense of accuracy and the ability to monitor it with computers, it seems like you're in the world of Big Brother.

Consistent with this sense of being closely watched were the beliefs that any remaining rule violation would be caught. Referring to the affirmative obligation, one specialist said, "It would be great to open a stock here and let it trade there. Just do whatever you want. But the Nazis with the clipboards would come down and find you later." At a subtler level are the everyday conflicts of interest created by information that a specialist receives. There is a temptation not to tell a customer information that might negatively affect the specialist's own account. "If somebody tells you something and you don't tell the interested third party . . . shame on you. But you can't operate that way. You are in a fishbowl down there. The third party sees the trade [on the tape] and comes over and says 'How the hell could you let it trade there if you knew I was . . .' All they have to do is call a 'blue stripe' [floor governor] over and say 'I got a problem here.'"

The most consequential basis of control for specialists is not the direct policing provided by the administrative hierarchy. Rather, it is the indirect control provided by the rating and allocation system. Since 1976 specialists have been rated using the Specialist Performance Evaluation Questionnaire and a variety of other less subjective standards that include timeliness of openings and speed of response to SuperDot orders. The questionnaire is filled out quarterly by a specialist's customers, the floor brokers. They evaluate the specialist in such areas as provision of continuity and depth in the market and use of his own capital to maintain orderly conditions. The ratings are reviewed by a Market Performance Committee and each specialist unit is ranked relative to all others at NYSE. The Committee sets numerical standards below which a specialist unit may not fall. Specialists are subject to performance improvement actions during which they are supervised by a monitoring team. They may also be denied allocation of new stocks, and in extreme cases, stocks may be reallocated to other specialists. Fear of missing a desired allocation for a newly listed stock is widely considered the major deterrent to rule violation and incentive for performance. Good allocations have become increasingly important as mergers and bankruptcies eliminate listed stocks.

The establishment of the rating system and its use in allocation decisions reflected a major change in the politics of the Exchange. Allocation had been traditionally an act of patronage among the floor elite. As one specialist put it, "It was hickory dickory dock, which Board of Governor gets the stock." Another specialist explained the change in more prosaic terms.

> The rating system came in about fifteen years ago, maybe a little more. In the old days there was an Allocation Committee but they made the decisions based on politics. Either you were in with them or you were in with the [listing] company. A lot of people

used to go out and get companies to list. Allocation was developing a relationship. *You* put in all that money and effort . . . *you* should be the specialist. Finally, the SEC said, "That is not a fair system. Come up with something else." That is why we have the rating system, so the Allocation Committee can say, "If they are rated number one, they deserve the stock at this time."

The rating system is credited with tremendous power by the specialists. It is widely seen to have changed specialist behavior. According to one observer, the rating system has "homogenized" the specialist community. "The very good used to be here, the very bad used to be here. Now I think they're all good." This sense of the rating system as a community purifier was expressed in a number of different ways.

> By the middle of the 1970s specialists began being rated by the people they dealt with every day. That acted as a tremendous force to make the specialist system more professional. There have been a million studies since 1987 and you can see that the politicians are dying to fix the system. But they don't know how to fix it. They have solutions but they haven't figured out whether it [the specialist system] has anything to do with the problem or not, or what the problem was to start with. The problem's not with *us* anymore.

Another trader described the change as a new attitude toward customer service: "We get rated every three months by the people that do business with us. In the old days there were some not very complimentary things that specialists did. In other words, they weren't always totally aboveboard and open in putting buyers and sellers together because that's how they made a living. So in the past fifteen years that's changed. We've changed."

Other changes attributed to the rating system are the deterrence of "trading ahead" and an enhanced customer orientation.

> If you came and told me that you had stock for sale, and I said that there were no bids and I didn't have any interest, and then a guy came to buy 5,000 and I sold it to him, after half an hour you would come running out and say, "Who bought that? Do they need more?" In the old days [they] wouldn't tell you who bought it. They wouldn't tell you if they needed more. They

traded ahead of the customer. They operated without communication . . . With the ratings system brokers now had a way to get at you. If you didn't perform you didn't get those stocks and if you don't have the tools you can't make any money. So it made a real difference. It took the politics out of it.

Specialists are very conscious of the contrast with behavior in the "old days." One might even say that they are particular about distancing themselves from their predecessors. But this cannot diminish the dramatic changes that have occurred in the culture of the specialists and rationalization of the market-making system over the last thirty years. Loss of power and control has been accompanied by a rather dramatic shift in identity. In my early days on the floor I was skeptical of the authenticity of this identity. Are the specialists authentically reverent or is reverence a collective self-presentation for the sake of customers and the broader public? I conclude that it is both. Reverence is a conscious but authentic self-presentation. Specialists are extremely aware of the presence of rules in their everyday life; discussing, interpreting, and using them. They are also highly aware of their predecessors' reputations for chicanery. But that awareness cannot invalidate the conformity that has become a part of their lives. The awarenesses are mutually reinforcing. The evident pride that my informants showed in their reformed market was sincere. The differences between them and their colleagues in the bond and futures markets are evident.

Specialists are surprisingly satisfied with their culture of restraint. They seem genuinely proud that the pressures of the rating system have forced on them a higher standard of behavior. As one specialist said, "The machines got good and the rules got good. And we got good." Although this pride in the rationalization of one's profession must be judged as commendable, it also seems somewhat disingenuous. Specialists, like so many professions, have lost considerable freedom. They have come under the sway of the Exchange administration, a bureaucracy. Their actions and even their failures to act, to intervene in the market, are constantly monitored. In this environment, where the incentives for rule adherence translate into continued opportunity for high levels of return on capital, veneration and pride are rational strategies for survival.

Specialists engage in continuing efforts to control their major sources of uncertainty. As conditions in the market and in the political environment change, they shift strategies, but continue their control efforts. In the beginning control meant the formation of a quasi-cartel in which they controlled access to the market and the price of each others' services. It continued as control of Exchange politics and later regulatory politics. Today, specialists are struggling to maintain control over daily operation of the market-making mechanism as both its technology and regulation are increasingly controlled by others. The identity of specialists has changed with the changing market and political conditions. Identity and control efforts seem to vary together. From empowered tough guys who dominated the Exchange and bullied customers, specialists have been transformed into defenders of price integrity.

But this transformation may be too little, too late. The specialist community is part of a larger institution, the New York Stock Exchange, which is caught in a classic dilemma of advanced capitalism. At its height, NYSE dominated America's financial markets even more than General Motors dominated auto production. As in other industries, institutional inertia set in. The conservative tendency at NYSE was created by a deep psychological as well as financial investment in the existing trading system, the interests of powerful groups resistant to change, and the existence of a complex and sedimented system of rules. The specialists anticipate that dramatic change in the organization of the market may be imminent.

COPING WITH THE THREAT OF EXTINCTION

6

I think the bottom line is specialist profitability. Someone else might say that the bottom line is extinction. Okay, but that is a thousand-year war. Always has been. They have been shooting at the specialist since 1792. You can find Institutional Investor articles that go back to the late sixties and early seventies that predict our demise. Well, it hasn't happened.

Specialist on the New York Stock Exchange

The specialist community at NYSE feels threatened. Some members of the community feel certain that the days of the specialist as market maker at NYSE are numbered. Others recognize the threat but feel that they can adapt to new conditions if they are allowed. All agree that there is no more room for inefficient specialist operations. They see market share falling and colleagues leaving the floor at an unprecedented rate. The river of profits is drying up. But as the specialist quoted in the epigraph points out, the frequent predictions of specialist demise seem remarkably inexact, if not premature. These predictions have relied upon observed dramatic changes in technology and the structure of competition in the market. The extent of these environmental changes is undeniable. But decline and even extinction are not fixed processes fully determined by market forces. Just as market institutions are constructed by human action, they can be deconstructed in diverse ways. What is ignored by technological and economic arguments is that NYSE and its market arrangements are social and political institutions. Decline is a process that is constructed by the action of powerful interests competing for control of a still-formidable domain.

Members of the specialist community experience the decline differently and will therefore respond to it differently. Coping with the threat of occupational extinction is not a monolithic process. This chapter identifies the dominant patterns of coping that are manifest among the specialists on the floor of NYSE. I begin by examining patterns of emotional response and causal attribution, followed by the coping strategies themselves and expectations for the future. I conclude by showing why, despite powerful trends in technological and economic forces, the pattern of decline and probability of extinction cannot be predicted.

The Texture of Decline

In Chapter 1 I found that the booming bond market of the 1980s rippled with expressions of self-reliance, risk-taking, and optimism. These strategies reflect a market at its peak. Several city blocks away and several years later, I found myself in a market with a decidedly different emotional resonance. Apart from the loss of control that developed in the 1960s and 1970s as described in the last chapter, more recently, specialists have experienced a significant decline in their market share and rate of profit. Most specialists entered the business at a time when NYSE had a virtual monopoly in the trading of shares that it listed. This dominance has been challenged by "third market" firms that trade NYSE-listed stocks away from the floor and "fourth market" automated transaction systems that match trades by computer. Toward the end of my fieldwork at the Exchange, the Wall Street Journal ran a lead story about the decline. "[E]ven as the Big Board celebrates its bicentennial, it is scrambling to protect its steadily slipping grip on U.S. stock trading. While other markets here and overseas and cheaper "off-exchange" electronic trading systems were growing, the Big Board accounted for only 59 percent of U.S. stock-trading dollar volume last year, down from 76 percent as recently as 1981."[1]

Many observers outside the specialist community agree that the days of the physical trading floor are numbered.[2] Not only are electronic trading systems cheaper, they can operate around the clock in a global market. As the pressure from these competitors increases, the commissions at the Exchange are forced lower and lower. Moreover, a big slice of NYSE's market share includes trades that have already been arranged between member brokerage firms. The specialist neither interacts with nor gets commissions from these trades. Finally, the increased volatility from program trading has made the specialists' trading riskier than it was before. The following elegy came from one of the specialist community's least sanguine members.

> It was always a great business because we earned a commission on whatever we acted as agent on. There is tremendous pressure on us to give up that business now. There are new types of competition from the regionals and even a firm that draws off the risk-free business and does it cheaper; in fact for free, and in some cases it gives rebates for sending order flow to [them]. They buy it at an eighth, sell it at a quarter. Our system, if the market is an eighth/a quarter, the public buys it at an eighth, sells it at a quarter. The public always did better with us and for handling it we got a commission . . . Market swings are as great as they've been since 1987 and the most recent statistics are that only twelve of the forty-six units were profitable last year and that's a first. So these guys were used to getting obscene returns on their capital and now they're losing money. They're not used to it. They don't like it. And they won't tolerate it. So the system's going to give.

The specialists' responses to decline are deeply felt. They reflect the extent of disruption wrought by changes that threaten their financial viability. Whether the threat of extinction seemed imminent or distant, specialists expressed strong feelings about their competitors and the changes occurring in their business. The texture of decline emerges in three patterns of response: "ressentiment," indignation, and fear.

Ressentiment

Specialists' strong feelings offer a somewhat ironic example of what Max Scheler referred to using the French term *ressentiment*.[3] Ressentiment is the sentiment experienced by a disadvantaged group against those who have assumed the advantage over them. It consists of feelings of envy and hostility that are exacerbated by the relative powerlessness of the subject to act on the hostility and the continued reexperiencing of the disadvantaged status. According to Merton, ressentiment smacks of sour grapes.[4] Specialists frequently ridicule the competitors who are displacing them, e.g. dealers in the over-the-counter market (OTC), specialists at the regional exchanges, and traders in stock index futures and options at the Chicago exchanges. They speak with great vehemence about the superiority of their system in terms of execution (getting the best price), information centralization, and fairness to the customer. This is always said against the backdrop of order flow (market share) that is shifting to these competitors.

The ressentiment of specialists was common, reflecting the constant experience of seeing order flow that used to come to them going to their competitors in the third and fourth markets. The following quotations reflect specialists' dismay at losing out to rival market makers who always act as the dealer, taking the trade for their own account rather than placing it in the market to compete with other orders. Note that the first speaker refers to the OTC as "screen trading," a nuanced slur referring to the fact that OTC dealers sit at terminals rather than face their trading partner on an exchange floor.

> The industry perception is that screen trading is modern. In most cases screen trading is really archaic. Behind that screen are really multiple traders competing for order flow rather than competing with each other. If your order goes to firm A, firm B is never going to see that order. Orders are not going to compete with each other. I think the value of the Stock Exchange is to have all the fairness of execution, where all orders are competing with each other. The best price. The specialist doesn't intervene unless there are no other bids or offers. The public's order is always executed before the dealers' are. It is just the converse of these other systems. In other systems it is always the dealer's order first and the customer's second, by definition. But this debate doesn't really come to the fore. Nobody bothers to look at the process behind the screen.

In the quotation that follows, the specialist emphasizes his superior knowledge of the market for a particular stock and the better price provided by specialists.

A customer comes in here, wants to know what XYZ is doing. The specialist knows what XYZ is doing. He knows where the buyers are. He *knows* where the sellers are. He *knows* what's happened to the stock in the last few hours, last few days. The same customer can go to the OTC guys . . . whether the OTC guy makes a bid or not is up to them. Of course, [the customer] can hit ten different dealers with the bid, but he may get 80 at one place, 80½ at another.

Not surprisingly, specialists believe they have a better system than their competitors. They talk disparagingly about a "dealerized market."

If you look at the London Stock Exchange, it was always a dealer marketplace. It's now been electronically hooked up, so there is no floor left. But there was never really public participation in the marketplace, so it makes sense it was a dealers' market. But if you come here [NYSE] you have democratic with a small "d," very reflective of our culture.

At one level specialists' ressentiment may be interpreted as sour grapes. At another level, its prevalence reflects the specialists' disappointment at having gone through a difficult behavioral transformation only to find things worse instead of better. Having abandoned the bullying, bluffing, and withholding of information discussed in the last chapter, they feel like the good guys who came in last. This sense of history is reflected in a comparison with futures traders.

The futures markets are structured such that you have that whole pit of people trying to get in between the public orders that are coming into the pit. That is just what floor traders did here [at NYSE] in the fifties and before, before the 1962 thing, before they got more and more restricted. You know the futures market consists mostly of floor traders trying to make money out of the orders coming in. It is very strange when you step into the futures world from the stock world. In the futures world it is really "devil take the hindmost" and the customer is sort of the enemy. Rather than you trying to get the best for the customer, *they are trying to gut him.*

The specialists have been forced to sanitize their behavior by forces beyond their control. Now they find themselves at a disadvantage to new competitors never exposed to those forces. Although specialists are unlikely to elicit the sympathy given to other disadvantaged groups, their ressentiment is often impassioned. It reflects the substantial change in their status vis-à-vis competitors they long thought of as inferior.

Indignation

Specialists believe current conditions are unfair. Decline is experienced not only relative to one's competitors but to one's sense of what is just. The rules of the game have changed and now even the profitability of the game is declining dramatically. Specialists are no longer sure what is appropriate, or how to play the game. It is clear to them that the current regulated system is too constraining, but it is ambiguous as to what should replace it. The current arrangement, with the specialist as the central market maker, is at the core of their identity.

> You take this tough old group that didn't work with the customers, that were basically loners, loners and cutthroats and great survivors; and then you break them down and teach them that they have to work with the community. We don't know if we're supposed to be *good guys* that work together with people and communicate and share information, or are we going to go back to [being] *cutthroats*? We can do great at cutthroat. We know that game. That comes *natural* to us. But then you can't rate me at every quarter and say, "He's a cutthroat." So we have this tremendous conflict that we work under. What the hell is the role? Go along and get along or cutthroat?

Specialists are indignant that the rules of the game have changed for them and not for others who now turn out to be their competitors. They see themselves engaged in a competitive struggle for existence in which they are forced to fight with one hand tied behind their backs. The targets of this indignation are the differences in rules and regulatory systems between them and their competitors. Specialists talk frequently of the need for "a level playing field" on which they feel certain they could compete successfully in the new trading environment.

What bothers me now is that the rules are different for some of my so-called customer/competitors than they are for me. An option trader. He can buy and sell options, and buy and sell stock. Any quantities he wants. He can set up straddles or whatever he likes. I cannot do that. I am restricted by the Exchange, because there are rules. Why not give me the same leeway that an option trader has? We are both doing the same thing and *I* have affirmative obligation. Those rules have to be changed so we are all playing on the same level field, not where everybody there has different rules that they live by.

The unequal rules are probably the biggest handicap to the specialist and the biggest threat to this institution. We've maintained a higher plane of rules. Let's at least make the rules so that everyone can play on the same playing field.

Another specialist emphasizes that it is NYSE's rules that have not kept pace with the larger trading environment.

If you have a professionalized trading environment but specialists are still operating under rules that were written prior to that, where we basically work under a set of rules that were designed to protect what we called the "little old ladies" of the world, then you end up needing change. Our customer base has changed and no one recognizes it. Or they don't address it. It's very difficult to remove rules and regulations.

It seems somehow ironic that this group which once made its own rules and dominated the market finds itself asking for a fair shake. The politics and economics of the market have turned circumstances around to make specialists feel victimized by the rules. Specialists have long believed their market-making arrangements to be superior to all others, yet the "higher plane of rules" is killing them. They look to the Exchange for guidance and leadership but only find their indignation intensified.

What the Exchange is telling us is, "We are not going to reward your risk. We are going to take away your commissions, we are going to throw a bunch of order flow at you that you can't interact with and you are going to do a whole bunch of things for free. We are going to bastardize the consequences of the auction market and in return for that you are going to make deep liquid markets at all times or we are going to take your stocks away."

Specialists feel abandoned by an organization they once controlled. They criticize its corporate philosophy and bristle at the fact that Exchange employees call it "the company." Forced to give up control of the Board, specialists soon found that the Exchange had transformed itself from an administrative support role to a governance system. In the 1980s the rift between specialists and administration grew. During the administration of Chairman John Phelan, a popular figure and former specialist, the alienation of the specialists from their Exchange reached its peak.

> John, having come from the floor, couldn't understand why we didn't see the big picture. We could see the big picture; we weren't part of it. And John forgot that we weren't part of that big picture. You know, as he introduced all these systems and the rates changed, rules changed, competition changed, demands changed, we saw that big picture, but he didn't think we ever got the full picture. We got the full picture, we just didn't see our picture there.

Many specialists are indignant over the compromises the Exchange makes with its other constituents. "The political powers upstairs look at the world and say 'I have a broad constituency out there. Who do I appease?' Some specialists feel excluded from the process. There is a large element of dissatisfaction. There is hurt and anger over being excluded."

Fear

Amidst the pattern of hostile bravado is a quieter, less obtrusive thread of fear. The dangers eliciting this fear lie in growing threats to profits and survival. Specialists anticipate danger from several sources: the continuing erosion of commission-based profits, increased market volatility as a result of program trading, and actions on the part of the Exchange or the government that might exacerbate these trends.

> We never had these kinds of *volatile* swings before. It used to be that you could get a feel for the market from one day to the next.

If the market in New York closed strong at four o'clock, nine times out of ten you would open up strong the next morning. It has no relationship now. What happens in the rest of the world overnight can change everything. What happens in Japan, what happens in London, what is happening in Kuwait right now. All of that is factored in. Secretary Baker, when he was Secretary of the Treasury, was in Germany and made a speech at two in the morning. Totally affected the opening of the marketplace. And that wasn't true years ago. So it is much more difficult to trade.

Another specialist attributes the volatility of the market to new trading strategies among investment banks and institutional investors.

Trading has become extremely difficult because of big hits. We have had stocks that swung like *this* [gestures in a big arc] instead of doing this [gestures in a little arc]. And we have good, stable companies. But even within the community of good companies you have investment money, short-term money, hot money, hedge fund money that sometimes pushes stocks to an extreme. And when you push them to an extreme there has to be a correction and you don't know where the correction is coming from. You don't know when it is coming.

Though traders are not by nature or training a fearful group, many of the specialists have held their wealth long enough to become risk-averse.

There are many people down here who were originally in the center of this marketplace, who inherited the business from their families, generations of specialists. Some of the incentives for them to remain aggressive don't exist because of the tremendous amounts of wealth that have been accumulated. They want to protect that wealth. They don't necessarily want to bet it every day.

There is also a latent fear of a crash, like the one in October 1987 or the less severe one in 1989. Many specialists saw their assets eroded in these crashes. Some specialist firms have protected their assets through incorporation or liquidation since then, but most still feel vulnerable. Even five years after the crash, there was still widespread speculation about how individuals would fare in the next one. Many insist that they cannot be expected to support a free-falling market at the risk of their solvency and they are especially angry that no other market makers are expected to do so.

> The specialists I talk to say, "Hey look, you think I actually lived through October 19 and 20, 1987 and didn't learn something? Let them take my stock away. But I am not going under." Now nobody on that sixth floor [the executive suite] got shot at in October 1987. Those were *bullets* down here. One guy lost his entire firm. That is how Merrill got the business. He lost his firm that day. A lot of others came up short and took another six or seven months to go out. A lot of others had the shock of their life. People do learn. They are not that stupid.

Discussions of the crash often illustrate all the cross-grained features of the texture of decline: ressentiment toward competitors who stopped making markets in the middle of the crash, thereby "dodging the bullets," indignation at officials who expected specialists to stand and take unlimited losses, and fear that the next crash could wipe them out. The 1987 crash and the continued market volatility seem to have exposed the limits of specialists' tolerance for pain. Although specialists have mostly been commended for their behavior during that crash, staying at their posts and fulfilling their obligations, many deny they would be so cooperative were it to happen again. Not only are specialists demoralized, there is less commitment to the institution. There is a sense that the world, or the set of relationships in which they have long been embedded, is falling apart.

Decline as a Social Process

This place is like Beirut . . . Christians shooting at Christians.
                                    Member of the New York Stock Exchange

An economic decline, like that of the specialist community, is most often understood as the outcome of competitive forces. In most accounts of decline, competition is portrayed as a natural or impersonal force, like gravity. Resources "gravitate" to new and more efficient organizations. In ecological models the environment is said to "select" particular organizations for survival.[5] In both these perspectives, competition is an asocial process. Competing actors are isolated units and social relations are "frictionless": there is no conflict.[6] The competitive decline of the specialist community has been neither asocial nor frictionless. Rather, competition appears more as a political process. Competitors are active agents mobilizing their scarce resources to shape their environment. The actors in the competition recognize each other as contestants. They are mutually oriented, adapting to each other's moves and mobilizing for collective action. In this view, decline becomes a form of conflict in which strategy and tactics determine outcomes. This is the way that most specialists experience decline: as a continuous battle, or as the specialist put it in the epigraph at the beginning of this chapter, "a thousand-year war."

Specialists feel beset by rivals who are nipping away at the order flow that has been their traditional meal ticket. A steady order flow means commissions on the one hand and trading opportunities on the other. Most of these rivals are also customers.

> There is a tremendous competition for order flow. The New York Stock Exchange, in terms of the listed stock market, has been the principal garner of order flow throughout the years. That is a tradition that is somewhat ending; there is severe competition, tremendous competition, for this order flow, and I think the biggest problem for the specialist industry is how the Stock Exchange deals with it . . .

Although market share has been declining as new rivals in the third and fourth markets offer lower commissions, perhaps the most significant rivalry for the politics of decline is with the member brokerage firms on the floor of the NYSE. These firms are the specialists' traditional customers, the agents who bring them commission-paying orders for execution. In the past most orders came from individuals who called their brokers. Today, most trading is done by institutions that are comfortable going to the third and fourth market where transaction costs are lower. As a result, in recent years member brokerage firms' trading for their own accounts has become an increasingly important contributor to their own bottom lines. Specialists find themselves competing with the trading desks of their customers, customers who also want an increasing amount of customer service. Referring to the member firms, one specialist said, "The competition has gotten more pronounced. As member firms' commission income has dwindled, they are more interested in actively trading. So they begin to look more like competitors than customers." Another specialist put it more vehemently: "You are my customer, fine . . . but now you are competing with me. Don't tell me I should treat you as a *customer*. You are a *competitor*." Specialists particularly resent that these competitors continue to rate their performance on a quarterly basis for the Exchange.

> They sometimes use the rating system as a club. They hit you over the head. So you must accommodate because of the rating system and you must accommodate because they are your customer but . . . you don't want to accommodate because they are your competitors. Sometimes it works, sometimes it doesn't, and friction does occur on the floor between the Merrill Lynch broker and you, and you feel he is overstepping his bounds and it just puts you up against the wall . . . they are pushing too hard.

Specialists' greatest ire is reserved for the specialists at regional exchanges. They routinely refer to them as "parasites" and "leeches." Not only do the regional exchanges lack the regulation of NYSE, but the regional specialists "feed off" the NYSE specialist by buying at the specialists' posted "bid" price and selling at his "offer."

> Regional specialists take what we call "the dealer turn." They buy on the bid and sell on the offer. We don't do that. Our rules don't permit it. We can buy higher or sell cheaper but we can't buy and sell at the same price and, in fact, trade for our own account ahead of public orders. The regulations put us in a bit of a corner because they require us to favor the customer first, our proprietary trading second.

Another trader gives a concrete example of "the dealer turn":

> Let's say the market is twelve to an eighth [i.e., the bid is 12, the offer is $12\frac{1}{8}$]. They can buy it at twelve, sell it at an eighth. If they buy too much at twelve they come in and sell it at the New York Stock Exchange. So, they are never at risk, or small risk, and they have the ability to make an eighth. And the larger a market the New York specialist makes, the more they can do this all day

long. That, now, is a competitor, but on the other hand, he is also your customer. You have to facilitate . . . you have to try to treat him as a customer.

The process of competitive decline is hardly asocial at NYSE. There is constant direct contact. Customers are also now competitors and the pressure as well as the resentment is constant. They are mutually oriented to each other. Each is trying to lower their commissions and attract the order flow. The specialists' rivals, with fewer regulations, would seem to have some advantage.

This rivalry reflects a condition in which a once-strong competitor has lost his edge. The edge was provided by Exchange rules that required members to bring all trades to the floor, by control over information about supply and demand in their stocks, and by a continuous flow of orders with which specialists could easily interact. These advantages were enhanced by the limited surveillance of the Exchange and the limited power of customers to complain, as described in Chapter 5. It is hardly surprising that specialists look to the Exchange with mistrust and disappointment as their position erodes further. The Exchange, no longer under their control, answers to a broad and demanding constituency. Its own politics lead it to put continuing pressure on the specialist community, both in terms of regulations and the commissions it charges customers.

When I started here, as recently as 1969, exchange employees were here to serve the members [gives an ironic laugh]. That's changed. They're not here to serve the members, they're here to cause them trouble, raise their dues. The whole attitudinal shift is phenomenal. You couldn't have a legitimate error today and say to a governor, "Look, this is ridiculous, this is what happened, get these guys with the clipboards to go on to something else." You can't do it. You have to let them continue their investigation. And in the end, very few guys are not on the up and up.

Pressures to reduce commission rates are considered even more insidious:

There are big meetings going on now with the Exchange for the specialist community as a group to give back something that approaches 11 percent of our commission income, through different charges and arrangements and stuff. Give it back to the customers: Shearson, PaineWebber, Merrill Lynch. The Exchange tells them, "Send your order flow here. Don't send it to regionals. Don't sell it to Bernie Mayduff [a non-member trading firm]. Keep using our system and we'll cut our commissions by about ll percent." Well, you can do that about ten more times. And so then you've bought us out of business.

One result of these pressures from the Exchange has been expanding mistrust on the part of the specialists.

I wish I knew whatever the agenda is up there, because the agenda seems to pay lip service to the specialist system on the floor, and in my view, they are giving every manifestation of killing it. Now there has always been a fear in this building that there was a secret agenda. And that the secret agenda was to turn this into the largest regulatory body in the world. The biggest computerized body in the world. Why? Because then "the company" survives.

For the specialists, decline is political and personal, as well as economic. They focus on that which is close to home, their most direct customers and the Exchange administration. They are certainly aware of the abstract threat of changing electronic technology and globalization of markets, but it is their own network of relations that is most salient. It is through these relations that they will influence the process of decline.

Coping Strategies

Specialists, like the other market makers discussed in this book, are aggressive traders who attempt to control their fate. The strong feelings of ressentiment, indignation, and fear, discussed above, have not resulted in paralysis. Rather, they have energized an array of coping strategies.

Getting Out

One of the surest signs of decline is when existing firms get out of a business. From my first contact with NYSE in the late 1980s through my exit from the field in 1992 the number of specialist firms declined from over fifty to forty. Informants remembered a

time when their were more than 100 firms. Some of the earlier decline in the number of firms is explained by mergers designed to
strengthen the capital position of each firm, but increasingly the
goal of the specialists is to get their equity out before it's depleted,
as this specialist describes: "Two more mergers just since I saw you
last. Neither one went out because they're broke. Both just wanted
out of the business. In the first case, it didn't fit the parent firm's
corporate structure to be a market maker, a specialist, and in the
other case, the partners just wanted their money out. So two different reasons for getting out. If the business was so terrific, why
wouldn't they look to expand it? That's my point."

Other firms went out because they failed to adapt to changing
conditions. With the rise of competition and without the cushion
provided by fixed commissions, some specialist firms were unable
to make a profit.

> The Exchange has been criticized because we have never actively
> put any of the specialists out of business. But passively there have
> been a ton that have gone by the wayside, which is really the best
> way to do it . . . You are going to lose stocks just by attrition.
> We used to have [XYZ stock]. It merged. There have been nu-
> merous stocks that we have lost over the years and you have to
> replace those. The Exchange has an allocation committee and they
> will allocate new stocks based on performance and if your report
> cards are continually bad—you don't do your job—you are not
> going to get any product. If you don't get any product, it is not
> going to take a long time to figure out that you have to get out
> or merge with somebody else. We've had a lot of mergers. You
> had a lot of guys who said, "I can't do this anymore, and I can't
> contend with it." You always hear, "It's too political now." Which
> is really a cop out, a rationalization because they couldn't do the
> job. So they are gone and they are gone for the right reasons.

In the early stages of the decline it was the least efficient who
were getting out. As the decline progresses, it becomes increasingly
difficult for specialists to find a buyer for their franchise. As one
specialist put it, referring to a recent sale of a firm, "You would
think that if you wanted to retire you would be at meetings
every day for three months deciding which offer to accept. They

couldn't give it away." But getting out is, of course, the last resort. Strong firms are coping with the threat of decline with more proactive strategies.

Rationalizing the Business

Specialist firms were traditionally small partnerships of two to five or six partners. Each specialist was responsible for a small group of stocks and the firm pooled the overhead costs. Profit margins were so high that partners were casual about such costs as clerical help, health insurance, accounting, food, and entertainment. With the end of fixed commissions in 1975, and the increasing competition, partnerships got larger and larger through mergers. Nevertheless the old habits die hard. Specialists are still struggling to rationalize the business.

> [Those specialists had a] total and complete lack of knowledge of capital or return on capital or anything else. No plans. Occasionally a partner who was making six figures would throw a ten-thousand-dollar bill back into the firm. No plan. No forced savings. Everybody doing their own thing, so to speak. I talked to my partners about incorporating, and they said, "What does that mean?" The specialist business is a business today. It wasn't then. Inventory management [is v]ery important now.

Some specialists think some firms are still not as streamlined as they need to be to compete in the new market.

> There are firms on the floor today that had really big franchises that are still poorly managed. Very, very poorly managed. They don't listen. I really think it is time. They are still running huge travel and entertainment accounts, cars, country clubs, limousines, all the nonsense, and not running this business. Putting up holding companies and investing in whatever other things . . . This sort of firm, they are going to get killed.

The specialists have adjusted to tighter profit margins not only by reducing operating expenses but by reducing the amount of capital they have at risk at any time.

> Over $100 million has been taken out of the business over the past year. Not through losses, but through restructuring of what

used to be partnerships into corporations and then only meeting the minimum capital requirements so that they have the least amount of money on the line. No one wants to be a terminal partner. You don't want to work all those years to accumulate wealth and have it at risk. So they're restructuring to protect their private lives.

Specialists in such a rationalized structure are now often asked to account for their trading to the firm.

> If you are a specialist with [a certain] specialist firm a senior partner will say to you, "The stock that you are trading trades 3500 shares a day. You are now long four days, that's 14,000 shares." That's not a lot, but they relate it to the buying in the stock. Which makes a lot of sense. Then they will say, "You can get long 50,000 shares of Exxon, but you can't be long 14,000 shares of X." No specialist firm ever did that in this business. And then you have a chance to tell a story as to why you are long. If your story isn't very good, either you will get out or someone will get out for you. That just wasn't done years ago.

These kinds of rationalizing strategies insure that there is less capital on the line and therefore reduced risk. Other, more aggressive specialists are choosing strategies to increase their risk on the theory that, "You gotta be in it to win."

Increased Trading

If a specialist is not content merely to survive, but wishes to grow and increase profitability, he must look for new sources of revenue. Some of this can be accomplished by getting new stocks as they are allocated by the Exchange. A growing number of specialists feel that this will not be enough. They believe that specialists must trade the stocks they already have more aggressively. As one explained, "If the specialist will not be a more active trader, he will not be in business in three to five years from now. You can't stand there and write commissions. So, the specialist will naturally have to become a trader." Most specialists can remember a time in the 1980s when 60 to 70 percent of revenue still came from commissions. In the early 1990s it was more like 30 percent. The need for trading profits is clear. Another specialist put it in similar terms: "We have increased our velocity of trading. I am a firm believer in specialists being much more active. Quicker profits. Quicker losses. The days of coming in at ten o'clock, when we opened at ten, and working until 4:00 and catching the 4:01 out of here are over and gone."

Collective Action

Specialists feel misunderstood. The Securities and Exchange Commission "has it out for us." Journalists still describe them as the power brokers of the Exchange long after their power has dissipated. Even the Exchange administration seems to have "a different agenda." There is a sense of powerlessness that is at odds with their previous dominance of the Exchange. Until recently, the specialist community, as a group, had not responded to its changed conditions: "We have never defended ourselves in any way, whatsoever. The over-the-counter market does all kinds of ads about this and that . . . [the s]pecialist system never really has . . . We've been the brunt of criticism. Whatever example I will give you of the good things we do, they will show you two examples of the bad. Only because those get publicized and the good don't. It's natural."

Although the specialists feel beleaguered, they have not remained passive. In the early 1990s they organized a Specialist Association. This association lobbies the Exchange and the SEC. It does marketing studies with the specialists' customers. It has even organized training sessions for the specialists in how to communicate with customers. Its founder and organizing force is a third-generation specialist, Terry Meehan, who is committed to specialists' survival.[7] He explains that forty separate specialist firms could not do much to influence the Exchange administration or the SEC. The Specialist Association represents a collective voice that is better able to pool its resources and get attention.

> The first time we called a meeting and we invited people from the Exchange, nobody showed up. They just didn't show up. When people don't show up you get the message. When you're taken out to dinner and lectured to, you get the message. When you ask to get together, nobody wants to see you, you get the message. Two years ago, a call may not have been answered. A year ago, the calls were answered, but what we're asking for never ar-

rived. Now they're responding. When they realized that forty out of forty-two specialist firms are contributing reasonable dollars to create a very professional organization, they had to pay attention. These people are not going to go away.

Customer Service

Ever since the customer performance evaluation was instituted in the mid-1970s, the specialists have been aware of the need to change their behavior toward customers. As profit conditions have worsened this awareness has increased. The arrogance that specialists were known for has been tamed. As one specialist put it: "The specialist cannot literally tell a guy to go shit in his hat anymore. That relationship has changed. The quality of conversation with the customer has changed." Some of my informants feel so strongly about customer service that they sound like true believers in the Total Quality movement that is sweeping American manufacturing firms. "The better specialists are the ones that are very, very customer aware. They are very aware of the customer needs. They don't have to be the biggest traders. They don't have to be the biggest risk takers. But they have to be aware of what the customer needs, what his wants are, what his demands are."

> The major issues are: "What service do we provide? Is there a need for us?" Those are issues which I think we have got to continually harp on and clarify and probably make ourselves obnoxious or more obnoxious about by making the world understand that we are a service-type business and that we do good things. We do bring buyers and sellers together. We do create transactions that might not otherwise happen. And we don't necessarily interfere with transactions. We don't, by nature, slamdunk the opponents, buy from the seller and automatically turn around and sell to the buyer and make a spread. The auction market tends to be the fairest pricing mechanism around.

Others have grown defensive about the importance of the service they provide.

> We are in a service business. Remembering where all the bodies are buried. Giving the information they want and not giving them something they don't want . . . I anticipate. We have several young partners and what I have tried to impart to them is, "If you see

somebody coming ask yourself, 'What do they want?' Do you have an order for them? Are you working an order for them? You see them walking toward you . . . You anticipate in your head what the perception is . . . you know what you're doing, you are in control." It is very, very important to be on top of it and not just stand there and react.

Specialists have been forced to make changes in their behavior toward customers. Some firms have partners who spend significant amounts of time and money to visit customers and the listing companies. Being a specialist has become a "relationship" business.

The five strategies discussed above suggest that specialists are trying to adapt to their changing environment. They are not passively waiting for extinction, yet there is no radical break with the past. Each of these strategies already existed in the repertoire or tool kit of available behaviors from which the specialist might draw. It has been adapted to current circumstances. There is no major ideological shift that unites all specialists with a single answer to their problems. Rather, individuals and groups call upon the available strategies selectively, bringing to bear their own styles and personal emphases. As one would expect with market actors, specialist's response to decline is largely constituted as the voluntary choice of individuals. The question remains, "Is it enough?"

The Future

Most specialists believed that the coming years would produce major changes in the specialist system. As one specialist put it, "The game cannot go on as it currently exists." But there is very little consensus about what the future will hold. A few think that specialists will be gone from the Exchange in a few years. Most talk vaguely about changes by the year 2000. Some specialists speculate about possibly extending the rating system to include a broader constituency of customers, while others imagine eliminating it completely. Some specialists continue to attack "dealerized" markets, others talk about the specialists becoming dealers themselves. No one knows what is going to happen and there is little evidence that the Exchange itself has a plan other than the status quo. The only thing specialists agree on is that the future is not something they will have much control over. The days of telling the SEC and the Exchange how to behave are long gone.

Nevertheless, most specialists believe that the future requires some sort of political or regulatory action. Although few are certain what changes will or even should be made, they all have some idea of the options. The major choice is between enhancing the existing auction market or becoming a dealer market in which market makers would be free to shift their capital to any stocks in which they had an interest. Most favor enhancing the status quo. "Should you concentrate to change the rules, so that we dealerize our marketplace? So that we can function better as a dealer within this dealerized marketplace? Or do you spend time trying to articulate it, trying to sell the agency auction, you know, and protecting the customer. I think the first thing you try to do is to lead into your strengths." Other traders advocate bolder action.

> So, here we have this national treasure that's being threatened. What do you do? Do you keep it ineffective and noncompetitive when you know the markets will go to London or Singapore because they're less regulated and it's less expensive to do business there? You can't lose the business to London. You have to keep the business in this country. So Congress and the SEC will have to take risks with the current system only because of the competitive nature of what's at stake and how fragile it all is . . . Do you replace us? Less regulation? Less capital requirement? Free up the margin requirements like you give your options and futures traders and you'll see a pool of talent and money hit this place that dwarfs the current specialist system.

Although the specialists expect change and have even organized through the Specialist Association, they are no longer powerful enough to shape that change themselves. They must depend on the powerful member firms and the complex regulatory regime that has pacified them. Specialists look to the more powerful actors in their environment. Chapter 8 will address why the SEC and Congress are unlikely to make radical changes in the market-making system at the New York Stock Exchange. As for the Exchange administration, it too is unlikely to make fundamental changes in the specialist system, its market-making structure. Everything about the Exchange administration is conservative. It was late to adopt computer technology, late to move into derivative instruments like options and futures, and slow to respond to the changes in its customer base. This conservatism reflects the competing demands placed on a membership association made up of coalitions with increasingly fragmented interests: the specialists, the member firms, the institutional traders, and the listed firms. The Exchange administration seems trapped in its own institutional inertia. This suggests a more likely scenario than radical change: incremental, persistent decline. Perhaps NYSE will become like the British Empire. The glory will be gone, but the institutions will endure.

The Social Construction of Decline

Despite strong economic and technological trends, it is not possible to predict the course of decline. That course will be constructed by a diverse group of powerful players with strong vested interests. The path that decline takes will be a product of their interaction. Over time these players will develop new rules, roles, and relationships that serve their interests. Market arrangements may continue just as they are, a more level playing field may be established, the specialists may change their functions, or they may disappear. Much depends on the role government chooses to take in reforming and protecting the market.

The decline will not be a simple linear process. Different elements of the institution will decline at different rates and in different ways. The number and diversity of buyers and sellers drawn to the market changes most easily. Cost and quality of the service provided will continue to be reflected in the economic and technological forces shaping demand. Institutional change comes more slowly. The market for the stocks of the largest corporations in the United States was effectively absorbed in the nineteenth century by the New York Stock Exchange. As a quasi-public institution, it became the legitimate provider of a regulated service. Civic culture and institutional inertia will make it difficult to eliminate that service or even change it very radically. Specialists have been on the Exchange since the 1870s. It should not be surprising if they once again reconstruct their identities, finding new ways to maintain their franchise.

There is no single response to the threat of extinction on the part of human communities. The specialists have more resources to fall back on than those in other occupations. Even in the face of technological and competitive forces, their decline is relatively gradual. With the help of the Exchange administration and government regulators, incremental adaptation to other forms of market making may be possible.

Even with a cushion of resources, the experience of decline is bitter. Ressentiment and indignation mingle with fear as specialists watch others take their market share. Many continue to deny that the current conditions are terminal, but a growing number choose to exit. The new Specialist Association recognizes that the problems are serious and that the government and even the Exchange are not necessarily committed to specialist survival. It seems likely that, even in the short term, specialists will have to change the way they play the game. They will have to become more like their competitors. This will require lifting some of the restraints discussed in Chapter 5. But whether the specialists become more like the OTC dealers they vilify or more like the floor traders of futures markets, they seem unlikely to regain their near-monopoly and the transition will be traumatic. The attrition during such a transition would probably thin the ranks of current specialists considerably. Will the specialists eventually disappear? The development of the automated trading systems and the institutional inertia of the Exchange are powerful forces against their survival. It's not a bet I would take any pleasure in winning.

OPPORTUNISM AND INNOVATION: AN INTERPRETATION OF THE MILKEN DRAMA

7

He emerged as the foremost villain of the age not merely by piling up a fortune; that was acceptable, even desirable, so long as one did it in the proper way with appropriate gestures toward convention. His rise to success followed the classic pattern of the rags-to-riches myth except in the crucial area of *method* . . . In business he was ruthless and devious, clever and unpredictable, secretive and evasive. Above all, he was imaginative, not only brilliant but thoroughly original.

Klein, The Life and Legend of Jay Gould

The previous six chapters have progressed from a discussion of the rampant opportunism described in Chapter 1 to the control and decline described in Chapters 5 and 6. I have described market makers caught in an ever-present tension between aggression and restraint. Each of the three markets examined managed this tension differently. Bond traders leaned more toward opportunism and specialists had gone furthest toward restraint. This chapter focuses on a small but notorious subgroup of bond traders: those who pushed and redefined the limits of normative behavior on the trading floor in the 1980s. I will discuss both the process of redefinition and the restraint this elicited. These actors, the best known of whom is Michael Milken, shared the self-interested goals of their peers in the market, but developed innovative means for their achievement.

As Robert Merton explains, such "innovators" are not uncommon in American economic history.

> On the top economic levels, the pressure toward innovation not infrequently erases the distinction between business-like strivings this side of the mores and sharp practices beyond the mores. As [Thorstein] Veblen observed, "It is not easy in any given case— indeed it is at times impossible until the courts have spoken—to say whether it is an instance of praiseworthy salesmanship or a penitentiary offense." The history of the great American fortunes is threaded with strains toward institutionally dubious innovations, as is attested by many tributes to the Robber Barons. The reluctant admiration often expressed privately, and not seldom publicly, of these "shrewd, smart, and successful" men is a product of a cultural structure in which the sacrosanct goal virtually consecrates the means. This is no new phenomenon.[1]

Such innovators are deviant in the sense that their *methods* (means, strategies) are outside the currently accepted practices, rather than implying any psychologically aberrant or irrational behavior. In fact, their methods eventually may come to define the new norm. Merton goes on to explain that those most predisposed to be deviant innovators are those for whom access to approved means is blocked. This suggests that in financial markets the deviant innovators will come not from the top tier firms nor from those that are already dominant, but rather from those firms with less access to the best customers and their pools of capital.

Merton also notes that these innovations are the product of a "cultural structure" in which the goal of extraordinary wealth "consecrates" normative violation. The study of bond traders in Chapter 1 suggests that an extreme version of this culture existed in the overheated bond market in the 1980s. It is worth noting that the culture of opportunism described in Chapter 1 was homogeneously distributed among the four investment banks studied. This is to be differentiated from the more radical and innovative behavior to be described in this chapter. Opportunism and innovation are not the same thing, although both share positive connotations in this culture and both thrive in conditions of high incentive and low restraint. The general culture of opportunism in the bond market at this time was probably a necessary and conducive condition for the success of the more radical innovative action by Milken.

What Merton fails to note is that much of this "institutionally dubious innovation" is accompanied by considerable conflict in the business community. Existing elites, defenders of the status quo, often fight the "innovators" tooth and nail. This chapter describes one such conflict. It illustrates the process by which an innovator's breach of norms captures the attention of community elites who feel compelled to respond. The resulting conflict threatens to undermine the position and legitimacy of one group or the other. Protagonists compete to define the newly emerging business reality. Outcomes are dependent on the interpretive skills of the conflicting parties, as well as their ability to mobilize resources. Deviant innovators are rarely able to compete with elites in such a conflict, resulting most often in the defeat or co-optation of the deviant.

The deviant innovators in such conflicts are often portrayed, and often portray themselves, as heroes.[2] They are the renegades who propose to shake up an industry or the corporate raider who has arrived to save a firm. On the trading floor they are the "entrepreneurs" who take the greatest risks, develop new instruments, and add most significantly to the firm's bottom line. But like all heroes, they run the risk of defeat and humiliation. The one-time hero may be redefined by his powerful opponents as a fraud and a public villain. In such a case, the hero's romantic image is exploded and the conventional social order is reaffirmed.

Michael Milken and Junk Bonds

Most readers will be familiar with the foremost deviant innovator in the financial markets in the 1980s. Michael Milken was a Wall Street hero who took what many in the community believe to be a tragic fall. I am less concerned with the criminal fraud for which Milken was indicted and found guilty than I am with the grand innovations he brought to bond trading, most of which were once resisted and are now accepted practice.[3] Michael Milken nurtured and controlled the junk bond market of the 1980s. His firm accounted for more than 50 percent of all junk bond trading during

most of those years. Eventually, it was the use of junk bonds to finance leveraged buy-outs and hostile takeovers that shook the financial community and brought the conflict to public attention.
My thesis is that the rise and fall of Michael Milken is a story of
deviant innovation and deep social conflict in the financial community. It is a conflict in which the protagonists continue to offer
competing and alternative interpretations of what happened.

We will focus our attention on these competing interpretations
and how their creators strategically succeeded or failed in defining
the situation and the outcome of the conflict. Michael Milken cast
himself as the underdog hero in a drama of societal change. As early
as 1970, in an op-ed article that was rejected by the New York Times,
Milken compared himself to other Berkeley graduates of that turbulent time. "Unlike other crusaders from Berkeley, I have chosen
Wall Street as my battleground for improving society. It is here that
the government's institutions and industries are financed."[4] Later,
at the height of his success, Milken became messianic. He told a
group of money managers in Boston in 1986, "We're faced with
change. And all of us have resisted this change. Our regulators have
resisted change, our politicians have resisted change, portfolio managers have resisted change, traders have resisted change, salesmen
have resisted change . . . The common perception is that capital is
scarce, but in fact capital is abundant. It is vision that is scarce."[5]
Milken led an increasingly large following into new forms of
financing. He used the model of crusading hero to guide his actions
and to influence others' interpretations and behavior.

Milken's exploits as a deviant innovator and the ensuing conflict
between Milken and those most threatened by him is a social drama
in four acts: breach, crisis, redress, and reintegration.[6] Referring to
the rise and fall of Michael Milken as a social drama is not to be-
little its significance in changing corporations and markets or in creating a huge new debt market in which mid-sized firms like Turner
Broadcasting and MCI financed their explosive growth. Major corporate restructurings were accomplished, among them RJR
Nabisco. Companies from Gulf Oil and TWA to Beatrice Foods
changed hands. The protagonists pursued such goals as changing
the way corporations are financed, ending the dominance of old

guard investment banks, and stopping the speculative mania of the raiders and their bankers on Wall Street.

Who are the protagonists in this dramatic social conflict? First, there is Michael Milken, head of the junk bond operation at Drexel Burnham Lambert. He and his colleagues at Drexel made the junk bond revolution possible. He was opposed by a series of increasingly important participants in the drama. In the early stages he was opposed by other bond traders and salespeople at investment banks inside and outside his own firm. Later he was opposed by actors in the wider corporate and political communities representing order, convention, and the status quo in corporate financing and ownership. Among these adversaries were chief executive officers of leading corporations as well as prominent members of the banking community. These leaders were joined by Paul Volcker, the director of the Federal Reserve Board, and several important Congressional leaders.

A final and extremely important set of actors in the drama was the media. In the early 1980s *Business Week* ran Milken on its cover. He was hailed as a hero. The media dubbed him the "King" of Junk Bonds and his customers as leaders of a revolution in corporate finance. By 1988 Connie Bruck, in her bestselling book, was calling his customers "predators," and by 1991 James Stewart, a Wall Street Journal reporter who won a Pulitzer prize for his reporting on Milken, described him as the worst of a "den of thieves." The media made this drama public and highly visible. All of these protagonists employed strategies designed to capture the attention and sympathy of various audiences. They grounded their performances in the myths and metaphors of the financial market and society at large.

The Breach

The drama begins with the breach of some crucial norm.[7] This violation is more than a faux pas, it is deliberate effort to challenge the establishment. The innovator sees himself as acting altruistically, as a representative of others, whether these others are aware of it or not. At least since 1970, Milken has cast himself as a crusader for change engaged in "the improvement of society."

Milken's first significant violation of the norms came very early in his career. During his years at Berkeley, he became interested in "fallen angels," bonds that had been downgraded by the rating agencies to "below investment grade." He came across a study by Braddock Hickman of every corporate bond issued between 1900 and 1943 showing that a portfolio of widely diversified low-grade fallen angels could be more profitable than a portfolio of high grade bonds, especially if you got in while they were undervalued. The barrier to selling fallen angels was the rating agencies, Standard and Poor's and Moody's. They controlled the definition of acceptable risk that investment firms used when recommending bonds to their customers. As a result most bond traders and salesman considered it unacceptable to trade in or offer such instruments.[8]

Milken took his first full-time job at Drexel Firestone in 1970. He soon asked to be moved from research to bond sales and trading. He began to focus on the low-grade (high-yield) bonds, doing meticulous research into the companies in order to promote what Stewart called "the gospel of high-yield bonds."[9] Milken's colleagues on the trading floor disliked the securities he traded and saw his behavior as a breach with tradition. As Connie Bruck explains, "Most of his colleagues looked askance at Milken and his low-rated bonds." She quotes a former Drexel executive who said, "The high-grade bond guys considered him a leper. They said, 'Drexel can't be presenting itself as banker to these high-grade, Fortune 500 companies and have Mike out peddling this crap.'"[10] Milken was segregated off in a corner of the trading floor but survived. By 1973 he was making a 100 percent profit on his trading position. The firm increased his capital and gave him increasing autonomy. They allowed him to keep one dollar for every three he made. He made $5 million in 1976.

During these years Milken built a clientele for low-grade bonds. He did this not only by convincing customers of the bond's high yield and underlying value, but by promising to bid on the bonds personally if the customer wanted to get out, i.e. he promised liquidity. Among Milken's early clients were small- and medium-sized insurance companies that bought for their portfolios, executives at the recently deregulated savings and loan associations, and aggressive fund managers looking for high returns. Among these customers was an inner circle who knew each other and traded in each other's debt and equity through Milken. As Stewart points out, among Milken's biggest clients were a small group of entrepreneurs—Saul Steinberg, Meshulam Riklis, and Carl Lindner—who had been rebuffed on Wall Street for their aggressive tactics or had been under investigation by the SEC.[11] For this group, Milken's breach of norms was recognized as a brilliant and useful innovation.

By 1977 Milken had established Drexel as the only firm willing to act as a market maker in below-investment-grade bonds. Milken stood ready to buy and sell throughout the day, albeit at a large mark-up of 3 or 4 points compared to the eighths and quarters in investment grade bonds. That same year, Lehman Brothers and Goldman Sachs underwrote the first important original issues of low-grade bonds for LTV, Fuqua, and Pan Am.[12] But it was Milken, who already had a ready group of buyers for such issues, who made it into a significant new form of financing. Fred Joseph, a partner in corporate finance at Drexel, brought Milken a client, Texas International, that wanted to issue low-grade bonds.[13] Milken helped Texas International issue $30 million in new debt. Drexel did seven more issues in 1977. By 1978 Drexel dominated the market for issuing what soon came to be known as "junk bonds." It completed fourteen issues that year. Its next closest rival, Lehman Brothers, did six. At its peak, Drexel held almost 70 percent of the market share in this business.[14] When the traditional "white shoe" investment banks became interested in this profitable market, Milken antagonized them by refusing to share initial offerings with a syndicate of firms.

The clients for this business were mostly mid-sized firms without previous access to such a market. The alternative for these companies had been the further dilution of their equity or taking on restrictive loan covenants. Milken felt strongly that these companies, and their entrepreneurial leaders, were being denied capital by the financial establishment. In an interview, Milken framed the issue as an ethical one: "To me it was a form of discrimination—to discriminate against the management and employees of a company which offered value-added products and services, all because [they] didn't get a certain rating. It seemed grossly unfair. So I would not have been true to myself if I didn't use the tools I had, to try and raise capital for these people."[15] Milken cast himself as the champion of the mid-sized firm. He used a charged word—"discrimination"—to attack the establishment banks and rating agencies for denying access to relatively cheap capital. Milken had clearly found his cause.[16]

The Crisis

Breaches of crucial norms in a community, whether those breaches are innovative or not, threaten the status quo and often elicit acts of repression. If such a breach is not "sealed off," it is likely to escalate into a mounting crisis.[17] The escalating nature of the breach seems to dare the establishment to deal with the menace. In the current instance, the breach was not repressed. The extension of junk bond financing to actors outside the traditional corporate elite escalated dramatically in the 1980s. Observers began to talk of a junk bond "revolution" as if it might be a turning point in corporate finance. In retrospect, it appears as a moment of suspense in which assumptions about corporate ownership and control were called into question.

The escalation of the breach is best represented by a single key innovation, one that threatened the corporate establishment and made Milken dangerous: using junk bonds to finance hostile takeovers. Although the breach was initiated in the corporate finance department at Drexel, it was made possible by Milken's ability to sell the debt. Milken is said to have feared that the extra risk involved in hostile takeovers might hurt the junk bond market he had created, but he clearly overcame any reluctance. He was widely perceived as the engine that made the rapid growth of the junk bond–financed hostile takeover possible.

The merger wave of the 1980s had begun with a series of friendly leveraged buy-outs in which large conglomerate firms were taken private and restructured. In some of the largest of these, such as Beatrice Companies, the deal would not have been possible without billions in junk bonds, sold by Milken. But it was the hostile takeovers that drew the greatest public attention and resistance. The hostile takeover itself was not a new innovation. Such takeovers have a long history. But they were always accomplished by a larger firm acquiring the stock of a smaller, attractive target. Milken's ability to sell large amounts of junk bonds made it possible for his customers to go after targets in corporate America that had previously been immune from the threat of takeover. Many of the most notorious raiders had strong alliances with Milken: Henry Kravis, Ron Perelman, Saul Steinberg, Victor Posner, T. Boone Pickens, and Carl Icahn. These men shared Milken's taste for innovative methods and his anti-establishment view of the existing corporate leadership. But, increasingly, it was Milken who was perceived as the man who made their dreams possible.[18]

It was the hostile offers for major oil companies, like Gulf Oil and Unocal, that extended the junk bond breach into a crisis. These actions revealed the extent to which entrenched senior managers would go to maintain their control and prerogatives.[19] More importantly, it revealed a vulnerability to disruption of their control for which these managers were unprepared. It was raiders like T. Boone Pickens who fearlessly taunted the corporate elite using the junk bond breach as their weapon. He argued that size should not protect stagnant management and that underachievers should not be safe just because of their size. In the Gulf deal, in 1984, Milken informed Pickens that he would be able to raise $1.7 billion for the campaign. This would enable Pickens' Mesa Petroleum to acquire a firm more than twenty times its size. Historian Robert Sobel believes that this deal was the turning point that established a sense of crisis and revealed the outlines of the ensuing conflict. "Later, those within the industry would recognize this interaction as a critical juncture in the history of the junk era—the moment Milken emerged as a superstar. Armed with such backing as Drexel could provide, raiders could go after just about any large, fat corporation. In his ability to raise enormous sums of money quickly, Milken had no peer—and major corporate targets had no greater adversary."[20]

Redress

Once a disturbance in the social order has become manifest, powerful members of a community may act to limit its spread. The means of redress include informal persuasion as well as recourse to formal legal restraints. There may also be a regression to the crisis

phase or the two phases may go on simultaneously. Although the leaders of the establishment may attempt to restore the status quo, this may not be possible. In the case of Milken and junk bonds, the corporate elite applied a broad cross-section of remedies in an effort to halt the escalating crisis. The initial remedy was simply for corporate targets to resist the raiders. This included both defensive and offensive strategies. As the crisis escalated, redress came to include action in the political arena.

Redressive action consists of both pragmatic techniques and symbolic action.[21] Early pragmatic techniques consisted mainly of defensive efforts by the target firms to either make themselves unattractive (changes in charter, taking on debt) or find a "white knight" to protect them from the raider by acquiring them on more friendly terms. Offensive strategies included threatening to acquire the raider (the Pac Man strategy), bringing injunctions against the raider, suing the raider, or paying off the raider (greenmail). Pragmatic action also included efforts in the political arena. The Business Roundtable, made up of the 200 largest U.S. corporations, began lobbying Congress in 1984 to pass legislation against takeovers. Several committees held hearings. A ban on mergers among the top fifty oil companies was proposed by Senator J. Bennett Johnson from Louisiana.[22] In response to T. Boone Pickens' raid on Unocal, its chairman, Fred Hartley, wrote to Paul Volcker, asking for an investigation by the Federal Reserve Board of "abuses by some banks and financiers that are feeding a takeover frenzy that strikes at the economic well-being of this country."[23] On December 6, 1985, the Fed curbed the use of junk bonds in acquisitions. By the end of that year more than thirty-one bills had been proposed in Congress to limit takeover activity. Individual firms lobbied in their home states. By 1987, thirty-seven states had passed laws restricting takeover activity.

Symbolic action played a significant role in the ultimate achievement of redress. The corporate establishment launched a rhetorical attack on Milken and junk bonds. They were attempting to shift his public image from hero to villain. Corporate lobbyists and corporate political action committees encouraged congressmen to investigate this latest form of financial innovation. Congressional hearings became the stage for the demonization of Milken and the "junk

bond bust-up hostile takeover." Nicholas Brady, investment banker for Unocal, and later Secretary of the Treasury, wrote an op-ed article for the New York Times entitled, "Equity Is Lost in Junk Bondage." He also told a reporter, "These are the people you want to keep off the streets . . . The best you can say is [that] they are gamblers and hustlers."[24] Felix Rohatyn, another investment banker, wrote an op-ed article in the Wall Street Journal called "Junk Bonds and Other Securities Swill."

The tone of the rhetoric against Milken is colorfully represented by Fred Mercer, CEO of Goodyear. "Let me tell you what's wrong with Mike Milken and company. You have to start by asking, what does he provide to society? What does he create? What actually happens in the way of building products that help our standard of living to be either maintained or improved? And the answer is nothing . . . and incidentally, it pays quite well. It pays a lot better than what I've been paid."[25] Leaders of the corporate establishment were clearly attempting to limit the spread of the crisis. They employed the powerful cultural frame of the outsider and speculator (gambler, hustler) who does not work for his wages, and does not deserve to be in the "game."[26] Drexel responded with a series of advertisements showing the mid-sized companies that Milken had funded, but the establishment's evocative anti-speculator imagery seemed more salient to a broader public.

Reintegration

The final phase of social drama involves either a reintegration of the violators or an irreparable schism. Neither is a return to the status quo ante: even reintegration suggests an altered community. There has been no schism on Wall Street or in corporate America. Rather, most of the radical innovators and most of their normative breaches have been reintegrated into the community. Junk bonds have become an accepted part of the financial world. After a short decline, starting with the demise of Drexel and continuing during the recession in 1990 and 1991, new issues of junk bonds returned to the market. In 1993, 341 new issues came to market, exceeding the 226 issues in the peak year of 1986. The amount borrowed

has grown from \$33 billion in 1986 to \$57 billion in 1993. Several of the junk-bond raiders joined the corporate establishment, actually running the firms they acquired; e.g., Icahn (TWA) and Perelman (Revlon). But the critical breach, the one that elicited the redress, has been curbed. Whereas 67.5 percent of junk bonds issued in 1987 were used in takeovers, only 11.2 percent were so used in 1993.[27] The largest corporations are once again safe from raiders and free to focus on the competition.[28]

Where do Milken's felony convictions fit in this drama? Like many dramatic heroes, Milken had a fatal flaw. Some saw it as greed. I think it was hubris. Milken had developed an exaggerated sense of himself in relation to the rules and norms of his community. His success was built on an escalating series of normative violations. There were no restraints for Michael Milken. The crimes for which he was imprisoned, all of which occurred during the takeover mania of the mid-1980s, reflect the recklessness of an overheated deal-maker: evasion of net capital rules, filing false statements with the SEC, concealing ownership of stock.

The crimes for which Milken was punished are of relatively small financial consequence when compared with the consequences of the breach he made possible: the junk-bond hostile takeover. This tool was the basis for widespread asset redistribution, large-scale corporate restructuring, and tremendous personal dislocation. Yet, it is hard not to see Milken's trial and imprisonment as the symbolic resolution of this social drama. By the time he was sentenced, Milken's breaches had become symbolic not only of speculative frenzy, but of corporate indifference and the disruption caused by a decade of corporate restructuring. Had Milken held himself to higher standards, thereby avoiding prison, the social drama might have had a slightly different denouement. Action by the Federal Reserve Board and the state legislatures had stopped the hostile takeovers anyway. What was missing was a ritual of censure and cleansing in the wake of a disruptive decade. Milken's personal fall and removal from the market served as symbolic redress and the basis for reintegration and reorganization of the community. Instead of the crusading hero of Wall Street, Milken became its foremost modern villain.

Milken in Context

The social drama we have explored here is representative of a turbulent decade in the financial markets. It was both a consequence and a cause of the volatility and change associated with the era. Although no one can predict the emergence of a deviant innovator who will transform market practice, the conditions under which deviant innovation is most likely to emerge are identifiable.

The bond trading floor of the 1980s was a relatively unrestrained environment, as I discussed in Chapter 1. Drexel, led by Milken, was perhaps the most extreme version. Many of the structural conditions shaping this environment were more exaggerated at Drexel than at other firms. Bonuses and participation in Milken-run investment partnerships made the incentive of potential income higher, and the restraining influence of reputational networks and interdependence with other firms less because of Milken's tendency to dominate markets and to go it alone in bond offerings. This same dominance of the market enhanced his ability to withhold information from customers and to mislead trading partners. Milken took the conditions conducive to opportunism and pushed them further. Like his predecessor Jay Gould, described in the epigraph at the beginning of this chapter, Milken's deviant innovation was mingled with his opportunism. In particular, high incentive and low restraint are contributors to both.

At the same time, Milken surrounded himself with a network of entrepreneurs who had built their fortunes by violating the norms of the business community. These included people like Saul Steinberg, who had attempted to acquire Chemical Bank in 1969, and T. Boone Pickens, who led the charge against entrenched management in the big oil companies. Like Milken, these men were outsiders committed to challenging the way business was done in America. They shared a belief that traditionally accepted modes of financing were inadequate. They successfully promoted these ideas, creating a new idiom in the business community. Together, their actions and their ideas redefined the culture of corporate finance.

Junk bond hostile takeovers were the most extreme threat to top management of large corporations in the decade and arguably in the century. Operating in a period of economic uncertainty and volatility, Milken took advantage of the government's low commitment to regulation, the heightened speculative interest in bonds due to the floating of interest rates, and the profit opportunities created by inefficient and entrenched systems of corporate governance and finance.

It is because of the previously conservative culture of bond dealers and the complacent condition of corporate governance that Milken was able to mount his frame-breaking innovations. He challenged the dominant definition of the market for corporate debt. He did this by first claiming that the rating agencies had mistakenly limited the market to those bonds they defined as "investment grade" and then proving that there was a market for debt that was below their designation. Milken's action showed that the definition of quality in the bond market is not absolute, but rather a contestable social construction.

Such acts of reconstruction are unlikely to be performed by employees of elite firms who already benefit from the status quo. Rather, deviant innovation is most likely to be the work of those who have less access to resources and customers but strong motivation to succeed. For these aspirants, the seductions of top-tier status are strong incentive to challenge the status quo. Milken, like other deviant innovators, must be understood in context as one who stood at the margin of the system and used its vulnerabilities to momentarily dominate it.

Deviant Innovators

It is worth noting that most innovative breaches never become full-blown social dramas, but are instead repressed. Their appearance, rapid repression, and demise signal the reaffirmation of the boundaries of acceptable behavior. The culture of Wall Street is fundamentally conservative, seeking to reproduce itself rather than change. But occasionally, a challenger of the status quo will mobilize sufficient support, despite the resistance of the elite, to change some aspect of the normative structure. If the breach is widely adopted, as junk bonds were, a new logic of action will be generated to legitimate the once-deviant behaviors.

It seems that the kind of deviant innovation described here is both addictive and blinding. It is addictive because each success encourages further deviance. But this escalating success at outsmarting the establishment can also be blinding. The innovator develops a distorted sense of his own power and position and begins to violate rules of transaction that get in his way by squeezing markets, exceeding limits, disguising ownership, and so on. At the same time, there are still lines to be crossed that may threaten establishment interests. The heroic innovator, through his own excess, gives his opponents the tools to demonize him. In the end, the redressive powers of the community are used to send a message to others about what happens to those who threaten the status quo.

History will always be ambivalent about such characters. It will paint them as both robber barons and industrial giants. Milken nurtured a new market in debt for mid-sized firms that is thriving today, but squandered his reputation on securities violations. Salomon built itself into a powerhouse of Wall Street, but its top leaders left in disgrace. Their downfall was in failing to heed their community's restraints. As long as incentives are high and restraints at a minimum, innovators will develop new and deviant methods to achieve wealth.

Conclusion

The story of Milken and junk bonds is a story of deviant innovation and the resulting social conflict within a community. Most of the scandals on Wall Street in the 1980s, however, were not social conflicts. They were about individuals engaged in deceit for the purpose of lining their pockets. Milken's fraud is only a small part of his drama, but Dennis Levine and Ivan Boesky offered no vision of change on Wall Street and threatened no establishment. Rather, they used their guile to garner "inside information," and then used this information to take advantage of others in the market. They were extreme opportunists.

But, as the Milken story suggests, there does seem to be an association between deviant innovation and deviant opportunism. Although most opportunists are not innovators, it may be that deviant innovations are more likely in opportunistic cultures and that, in turn, successful deviant innovation creates an environment conducive to even greater excesses of opportunism. The innovations themselves may balance out as either positive or negative from the perspective of society's greater welfare. They will be tested by time. But the opportunism associated with such activity is clearly negative in the sense that deceptive practices reduce the credibility of the market as an institution. Nevertheless, both deviant innovation and opportunism seem to be inherent in the system. Their recurrence on Wall Street throughout its history suggests that it is a conducive environment for both. The dilemma for society is to identify a degree of restraint that will inhibit the opportunism without forestalling the innovation.

CYCLES OF OPPORTUNISM: PROFITS, PRUDENCE, AND THE PUBLIC INTEREST

8

In this concluding chapter I will attempt to account for some of the differences in the trading floors studied in this book. The arrangement of the preceding chapters suggests a continuum from the most opportunistic context (the bond market) to the most restrained (the New York Stock Exchange). But there is nothing intrinsic in the commodities being traded or the people doing the trading that would explain the ordering along this continuum. In the bond market, older traders remembered a time when opportunism was low and trust was the widespread currency of transaction. At NYSE, the older specialists remembered their early days when bullying and bluffing were expected. These reversals suggest that financial markets swing between periods of greater opportunism and greater restraint. Put another way, market makers are pulled between the short-term attractions of extraordinary profits and the long-term benefits of prudence. This chapter examines the nature of this dynamic process and the factors that influence a market's position along the continuum from opportunism to restraint.

The Many Faces of Self-Interest

Right now I'm short thirty silver. So I'm looking for the market to break. I will wait and wait and wait until either they get me or

I'm going to get them. But you have to know the players, whether they squeeze orders or let go . . . If I know a certain guy who'll offer a few out when he usually has more [He's trying to squeeze the order] . . . well, I might bid him up a penny because I know I can get him. But if I'm wrong, I've exposed my position to the pit, my anxiety to the pit. I would rather have kept quiet . . . Everybody in the pit has an interest. People will stab you in the back. Say one thing and do another. It's part of the game.[1]

The words of this highly successful futures trader paint a picture of extreme competitive aggression; a world where deceit and even "back-stabbing" are possibilities in every transaction. Each trader is competing with all the others, and must strategize not to reveal his position, his "anxiety," to them. Survival requires that he aggressively pursues his self-interest; that he watches his back and "gets" the other guy when he can because that is where he'll earn his profit.

Every market has some degree of aggression. But few occupations offer the continuous opportunity, the tremendous incentives, and the repertoire of strategies available to the market makers. Few are as openly accepting of such behavior. But even among the markets studied here there is considerable variation. On the bond trading floor between 1987 and 1989, there was greater acceptance of such strategies as "laying off bonds" on unsuspecting customers, "showing a bid" to bluff others into buying what one needs to unload, and "front-running," where the trader uses knowledge of a customer's intention to trade ahead of the customer. On the floor of the stock market such strategies, which had once been fairly common, have been replaced by a more consistent ethic of "customer service" and "the rule of agency."

Economists since Adam Smith have believed that economic actors are self-interested and rational. They suggest that these attributes are intrinsic to human nature. The idea that the attributes of economic man are rooted in his reason, drives, or instincts makes them seem fixed and immutable. The studies in this book suggest that these attributes are stylized interpretations of human nature that are skillfully crafted by economic actors for specific contexts. My intention is not to deny the existence of self-interest in human behavior, or even to deny the existence of instincts or drives, but rather to suggest that ". . . such drives are highly unspecialized and undirected."[2] It is only in a social context that such drives are defined and given meaning. As a result, they find their expression in the social world; so-called human nature is context-dependent.

How self-interest is translated in particular situations is a product of social interaction and the context in which it occurs. In a rural farming commune or an urban consumer cooperative, self-interest is going to have a different meaning than it does in a used car dealership or on a trading floor. In each context the pursuit of self-interest will take different forms. Self-interest may lead to cooperation in one context and individualistic opportunism in the other. Individuals in each context experience local behaviors as appropriate. From the point of view of the traders studied in this book, aggressive behavior has been defined as appropriate for this context. Aggressive and/or opportunistic strategies are part of the common stock of knowledge available to members of each trading floor community. This shared background of mutual understanding enables the orderly reproduction of exchange relations on each trading floor.

Settings are constructed to maximize profits by rewarding aggressive behavior. In the bond market, the bonus system for traders at investment banks provided the incentive for aggressive trading. The relative absence of restraints and the tacit approval of strategies in "the gray area" provided conditions conducive to opportunism. The extraordinary personal income derived from opportunistic action and the low level of restraint by the firms employing these traders signaled the local parameters of self-interested behavior. In the futures market, the rapid growth of financial futures produced a similar scenario. In this case it was the exchanges, anxious for growth in these new markets, that allowed young, under-capitalized traders to create an environment of extreme aggression. Informants in older markets spoke derisively of these new markets. An FBI sting operation in 1989 suggested the extent to which the formal self-regulatory structure may overlook violations of its rules.[3] FBI agents uncovered commonplace frauds that involved pre-arranged trades and false trades as well as trading ahead of customer orders. What constitutes an opportunity for bluffing, deceiving, or abusing a customer's trust is defined on each trading floor. Those with supervisory responsibility over traders send signals as to what is appropriate through their supervision or lack thereof; those who trade interpret these signals and transform them through aggressive action. What constitutes appropriate self-interest is socially constructed through the interaction of traders and their supervisors.

In each trading floor community, self-interest is transformed into the strategies discussed throughout this book. These are technically complex operations learned by the novice trader from mentors, peers, and exchange partners. Although new variants may be adopted, as I showed in the discussion of Michael Milken, fundamental forms are taken for granted in the environment of the trader. They are central aspects of the culture of the trading floor. Each strategy is a resource that is learned and may be perceived or not perceived, used or not used in organizing behavior. Floor culture is a "tool kit" traders use to solve different kinds of problems. It provides a "repertoire of capacities from which varying strategies of action may be constructed."[4] In this sense the strategies for market makers represent a cultural resource that facilitates particular patterns of behavior and discourages others. They allow actors to channel "unspecialized and undirected" drives into locally scripted means of goal attainment.

The perspective developed here is not meant to portray strategies as a kind of cultural straitjacket, implying that all members of the same trading floor automatically enact the same cooperative or competitive strategies. It emphasizes the extent to which the "cultural tool kit" is remade by its users, often in response to new situations. The knowledge of strategies does not condemn the individual to predetermined behaviors. As Biggart notes, "[T]here is no necessary law of marginal utility or other impersonal system of laws that works to produce the economy."[5] Rather, consciously and unconsciously, individuals choose strategies that are useful or appealing to them from the cultural repertoire. They must assemble the elements of the strategy to fit their situations, advance their careers, and construct a coherent identity. An individual may choose his or her occupation because of an attraction to elements of the script. Once in the occupation, the incumbent may accept or reject various elements of the script and interpret others to fit situational contingencies. In the case of the bond market in the 1980s, freshly minted MBAs found themselves exposed to strategies of business found in no textbook. They redefined themselves as "entrepreneurs." At the New York Stock Exchange, specialists were able to reject elements of the old script and remold their identities when the context changed.

Although self-interest may be instinctual, the forms which it takes are socially defined, as are the levels of acceptable aggression and deceit. But why do different market cultures, even subcultures as closely related as the three studied here, define these levels differently? How can the differences in the levels of self-interest revealed in these studies be explained? It cannot be explained by incentives, because extraordinary ones exist in each of these markets. The answer lies in the systems of restraint.

The Paradox of Restraint in a Free Market

> Traders, as a group, police themselves. Certain behavior is acceptable. Certain behavior is not acceptable. I think you learn the rules by people yelling at you. When you do something wrong, or what somebody else thinks is wrong, they generally let you know. They just tell the guy, "You better not do this again. If you do this again we'll take you downstairs or we'll just freeze you out." . . . So, first it's done privately, then it's done publicly in the pit to let other people know what's going on, what he's been doing. You might tell a member who's on the Business Conduct Committee. As a last resort, you would tell somebody downstairs in Investigations and Audits. The guy can be warned, fined, or suspended.[6]

Restraint is a social process. What is acceptable and what is not acceptable is established within the trading floor community. It is communicated to the novice by mentors, but more importantly it is reinforced by what is sanctioned and what is not sanctioned on the trading floor. Through informal means, traders "police" each other. By yelling at the miscreant publicly or by freezing him out of trades, the boundaries of appropriate behavior are defined for individuals and the community. Norms about how much information a market maker reveals to his customers, how widely he distributes this information, how and when he disguises his intentions and even how far he pushes his advantage are enforced by group pressure and the power of reputation in the market. These informal modes of control have been crystallized into more formal modes of control and enforcement. The chapters in this book have revealed a system of control that is highly institutionalized; a world of norms, rules, and procedures to which members of the trading community are habituated.

It seems more than a little ironic that markets that are often cited as exemplars of "the free market" should exhibit such elaborate systems of restraint. Market makers do not allow their competitors' self-interest to be the sole director of economic action. Rather, they take cooperative countermeasures to control each other. Market makers have created self-regulatory associations that restrain market behavior. In both stock and futures markets, they created these restraints before there were powerful government agencies to oversee them. This is what is meant by the paradox of restraint in a free market. Financial markets will not exist for long before individuals take action to collectively restrain excesses that may undermine the market's long-term viability. The configuration of the resulting institutions changes as a result of the action of powerful interests competing for control. Shifts in the balance of power among groups on the trading floor determine who may design or redesign these restraints to benefit themselves.[7]

The studies in this book have shown that stock markets, bond markets, and futures markets are laden with formal and informal modes of control. Too little attention has been paid to these market-based (non-governmental) systems of restraint either in academic journals or in the press.[8] Such restraints seem illogical to financial economists: they would (theoretically) interfere with the market mechanism. This theory is but an academic amplification of the ideology of free enterprise. The market makers themselves and their self-regulatory associations have only recently begun to draw attention to their self- regulatory efforts.[9] Much self-regulatory action is handled informally and/or confidentially through the moral suasion and containment strategies discussed in Chapter 3. The government, of course, maintains its legitimacy by creating oversight regulatory agencies like the Securities and Exchange Commission, but few realize and the agency rarely reveals that enforcement is largely dependent on the data and investigations of these market-based self-regulatory associations. As a result, the operation of these systems of restraint, as they effect the process of market making, is nearly invisible to the public.[10]

Institutionalized Markets

The strategies, rules, and more formal procedures discussed in the preceding chapters are largely taken for granted by market makers. Institutionalized markets, in which traders are habituated to particular arrangements, consist of three nested layers, which I will call *individual, transactional, and regulatory,* respectively. The levels build on each other. At the core of the institutionalized market is the individual trader driven by his own self-interest. This would seem to be the least institutionalized aspect of the market in that the buyers and sellers operate as relatively autonomous actors. Nevertheless, self-interest is transformed into situationally specific, culturally proper strategies enacted from a preexisting repertoire. This repertoire, or tool kit, defines the range of appropriate behaviors on the trading floor. The likelihood of opportunism in a market is increased when opportunism is culturally approved and available.

The individual trader exists within a set of formal and informal social arrangements at the transaction level. Exchange relations in financial markets often appear spontaneous and chaotic. But even in competitive financial markets, exchange is often ritualized and enacted as "programmed action"[11] through an intricate but standardized sequence that brings money and information into the market and passes it back out. In this sequence buyers and sellers differentiate into institutionalized roles with specialized functions (brokers, dealers, agents, and other middle men). Transactions differentiate into institutionalized processes (matching, sorting, distribution, and referral).

To the extent that transactions recur between parties day in and day out, norms of exchange and reputations for trustworthiness are established. Transaction opportunities come to be shaped by each actor's reputation in a network of other traders. In high-density competitive networks, such as those on stock and futures trading floors, a reputation for normative behavior may be essential for survival. Those who fail to conform may find themselves outside the network.

The transactional level of institutionalized markets includes the more formal set of organizational arrangements created by the self-regulatory association. These arrangements are created and maintained by the collective action of the most central and powerful market participants. Market norms are formalized into rules and standards, and exchange sequences into required procedures. Elements of surveillance and enforcement are added. What was initially created in interaction comes to seem external and objective. Adherence becomes a strategy for success. Self-regulatory bodies assume or delegate responsibility for setting standards, monitoring behavior, arbitrating conflicts, and enforcing rules. Within these organizations market participants organize lobbying efforts to obtain the benefits of regulation or to respond to threatening actions by the state.[12]

The third level of an institutionalized market, the regulatory level, has become increasingly important over the course of the twentieth century. Its role varies from market to market, ranging from loose oversight to active intervention. Early self-regulatory associations in the nineteenth century sought charters to legitimate their standardizing and rule-making functions. In the twentieth century, antitrust legislation and the court decisions that followed defined and restricted the rights and duties of these membership associations. In recent years, increasing regulatory attention has led to enhanced self- regulatory enforcement at the exchanges. Patterns of interaction between associations and the state have refined the institutions of market restraint.

The notion that some degree of restraint in the market may be desirable was tested in the Supreme Court in the early part of the century, where it found support. The Court found that the power of an association to restrain its members may be used for positive or negative purposes. Justice Brandeis, in defining reasonable self-regulatory restraint by the Chicago Board of Trade, wrote that, "The true test of legality is whether the restraint imposed is such as merely regulates and perhaps thereby promotes competition or whether it is such as may suppress or even destroy competition."[13] This decision kept the state at arm's length from financial exchanges.

As the twentieth century progressed, the federal government created independent regulatory agencies and other bodies to oversee markets. The Securities and Exchange Commission was created in 1934 and the Commodity Futures Trading Commission, in 1974. But the SEC and CFTC did not replace the self-regulatory associations. Each new aspect of oversight further institutionalized the existing self-regulatory arrangements. The intensity and rigor of oversight by government regulators has varied.

It seems reasonable to assume that traders' perceptions of regulatory rigor shape their behavior and the behavior of their self-regulatory associations. The fifty-four bond traders at investment banks in my sample were largely unconcerned with regulation. Most felt that there had been a general loosening of the regulatory regime in the 1980s. The futures traders in the early eighties were more aware of regulation and feared that the relatively new CFTC would change the "free market" environment on which they depended. Most agreed that the agency didn't have much bite yet, but they feared that it might. The futures exchanges established some of the nation's richest political action committees (PACs) during the 1980s. Specialists at the New York Stock Exchange were highly aware of the SEC and believed that SEC pressure on NYSE as a self-regulator had increased markedly in the 1970s and continued into the 1980s. During this time the Exchange administration had professionalized and internalized strong regulatory values. Regulatory regimes vary widely in the financial markets. The history of shifting government policy toward market makers plays a critical role in the institutionalization of their markets and in the levels of opportunism found there.

The Dynamics of Profit and Prudence

The three groups of market makers studied in this book occupy different positions on a continuum of strategies from highly opportunistic to highly restrained; positions which change over time. The market makers in stocks and bonds, for example, move in reverse directions. Why does this movement occur? My answer is based on the dynamic relationship between profits and prudence in these markets. It requires consideration of interests and power at all three of the levels discussed: the traders, their formal and informal social organization, and the regulatory regimes in which they are embedded.

To understand this change process I will first examine the pressures shaping market-maker behavior. Market makers are pulled in contrary directions. On one hand, self-interest, as well as competitive pressures, compel traders to maximize profits in the short term through the locally available strategies of aggressive trading. This aggression may sometimes slip over the line into opportunism. The goal, of course, is accumulation of assets. On the other hand, self-interest, as well as social pressures, compel traders to preserve their income stream in the longer term by maintaining interpersonal relationships and attractive markets. This elicits strategies of restraint and the elaborate organizational arrangements described throughout this book.

In financial markets the pressure to generate substantial and sustained profits and capital growth is in a state of ever-present tension with institutional pressures for legitimacy at all levels of the system. Cognate pressures are to be found at all three levels of institutionalized markets. These pressures reflect the logic of markets in capitalist economies and have been noted by both institutional economists[14] and Marxist theorists.[15] At the individual level these pressures manifest as a tension between the temptation to press one's short-term advantage versus the benefits of sustaining long-term exchange relationships with transaction partners.[16] At the transactional level the tension is between the individual and the collectivity, i.e. maximizing an association member's profits or exercising prudent mechanisms of restraint on him. At the regulatory level this appears as the contradictory pressures on the government for enhanced market growth and capital formation versus the pressures for the continued legitimacy of the market and protecting the assets of investors. At each level, an increase in one type of pressure may threaten the other.

Polanyi Cycles

The dynamic tension in financial markets between the interest in profits and the interest in prudence does not result in stasis. The trading floor community is drawn from one side of the continuum to the other over the course of time. There is a self-correcting process through which traders and other market stakeholders recognize that behavior has pushed too far in one direction or the other. The process is one in which strategic behavior in the institutionalized market swings back and forth between the poles, never quite finding equilibrium. I refer to this movement as a "Polanyi cycle." Its logic was identified by the economic historian Karl Polanyi who observed that markets contain a "self-destructive mechanism" that communities protect themselves against.[17]

Polanyi identified a dynamic relationship between periods of relatively low restraint in markets and periods of interventionism. Consonant with our findings, Polanyi found that low restraint yielded "pernicious effects" for the less powerful market participants. The result was often interventionism on the part of government. He noted that in the nineteenth century, early industrialized nations developed factory laws, tariffs, and social insurance to protect themselves against the perils inherent in the free market system. In the wake of World War I, when many nations' economies lay in waste, efforts were made to reestablish unfettered markets as a goad to productivity.[18] These efforts dissolved with the Great Depression and renewed interventionism. We are currently in the latest cycle of this master trend as developed nations deregulate, privatize, and negotiate free trade treaties. In each cycle, a period of massive dislocation is followed by efforts to re-regulate the market. Dislocation is never long tolerated. The "pernicious effects" of the market are restrained. Then, once the dislocation is forgotten, the problems of market society are increasingly blamed on interventionism. Economic liberals attempt to remove the restraints and set the markets (nearly) free.

This tension between unfettered market relations and interventionism is the dynamic that underlies change in institutionalized markets. Each market has its own dynamic, not necessarily tied to Polanyi's master trend for national economies or the kind of business cycles described by economists. Rather, the dynamics of a market are determined by the historical conditions of its founding and its subsequent institutional and economic development. Although all institutionalized markets are expected to exhibit a long-term trend toward rationalization, each is likely to be on its own historically contingent schedule. Such dynamics exist in microcosm in stock, futures, and bond markets.

Opportunism Cycles

In financial markets the dynamic identified by Polanyi manifests itself in cycles of opportunism (see Figure 4). These cycles exist at both the transaction and regulatory levels of the institutionalized market. At the informal transaction level, some individual traders, driven by self-interest, engage in opportunistic behavior. The level of opportunism on the trading floor grows as traders observe the benefits of opportunism accruing to others. Individual traders will test the limits with increasingly extreme strategies. Members of the transactional network on the trading floor come to perceive that these acts have gone beyond what the group is willing to tolerate. Pressures rise to restrain the extremes of opportunistic behavior. As restraints increase, the level of opportunism is forced to decline, and eventually members of the network come to believe that they can relax their vigilance. Restraint subsides to the minimal levels favored by market participants. Eventually, this level of control is no longer high enough to inhibit opportunism and the sequence be-

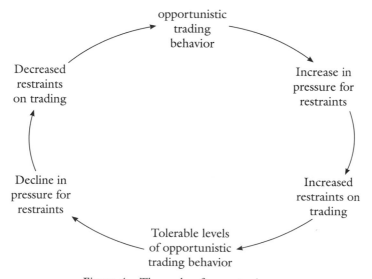

Figure 4. The cycle of opportunism

gins again. This same causal series occurs within the formal self-regulatory association, but with lower frequency and more slowly. This kind of opportunism cycle was observed in the cases of manipulation discussed in Chapters 3 and 4.

The self-regulation of the trading floor is nested in another layer of control, the regulatory system (see Figure 5). The ebb and flow of the informal and formal mechanisms of self-regulation account for most of the control on the trading floor. But on occasion extremes of opportunism exceed the level of tolerance of various powerful stakeholders inside and outside the market, which may lead to a rising perception of opportunism in the legislative or executive agencies. Members of the regulatory regime, i.e. legislators and regulatory officials, come to recognize that these acts have gone beyond what they are currently willing to tolerate. Pressures rise for government intervention. Once the regulatory controls are set in motion, the extreme level of opportunism declines. Eventually, the regulators come to believe that they can relax their restraint. Restraint subsides in keeping with the ideological and political preference for minimal control on economic activity. Ultimately, the visibility of the regulatory regime is no longer adequate and the testing of limits is renewed.

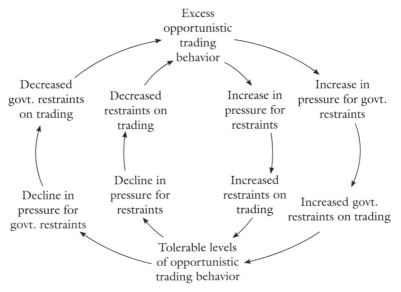

Figure 5. Nested cycles of opportunism

The timing, or oscillation, of these cycles of opportunism is not fixed or predetermined. It is shaped by the action of the traders, networks, self-regulatory associations, and regulators. The actors, at all levels, are embedded in cultures that define levels of tolerance for opportunism and for regulation. Such definitions will vary from trading floor to trading floor. The time it takes for perceptions of opportunism to gel will also vary. Visibility of the behavior and the density of interaction will shape traders' tendency to restrain others' behavior. At the self-regulatory and regulatory levels, the existence of formal procedures and informal norms will influence the recognition of opportunism. In the wider society, political trends favoring either conservative or liberal economic policies will shape the level of tolerance for opportunism, but such trends have an uncertain influence on tolerance at lower levels.[19] Oscillation in the cycles at one level may affect the oscillations at other levels, but not in perfectly predictable ways. Regulation will never be fine-tuned and regulatory action, even in the presence of political consensus, will remain part science and part craft.

Market Breaks and Market Politics

Many of the most profound examples of regulatory action seem to coincide with major breaks in the market, precipitous drops, and crashes. In financial markets, which are notoriously fragile, movement seems to be related to the recognition of crisis that undermines the faith of customers and other stakeholders. As in the case of the silver futures market in Chapter 4, market breaks (panics) are often preceded by periods of mania during which opportunism is at its height. The result is increased government attention and regulatory intervention in the market. It is not so much the crisis event, but rather the accumulating recognition and pressure that leads to regulatory action. Among regulators the dominant logic of action changes from the facilitation of *efficient* markets to the maintenance of *socially legitimate* ones. Actors at all levels respond to these changing pressures by developing effective and appropriate programs. The prevailing logic at each level appears as a binary choice, such as efficiency versus fairness, reflecting the tension of dual pressures. This logic shapes the specific strategies available to actors at that level. The choices made at one level, in turn, shape the pressures at other levels.

But government attention and even regulatory action does not lead inevitably to changes in behavior at the individual and transaction levels. Market makers in the pursuit of profits are likely to resist outside efforts at restraint even in the wake of a major market break. The probability that the logic of prudence will come to dominate that of profits is shaped by the relationship between the strength of the regulatory regime and the strength of the self-regulatory association. I will use the differences in two examples drawn from our study of the New York Stock Exchange in Chapters 5 and 6 to illustrate this point. In the first period the market break is followed by little if any behavioral change by the market makers. In the second, the market break was the precipitant to significant change.

Period One—1929–1962

Following the Crash of 1929, the Securities and Exchange Commission was established in 1934 to oversee the securities markets. In Period One there was very little evidence of increased regulation on the floor of the New York Stock Exchange. Unlike securities firms that had to divest their banking operations and meet a variety of new requirements as a result of the legislation in 1933 and 1934, New Deal regulation had little effect on specialists. Specialists successfully defended themselves against the efforts of the regulators. When the third chair of the SEC, William O. Douglas, declared that specialists could no longer be both brokers and dealers the Exchange threatened to close. The SEC backed off. At the transactional level, there was very little disruption as a result of the crash. The Exchange continued to serve the interests of its insiders. The floor community was dominant and it continued to operate as a cartel. Allocation of stocks was political and self-regulation of specialist conduct was limited. Specialists enjoyed nearly unquestioned power from the 1930s through the 1950s. During this time specialists were among the most powerful traders in the markets they made. At the individual level, specialists traded ahead of their customers and used the information available to them for personal advantage.

Period Two—1962–Present

Following the severe market break in the spring of 1962 and the "Special Study of Securities Markets" completed by the SEC in early 1963, the controversy over specialists' power was rekindled. It was found that specialists had not performed their market-stabilizing function during the drop in prices. *Fortune* magazine called the SEC's efforts to reform the specialists "Wall Street's Main Event."[20] The result was that the first explicit rules for specialists were enacted, including the "affirmative" and "negative" obligations to intervene in the market. Faith in specialist performance was further eroded following the "back-office" crisis of the late 1960s and the SEC's "Institutional Investor Study" of 1971. This study showed that specialists were clearly unable to offset the majority of large institutional trades that were increasingly dominating trading on the floor. Both the SEC report and Congressional hearings concluded that the specialists should be forced to compete with market makers in other marketplaces.[21] The specialists might have been able to fight the conclusions of these hearings and reports if they had retained their power at the transactional level. As volume at the Exchange accelerated through the 1960s and 1970s, it was the large securities firms and the institutional investors that came to dominate trading. As the power of these two groups grew they demanded better service from the specialists and more representation from the Exchange. There were changes in floor culture, especially the move toward customer service, and there were changes in Exchange governance. In 1972, specialists' political dominance of the Exchange was ended when seats on its Board of Directors were reapportioned. In 1976, control of stock allocation was shifted to a performance-based system. Throughout the 1970s and 1980s the Exchange staff became increasingly professionalized and active. At the individual level, specialists experienced the affirmative and negative obligations and the performance evaluation as powerful controls in their work life. They now consider themselves part of a quasi-public, highly regulated institution.

The dynamics of the model described above suggest that if and when Period Three comes for the specialists at NYSE, it will include a lessening of regulatory control. The precipitant to such a new era may come from a market break or crash, but more likely it will come from a competitive challenge to NYSE's dominance of its market. Most informants predict that the future of specialists lies in a level playing field where specialists can compete equally with all other markets makers who now have access to their stocks. This field will be cleared of the current regulatory constraints but freshly seeded with increased incentives that will be provided by a freer use of specialist's capital. Specialists would be allowed to trade in any stock on the Exchange, thereby enhancing profit opportunities. Many believe that such a change is necessary for specialists' survival.

But market crises and government action are not definitive in shifting market behavior. Powerful market participants and the balance of power between these participants are the critical factors. Even then, the structure of market arrangements cannot be predicted by what would be most efficient or effective.[22] Market institutions, like those studied in this book, are constructed and reconstructed through the interaction of these powerful groups. Such groups take advantage of opportunities to advance their agendas. This is true over long periods, as in the examples discussed, and it is true in smaller crises, as in the futures market manipulations discussed in Chapters 3 and 4, where the status of the actors involved (insider versus outsider) was critical in determining self- regulatory outcomes. Although prediction is beyond the scope of this book, it seems safe to say that prospective market arrangements on all the trading floors studied here will be shaped more by institutional investors and large securities firms than by individual market makers whom they have eclipsed.

The Public Interest

I began this chapter by showing that self-interest, the underlying motivation of economic behavior, is socially constructed and that its manifestations differ from context to context. I proceeded to explore some of the reasons why this might be true even in closely related markets. This reasoning and the evidence behind it suggests that the strategic and sometimes opportunistic individual behavior in these markets is strongly shaped by the institutional contexts in which it occurs. The reliance on opportunism as an explanation can only take us so far, however. It is the site-specific institutions of restraint and the power relations that underlie them that explain the observed differences in various markets.

At a more fundamental level, I'm suggesting that opportunism and restraint exist in a cyclical relationship with each other. As much as extremes of self-interest may be inhibited, the logic of the market suggests that they will be back. Although trading floors have been rationalized, periods of opportunism return. The investors' problem is that they want to have it both ways. They want the accumulation of profits that the aggressive pursuit of self-interest can bring. They also want the fairness and legitimacy that come from restraint. There is no optimal point, only contradictory forces that are in a constantly moving disequilibrium.

But the cycles of opportunism that result are not fixed either. Regulatory intervention may dampen or amplify the oscillation of these cycles. In the early 1980s, as stagflation gripped the American economy, leaders responded with a lessening of market restraints—deregulation. The deregulation was accompanied by a wave of rhetoric that washed over the financial markets sending strong signals to the trading community. Even during my research in the bond market at the end of the decade these signals continued to echo in the minds of my informants. The strength and content of such signals affected the oscillation of the cycle. Signal strength and content are political acts performed by leaders. This suggests that the message sent to traders needs to be nuanced. Restraints may be lifted without giving the impression that extreme behaviors will be tolerated. The threat of enforcement at the margins must retain its bite even as some rules and procedures are changed to attract investment.

Regulation can never replace self-regulation on the trading floor. Bureaucrats are simply too far from the action. But regulators can do better at stimulating self-regulatory vigilance in areas of extreme opportunism. Annual audits of self-regulatory statistics and procedures are inadequate. Excessive opportunistic strategies suggest the need for occasional unscheduled spot checks of market making by savvy investigators who can bypass the self-regulatory structure. This could be accomplished by increased investigation of complaints and even undercover work by "moles" who can gain access to the culture. The negative publicity that accompanies the results of such

action can be used to pressure self-regulators to focus on opportunistic strategies they have been ignoring.

Financial markets are competitive arenas with winners and losers.
It is hard to know where to draw the line. If the behavior of the
players is too circumscribed, there are several potential outcomes
that are undesirable: 1) the costs of trading are increased by compliance, 2) the incentives for participation and innovation are de-
creased, and 3) those with capital may choose to play elsewhere. In
short, you risk killing the goose that is laying the golden eggs. None
of these outcomes is in the public interest. The result is that the
public is forced to tolerate more opportunism than it would like.
Financial markets, as arenas of competition, are designed to elicit
aggressive behavior. That is their logic. Though increased pressure
on self- regulators, especially in the over-the-counter markets, may
be beneficial, I am forced to conclude that dramatic increases in direct government regulation are unwise.

Ironically, the question of regulating the trading floor will
probably be moot in the not-too-distant future. Advances in
technology are making possible an electronic market without
human market makers. Trading can be done through computers
that match bids and offers anywhere in the world. The cost per
transaction is a fraction of what it costs when there are human
intermediaries. Market makers are already resisting the trend but
the outcome seems inevitable. Increasingly, market making with
a human touch will be limited to those stocks, bonds, and
futures in which there is the least interest.[23] Most trading will
flow to low cost networks.

Other Markets, Other Industries

Criminogenic Market Structures

This book has taken the position that the tendency of economic
actors to pursue their self-interest is a drive that is common to the
species. On the other hand, the level of opportunism found in any
particular market is a product of the specific social context in which
the economic action occurs. There are patterned conditions asso-

ciated with the likelihood that economic actors will use illegitimate means to achieve their goals. Four major categories of criminogenic conditions are suggested: incentive, opportunity, and the structure and culture of restraint. Although most other studies of criminogenic factors in markets have focused on incentive and opportunity, my book emphasizes the nature of restraint.[24]

The incentive for opportunism seems obvious. As Phillip Selznick recently put it, "People want more money and more of what money can buy."[25] There is no need to posit any form of psychological abnormality. Some organizations create extreme pressure for performance, such as when top management puts pressure on middle management or when manufacturers put pressure on the profit margins of dealers and wholesalers. The threat of termination or reduced profits may provide incentive for the use of illegitimate means. At the other extreme, extraordinary bonuses, such as those in the bond market in the 1980s, may contribute to raising the level of opportunism. When bonuses are in the millions of dollars, there are strong rational reasons to push the limits of normative behavior.

Market arrangements, the systems that coordinate the movement of capital between buyers and sellers, create opportunities for delinquency. Arrangements which foster the anonymity of the exchange partners, such as those in the bond market or in electronically mediated exchange, increase the probability of the use of illegitimate means. Market arrangements that isolate, buffer, or mask the parties, reduce the risk of detection. Situations in which one party has better access to information than the other create similar opportunities for deception. Knowledge of the market systems' routines and limits is frequently not evenly distributed among their users. All of these situations create opportunities.

The studies in this book suggest that even in the presence of high levels of incentive and opportunity, social controls may inhibit the use of illegitimate means. Such controls may be the product of reputational networks, informal norms and their enforcement through group pressure, organized surveillance by firm and industry, or strong legal sanctions and regulatory vigilance. The absence of such restraints, or their sudden reduction, creates a climate of tolerance that may be criminogenic. At the informal level, the threat of one's reputation for opportunism being spread to a broad network of customers and potential customers is a primary but imperfect source of restraint. Reputation is an imperfect restraint because the opportunistic action may be invisible to customers, customers may not be part of the relevant networks signaling reputation, and some customers may choose to ignore a reputation for opportunism in return for special information or access possessed by the opportunist. In the presence of such imperfect networks, opportunism is more likely.

Restraint comes also from in-group norms and pressure for conformity. Floor traders learn appropriate norms during their early and often lengthy socialization. These norms are continually reinforced. They accomplish this in face-to-face interaction on the floor and after hours. Community pressure is often a potent force in limiting opportunism. Business forums, chambers of commerce, and even elite social clubs are vehicles for setting and maintaining minimum norms of commerce. Nevertheless, in markets in which there is limited interaction between sellers and between buyers and sellers there is also little opportunity for such informal social control.

At a more formal level, established agents of control must provide more than symbolic window dressing. Organized surveillance by firms and industries must have efficacy and legitimacy. Compliance offices with little staff, budget, or visibility in the organization create cynicism. Compromised systems of industry self-regulation in which insider elites have an advantage over outsiders encourage opportunism. Self-regulatory systems in which it is generally known that certain violations are not enforced, such as those in the futures markets, must be considered compromised. At the government level, legal restraints and regulatory intention must be matched by enforcement power. Symbolic statements about de-regulation may send a message of tolerance that increases the willingness of actors to test the limits. De-regulation should be clearly decoupled from continuing enforcement of remaining rules. This perspective on restraint suggests that the moral order of the market is precarious and that it requires community vigilance.[26]

The Market as a Moral Community

Although some might maintain that the notions of "market" and "moral order" are antithetical, I reject this undersocialized view of economic activity. Rather, financial markets operate as complex communities that include not only buyers and sellers, but subgroups of buyers and sellers who recognize each other and may act collectively in their common interest. They also include interested outsiders who are influenced by and attempt to influence market affairs.[27] The stability, vitality, and survival of these groups is dependent on protection of their market from extremes of opportunism. As in other communities, self-interest is weighed against community stability.[28]

This book has identified characteristics which facilitate market participants' ability to act as a community. Markets differ in their possession of these characteristics, but the view of markets as atomized crowds of buyers and sellers has kept us from exploring the extent to which market communities exist. Apparent social disorganization may be an illusion. Those markets with networks of social ties among the participants provide both trust and peer pressure when trust breaks down. The formal organization of markets and industries into active associations provides a sense of inclusion. Voluntary participation in governance and administration develops commitment to superordinate goals. Even regulation and the related pressures of external stakeholders serve the cause of integration and community-building as the internal participants claim moral and administrative autonomy. Although such organization may be used to defeat rather than serve the wider public interest, there may also be strong pressure not to "foul the nest" with illicit and disruptive behavior. In the presence of government restraints, such as antitrust enforcement, formal organization has yielded industry-wide standards that frequently afford effectiveness and protection for the consumer.[29]

It is worth noting that as markets develop from local to national to global dimensions, the social fabric is drawn thinner and thinner. Markets by phone, computer, and satellite may lose their sense of moral community. Exchange is governed more by formal contract than personal trust.[30] Norms of transaction may vary from region to region and culture to culture. Global markets may include participants, especially major ones like China, that resist normative pressure and legal sanctions. The sense of community will be increasingly difficult to maintain.

The Social Construction of Markets

The perspective developed in this book may be usefully extended to the study of other markets. Economic actors produce a social world that shapes their future transactions. The structure and culture of transaction will vary by the social conditions of the actors. Among the most important social conditions to be considered are the strength and efficacy of reputational and trust networks among buyers and sellers, the shifting balance of power among stakeholder groups in the market, the strength and efficacy of institutionalized norms and rules of exchange, and the role of state intervention in shaping market relations.

Embeddedness

Every market actor is part of a community of actors and all economic activity is shaped by the social relationships, cultural idioms, and institutions in which that activity is embedded. This principle suggests three approaches to the study of markets in which the analyst looks beyond individual buyers and sellers as the unit of analysis. A structural embeddedness approach focuses on the network of relationships of which every buyer or seller is a part. Stable networks of relationships are expected to produce trust, low opportunism,[31] and relative efficiency.[32] Cultural embeddedness focuses on the culturally available scripts and strategies that define who may transact and how they may do it. These scripts and strategies include locally defined goals and the prescribed means for attaining them.[33] They are distinct to every market. Finally, institutional embeddedness alerts us to the existence of more formal market arrangements that shape and control transactions. These market arrangements, from local flea markets to markets negotiated under the General Agreement on Tariffs and Trade (GATT), constitute a market control system such as the one discussed in Chapter 2.

Dynamics of Profit and Prudence

The forces of self-interest and the forces of restraint are expressed by social action beyond the pricing mechanism (the invisible hand). Self-interest and restraint are not absolutes, but vary from market to market and are defined through the interaction of market participants. Self-interest and restraint move in a cyclical relation to each other, never quite reaching equilibrium. Much remains to be learned about the changing behavior of market participants during the various phases of these cycles.

Dynamics of Institutional Change

Market institutions are produced and redefined as a result of the purposeful action and interaction of powerful interests competing for control. Participants and stakeholders are not passive. They organize informal and formal coalitions to get their interests met. This ongoing conflict often produces incremental change in the institutions. Government, and in particular its regulatory regimes, plays a significant role in determining the parameters of this change. Antitrust laws, regulatory legislation, and administrative action limit the strategies available to the competitors. At the same time, market participants actively lobby to influence these parameters. Large scale institutional change is most likely when depressions, deregulation movements, and the like create opportunities for a realignment of the players and redesign of their institutions.

The social construction perspective also suggests that when systems of restraint are created to govern opportunism, those systems are not necessarily the optimal solution to the problem. Rather, they reflect the efforts of powerful coalitions to maintain their legitimacy, control their domains, and deny existing opportunities to their competitors. Understanding of control mechanisms in the market requires historical analysis of the struggles of competing stakeholders and the events shaping the struggle.

Traders and Trading Floors

What can be concluded about market makers as representatives of the species homo economicus? Trading floors may include both the twenty-five-year-old opportunist in the bond market and the sixty-year-old specialist worrying about customer service and extinction at NYSE. Both are hyper-rational risk-takers facing the trading day with speculative gusto, but the structural conditions on their respective trading floors differ. Both are embedded in social relations that facilitate and restrain their opportunism.

What can be concluded about the trading floor as a social institution? Like most other institutions, it is imperfect. But it provides benefits for which there is currently no substitute. The trading floor, in the three guises studied here, provides efficient coordination of buyers and sellers. But like other institutions, including representative democracy, it teaches us to settle. It teaches that uncertainty, opportunism, and occasional severe dislocations must be tolerated in order to benefit. It teaches that these benefits will be unevenly distributed and that the unevenness will be explained by the distribution of power. Technological change and globalization of markets will undoubtedly change it further. But whatever changes may occur, there will always be self-interested actors who will find ways to use and misuse these markets. It is part of their logic and allure.

NOTES
INDEX

—

NOTES

—

Introduction

1. "How Salomon's Hubris and a Quiet U.S. Trap Led to Downfall," *Wall Street Journal,* 19 August 1991, p. 1.

2. "Salomon Reveals It Had Control of 94% of Notes at May Auction," *Wall Street Journal,* 5 September 1991, p. C1.

3. "SEC Sets $5 Million in Penalties," *New York Times,* 17 January 1992, p. D1.

4. Oliver Williamson has defined opportunism as "self- interest seeking with guile." Although this is a useful working definition, in practice the point at which self-interest becomes opportunism is a social construction, determined by the collective tolerance of a community for self-interested behavior. See Oliver Williamson, *Markets and Hierarchies: Analysis and Antitrust Implications* (New York: Free Press, 1975), p. 25.

5. There are several useful accounts that discuss the changing financial environment of the 1980s. See A. W. Samatz, "The New Financial Environment," in *The Emerging Financial Industry,* ed. A. W. Samatz (Lexington, Mass.: Lexington Books, 1984) and J. O. Matthews, *Struggle and Survival on Wall Street* (New York: Oxford University Press, 1994).

6. I will use masculine pronouns to describe market makers throughout this book. This was a difficult decision. There are very few women market makers in the markets I studied. I met no women traders in the futures markets I studied in the late seventies and early eighties. There were two out of fifty-four in my bond trader sample. There was one women specialist out of four hundred on the New York Stock Exchange. Given the level of discrimination reflected in these numbers, it seems inappropriate to imply that my statements apply to a mixed-gender group. The gender discrimination on the trading floor is remarkable by current business standards.

7. See James F. Gamill, "The Organization of Financial Markets," paper presented at the Annual Meeting of the American Sociological Association, 1 September 1986.

8. H. Stoll, "Alternative Views of Market Making," in *Market Making and the Changing Structures of the Securities Industry,* eds. Y. Amihud, R. Schwartz, and T. S. Y. Yo (Lexington, Mass.: Lexington Books, 1985), p. 67.

9. R. Ney, *The Wall Street Jungle* (New York: Grove Press, 1970).

10. Stoll, "Alternative Views of Market Making," p. 77.

11. Economists often assume that economic arrangements, such as market making, exist because they are the most efficient solution to the problem of matching buyers and sellers. This study will focus instead on the powerful actors involved in constructing this solution and the interests that are served by existing arrangements. Organizational economists assume that governance structures are a result of the most efficient solution to the problems of transaction cost and moral hazard. The perspective developed here maintains that such structures reflect the struggles over power and control within the market as an institution.

12. The themes guiding this study are those of the growing field of economic sociology. For useful discussions of this recently reborn field see R. Swedberg and M. Granovetter, introduction to *The Sociology of Economic Life,* eds. M. Granovetter and R. Swedberg (Boulder, Colo.: Westview Press, 1992); N. Smelser and R. Swedberg, "The Sociological Perspective on the Economy," in *The Handbook of Economic Sociology* (Princeton: Princeton University Press, 1994).

13. The history of the founding of the New York Stock Exchange and the Chicago Board of Trade show that merchants came together to design institutions that would give them decided advantages and define a new market. For the history of NYSE, see R. I. Warshow, *The Story of Wall Street* (New York: Greenberg, 1929). For the history of the CBT, see J. Lurie, *The Chicago Board of Trade 1859–1905: The Dynamics of Self-Regulation* (Urbana, Ill.: University of Illinois Press, 1979); M. Y. Abolafia and N. W. Biggart, "Competition and Markets: An Institutional Perspective," in *Socio-Economics: Toward a New Synthesis,* eds. A. Etzioni and P. Lawrence (Armonk, N.Y.: Sharpe, 1991). Neil Fligstein shows that a similar dynamic is at work in industrial markets. See N. Fligstein, *The Transformation of Corporate Control* (Cambridge, Mass.: Harvard University Press, 1990).

14. Although over-the-counter trading existed prior to the twentieth century, the National Association of Securities Dealers (NASD) and its institutionalized structure of trading are twentieth-century creations.

15. The process of social construction is not random. Outcomes are guided by the distribution of power in the community. As Berger and Luckmann put it, "He who has the bigger stick has the better chance of imposing his definitions of reality." See P. L. Berger and T. Luckmann, *The Social Construction of Reality: A Treatise in the Sociology of Knowledge* (New York: Anchor Books, 1966), p. 109.

16. This view of economic behavior corresponds to the theories of social embeddedness developed by Granovetter and of cultural embeddedness de-

veloped by DiMaggio. See M. Granovetter, "Economic Action and Social Structure: The Problem of Embeddedness," *American Journal of Sociology* 91 (November 1985), pp. 481–510; P. DiMaggio, "Cultural Aspects of Economic Action and Organization," in *Beyond Marketplace,* eds. R. Friedland and A. F. Robertson (New York: Aldine de Gruyter, 1990).

17. The view that economic behavior is exclusively the product of individual choice reflects its methodological individualism. It is represented in the vast majority of economic literature. Work on opportunism by economists, most prominently Oliver Williamson, considers the economic and cognitive environment of actors (e.g. asset specificity and uncertainty), but reflects an undersocialized view of economic actors in which opportunism is not at all mediated by work group association or local culture. See Williamson, *Markets and Hierarchies;* and Oliver Williamson, *The Economic Institutions of Capitalism* (New York: Free Press, 1985).

18. Peter Bernstein, *Capital Ideas* (New York: Free Press, 1992), p. 7.

1. Homo Economicus Unbound

1. Because I was accustomed to teaching women MBAs, it was surprising to see that there are still occupations, even in major banks, where women are so under-represented. Male pronouns are used to maintain realism.

2. C. Geertz, *The Interpretation of Cultures* (New York: Basic Books, 1973), p. 433.

3. This finding is similar to the interpretation of deviant behavior developed by Katz. See Jack Katz, *The Seductions of Crime: Moral and Sensual Attractions in Doing Evil* (New York: Harper Collins, 1988).

4. Oliver Williamson, *Markets and Hierarchies: Analysis and Antitrust Implications* (New York: Free Press, 1975), p. 26.

5. The bond traders were clearly aware that although their behavior may have been locally within bounds, it would be frowned on by those outside the trading floor culture. See J. Van Maanen, "The Fact of Fiction in Organizational Ethnography," *Administrative Science Quarterly* 24 (1979), pp. 539–550.

6. M. Lewis, *Liar's Poker: Rising through the Wreckage on Wall Street* (New York: Norton, 1989), p. 34.

7. See Williamson, *Markets and Hierarchies;* Williamson, *The Economic Institutions of Capitalism;* A. Sen, "Rational Fools," *Philosophy and Public Affairs* 6 (1977), pp. 317–334; T. Scitovsky, *The Joyless Economy* (New York: Oxford, 1976); H. Leibenstein, "Allocative Efficiency vs. 'X-Efficiency,'" *American Economic Review* 56 (1966), pp. 392–415.

8. See H. Simon, *Administrative Behavior,* 3rd ed. (New York: Free Press, 1976); J. March and H. Simon, *Organizations* (New York: Wiley, 1958); J. March and J. Olsen, *Ambiguity and Choice in Organizations* (Bergen, Norway: Universitetsforlaget, 1976); and A. Etzioni, *The Moral Dimension: Toward a New Economics* (New York: Free Press, 1988).

9. A. Tversky and D. Kahneman, "Judgment under Uncertainty," *Science* 185 (27 September 1974), pp. 1124–1131.

10. Sen, "Rational Fools."

11. R. Thaler, *The Winner's Curse* (New York: Free Press, 1992).

12. J. M. Keynes, *The General Theory of Employment, Interest, and Money* (New York: Harcourt, Brace, 1964), p. 154.

13. For a model of how this works, see H. White, "Where Do Markets Come From?" *American Journal of Sociology* 87 (March 1981), pp. 517–547.

14. For a discussion of establishing value in other markets, see C. W. Smith, *Auctions: The Social Construction of Value* (Berkeley: University of California Press), 1989.

15. Jerome Bruner, *On Knowing* (Cambridge, Mass.: Harvard University Press, 1962).

16. M. Polanyi, *Personal Knowledge* (Chicago: University of Chicago Press, 1958).

17. P. L. Berger and T. Luckmann, *The Social Construction of Reality: A Treatise in the Sociology of Knowledge* (New York: Anchor Books, 1966), p. 62.

18. Max Weber, *The Protestant Ethic and the Spirit of Capitalism,* trans. Talcott Parsons (New York: Charles Scribner's, 1958). The spirit of capitalism may be thought of as a typification of the strategies of the early Calvinists. These Calvinists would likely be shocked by the behavior of the bond traders, particularly their materialism.

19. Lewis, *Liar's Poker.*

20. W. Baker, "The Social Structure of a National Securities Market," *American Journal of Sociology* 89 (January 1984), pp. 775–811; and M. Y. Abolafia, "Self- Regulation as Market Maintenance," in *Regulatory Policy and the Social Sciences,* ed. R. Noll (Berkeley: University of California Press, 1985); and Chapter 5 of this book.

21. D. A. Vise and S. Coll, *Eagle on the Street* (New York: Charles Scribner's, 1991).

22. D. P. McCaffrey and S. Faerman, "Shared Regulation in the United States Securities Industry," *Administration and Society* 26 (August 1994), pp. 204–235.

23. Abolafia, "Self-Regulation."

24. In contrast, a study of specialists on the floor of the New York Stock Exchange found that the specialists were conscious of regulation, easily citing three regulations that constrained their trading on a daily basis. For more information on this study, see Chapter 5.

2. Structured Anarchy

1. Frank Norris, *The Pit: A Story of Chicago* (New York: Doubleday, Page & Co., 1903), p. 98.

2. Paul Samuelson, *Economics: An Introductory Analysis,* 6th ed. (New York: McGraw Hill, 1964), p. 69.

3. See W. R. Ashby, *An Introduction to Cybernetics* (New York: Harper & Row, 1965); W. Buckley, *Sociology and Modern Systems Theory* (Englewood Cliffs, N.J.: Prentice-Hall, 1967); M. Cadwaller, "The Cybernetic Analysis of Change in Complex Social Systems," in W. Buckley, ed., *Modern System Research for the Behavioral Scientist* (Chicago: Aldine, 1968); T. Parsons, "Three Levels in the Hierarchical Structure of Organization," in W. Evans, ed., *Interorganizational Relations* (Philadelphia: University of Pennsylvania Press, 1978).

4. Chicago Board of Trade, *Commodity Trading Manual* (Chicago: Chicago Board of Trade, 1979), p. 403.

5. Merrill Lynch suggests to prospective futures clients that they have at least $50,000 in speculative capital before they begin. It is not unusual for commission houses to keep Treasury bills and other easily liquefiable assets on deposit as part of the margin account. Smaller houses may ask for only the minimum required by the exchange.

6. M. Powers, *Getting Started in Commodity Futures Trading* (Waterloo, Iowa: Investors Publication Inc., 1980), p. 253.

7. Ashby, *An Introduction to Cybernetics;* H. Simon, *The Sciences of the Artificial* (Cambridge, Mass.: MIT Press, 1981).

8. Simon, *The Sciences of the Artificial,* p. 12.

9. J. Lurie, *The Chicago Board of Trade 1859–1905;* C. Taylor, *History of the Board of Trade of the City of Chicago* (Chicago: R. O. Law, 1917).

10. The perpective on market control developed here is in substantial agreement with the idea in organizational economics that such structures are a response to the threat of opportunism. But whereas organizational economists assume that the design of such structures is the result of the most efficient response to the problems of transactions costs or moral hazard, this perspective maintains that the design of these structures reflects struggles over power and control within the organization.

11. J. S. Commons, *Institutional Economics* (Madison: University of Wisconsin Press, 1959), p. 713.

12. T. A. Hieronymus, *Economics of Future Trading* (New York: Commodity Research Bureau, 1971).

13. New York Mercantile Exchange, *By-laws and Rules* (New York: New York Mercantile Exchange, 1979).

14. Ibid., pp. 2–20b.

15. On the four largest exchanges, which account for more than 90 percent of trading, the staff was between 13 percent and 18 percent of the size of the total membership in 1980. The largest of the four had 254 staff, the smallest had fifty.

16. Chicago Board of Trade, *Commodity Trading Manual.*

17. Competition began to heat up in the mid-1970s over the development of futures contracts in financial instruments, such as Treasury bills and bonds, Government National Mortgage Association Certificates, and most recently,

stock indexes. It appears that existing economies of scale at the CBT and Chicago Mercantile Exchange will eventually allow each to overcome competition from the New York exchanges and to dominate in particular commodities.

18. The establishment of the federal Commodity Futures Trading Commission in 1975 has inhibited their freedom in rule-changing to a degree, in that the exchanges must now submit all rule changes for approval.

19. M. Y. Abolafia, "Taming the Market: Self-Regulation in the Commodity Futures Industry" (Ph.D. diss., State University of New York at Stony Brook, 1981).

20. In my doctoral dissertation, "Taming the Market," I have discussed the agency's reluctance to intervene in the exchange's market control system. Recently, the agency has been forced by events covered in the press to attend to conflicts of interest which may occur when members of the board of directors use their rule-changing power to affect trading in a contract in which they hold positions. See Chapter 4 in this book for an example.

21. C. B. Cowing, *Populists, Plungers, and Progressives* (Princeton, N.J.: Princeton University Press, 1965); Lurie, *Self-Regulation*.

22. "Board of Trade Fines Clayton Brokerage," *The Wall Street Journal*, 21 February 1979, p. 24.

23. This account of the bucket shops is based on the historical account in Lurie, *Self-Regulation*.

24. Ibid., p. 80.

25. "Chronology of Activities Relating to the Silver Market from September 1979 through March 1980" (news release, Commodities Exchange of New York, 1980).

26. "CBT, CME, and Comex Join Forces," *Futures Industry: The Newsletter for Futures Market Professionals* 3 (2 June 1980), p. 4.

3. Taming the Market

1. See C. Taylor, *History of the Board of Trade of the City of Chicago* (Chicago: R. O. Law, 1917); G. W. Hoffman, *Futures Trading upon Organized Commodity Markets* (Philadelphia: University of Pennsylvania Press, 1932); H. S. Irwin, *Evolution of Futures Trading* (Madison: Mimir Publishers, 1954); J. Lurie, *The Chicago Board of Trade 1859–1905: The Dynamics of Self-Regulation* (Urbana: The University of Illinois Press, 1979).

2. Taylor, *History of the Board*.

3. Irwin, *Evolution of Futures Trading*.

4. Hoffman, *Futures Trading*.

5. The notion that some degree of restraint in the market may be desirable was tested in the Supreme Court, where it found support in the early part of this century. One of the earliest and clearest statements of the principle was given in *Chicago Board of Trade v. United States*. In this case the Supreme

Court found that the CBT's call rule was a reasonable restraint of trade. The rule prohibited members from purchasing or offering to purchase grain to arrive after the close of trading. The rule was little different from a variety of others that restrained behavior in the markets. The Court found that the power of an association to restrain its members may be used for good or bad purposes. Justice Brandeis, writing for the Court, made the point that all commercial actions contain some degree of restraint: "Every agreement concerning trade, every regulation of trade, restrains. To bind, to restrain, is of their very essence. The true test of legality is whether the restraint imposed is such as merely regulates and perhaps thereby promotes competition or whether it is such as may suppress or even destroy competition." See U.S. Supreme Court, *Chicago Board of Trade v. United States,* 246 U.S. Reports 231 (1918).

6. S. Peltzman, "Toward a More General Theory of Regulation," *Journal of Law and Economics* 19 (1976); G. Kolko, *Railroads and Regulation 1877–1916* (New York: Norton, 1965); G. Stigler, *The Citizen and the State* (Chicago: University of Chicago Press, 1975).

7. It is important to note that the terms competition and conflict are used here in the sociologist's rather than the economist's sense. Competition refers to mutually opposed efforts to secure some valued object. Thus, futures trading is competitive in the sense that two or more buyers (or sellers) seek the same limited number of bids (or offers). Futures trading is almost ideally competitive in that it occurs at open auctions on the floors of exchanges where all bids and offers are made. This behavioral definition of competition differs considerably from the formal economic definition. When the economist refers to a competitive market, he or she is likely to emphasize the large number of buyers and sellers, which insures that no single buyer or seller is able to influence the prices being established. Thus, the economist would emphasize the independent nature of each individual's actions. The sociologist looking at the same event is concerned with the behavioral rivalry involved in market relations and its implications for the distribution of economic rewards. See F. M. Scherer, *Industrial Market Structure and Economic Performance* (Chicago: Rand McNally, 1970). A second social process that will be central to this study is conflict, especially market conflict. Sociologists use the term to include situations in which two or more actors attempt to realize their opposing interests. Weber defines conflict as a relationship "insofar as action within it is oriented intentionally to carry out the actor's own will against the resistance of the other party or parties." See M. Weber in *The Theory of Social and Economic Organizations,* ed. T. Parsons (New York: Free Press, 1947). This sort of situation arises in futures markets, particularly as the delivery date of a contract approaches, when a large portion of the contracts (bought or sold) is held by one or a few interests. Typically, these dominant interests will push their advantage by squeezing a more advantageous price out of those on the other side of the market who need an offsetting trade to close out their position. Conflict, then, is inherent when people use their bargaining power to estab-

lish price. See T. A. Hieronymus, "Manipulation in Commodity Futures Trading: Toward a Definition," *Hofstra Law Review* 6 (1977), pp. 41–56.

8. T. A. Hieronymus, *Economics of Futures Trading* (New York: Commodity Research Bureau, 1971).

9. Agricultural economists, notably Thomas Hieronymus and Roger Gray, generally argue that what is called manipulation is most often just extreme risk-taking. As Hieronymus has shown, deliverable supply, because of its expectational character, is not easily defined. See T. A. Hieronymus, "Manipulation in Commodity Futures Trading." If longs are squeezing shorts on the basis of a limited deliverable supply, they are taking the risk that more of the commodity can be certified or moved into position for delivery. Such risk-taking is part of competition, and it is not surprising that differences in expectations and attitudes toward risk often result in dominant positions at the end of a contract. Moreover, aggressive trading and manipulation have the same intent, i.e., profit. So where does one draw the line?

10. *Board of Trade v. Commodity Futures Trading Commission,* U.S. District Court, Northern Illinois, p. 81 (18 March 1979). Emphasis is my own. The subjectivity of the standard for artificial prices is signaled by the basis for evaluation: "if people get nervous."

11. Ibid., p. 58.

12. U.S. House of Representatives, *March Wheat Futures Trading on the Chicago Board of Trade,* 96th Cong., 1st sess. (Washington, D.C.: GPO, 1979b), p. 61.

13. I was able to gather case studies on only two such actions in the last twenty years and only bits and pieces of several cases before that.

4. Responding to External Threats

1. U.S. House of Representatives, *Silver Prices and the Adequacy of Federal Action in the Marketplace, 1979–1980,* Committee on Government Operations, 96th Congress, pp. 291, 297.

2. Portions of this chapter are taken from Mitchel Y. Abolafia and Martin Kilduff, "Enacting Market Crisis: The Social Construction of a Speculative Bubble," *Administrative Science Quarterly* 33 (June 1988), pp. 177–193.

3. S. Fay, *Beyond Greed* (New York: Viking, 1982), p. 138.

4. C. P. Kindleberger, *Manias, Panics and Crashes: A History of Financial Crises* (New York: Basic Books, 1978).

5. M. H. Wolfson, *Financial Crises: Understanding the Postwar U.S. Experience* (Armonk, N.Y.: M. E. Sharp, 1986), p. 6.

6. N. F. Brady, *The Presidential Task Force on Market Mechanisms* (Washington, D.C.: GPO, 1988).

7. Commodity Futures Trading Commission, *Report on Recent Events in the Silver Market, May 29, 1981* (Washington, D.C.: Commodity Futures Trading, 1981), p. 8.

8. The information in this section is drawn from several sources: U.S. Securities and Exchange Commission, *The Silver Crisis of 1980: A Report of the Staff of the U.S. Securities and Exchange Commission* (Washington, D.C.: U.S. Securities and Exchange Commission, 1982); U.S. House of Representatives, *1980 Silver Prices and the Adequacy of Federal Actions in the Market Place, 1979–80,* Committee on Government Operations, 96th Cong. (Washington, D.C.: GPO, 1980); Fay, *Beyond Greed;* P. Sarnoff, *Silver Bulls* (Westport, Conn.: Arlington House, 1980); and interviews conducted by the author with participants during and after the crisis.

9. "Long" and "short" refer to the positions held by a trader in the market. The Hunts would be called "longs." Being long in silver futures means that the trader holds a contract that entitles him or her to buy a specific grade and quantity of silver at a fixed price on a set delivery date in the future. Being short in silver futures means that a trader is entitled to sell a specific grade and quantity of silver at a fixed price on a preset delivery date. Speculators may be either long or short depending on whether they expect the price to go up or down. Only 3–5 percent of traders ever demand or tender delivery. Most traders offset their position before the delivery date by making an equal but opposite transaction at the current price and accepting their subsequent loss or gain.

10. Fay, *Beyond Greed.*

11. Margin is the cash funds every trader must deposit with a broker for each contract as a sign of good faith in fulfilling contract terms. A margin call is a demand for additional cash because of adverse price movement. In the silver crisis, as the price went up, increasing the value of the Hunts' position, it had an equal and opposite effect on the position of the silver firms. Each day's adverse price movement required an additional margin payment to the broker who was legally responsible for insuring that the contract terms could be met at all times.

12. See I. O. Glick, "A Social Psychological Study of Futures Trading" (Ph.D. diss.: Department of Sociology, University of Chicago, 1957); J. K. Galbraith, *The Great Crash* (Boston: Houghton Mifflin, 1961); M. Y. Abolafia, "Taming the Market: Self-Regulation in the Commodity Futures Industry" (Ph.D. diss.: State University of New York at Stony Brook, 1981).

13. Futures exchanges have the legal right to restrain trade when that restraint is intended to maintain the stability of the market and thereby promote competition. This justification for restraint in the context of free markets was formulated by Justice Brandeis in U.S. Supreme Court, *Chicago Board of Trade v. United States,* 246 U.S. 231 (1918). Exchanges are now obligated to maintain market integrity by the Commodity Futures Exchange Act of 1974. See M. Y. Abolafia, "Self-Regulation as Market Maintenance," in *Regulatory Policy and Social Sciences,* ed. R. Noll (Berkeley: University of California Press, 1985), for a detailed discussion.

14. "Reserve Board in New Attack on Inflation Is Stressing Restraint on Debt," *Wall Street Journal,* 17 March 1980, p. 1.

15. See Commodity Futures Trading Commission, *Report on Recent Events*.

16. Ibid., p. 10.

17. The CFTC showed, through its intervention, its concern with the non-price issues (i.e., legitimacy of the market and the agency) involved in the crisis, yet, for public consumption, it limited itself to supply-and-demand conditions. Both the exchange members and the regulators were unwilling to say publicly that the markets did not work as advertised, despite their own telltale actions. The legitimacy of both institutions rests on the maintenance of open markets.

18. Glick, "A Social Psychological Study," p. 127.

19. Many months later this decision was reversed, and its reversal was upheld by the U.S. Supreme Court in April 1980.

20. R. Michels, *Political Parties* (New York: Free Press, 1962).

21. H. Demsetz, "Perfect Competition, Regulation, and the Stock Market," in *Economic Policy and the Regulation of Corporate Securities,* ed. H. Manne (Washington, D.C.: American Enterprise Institute, 1969), pp. 4–5.

22. Noll has argued that futures exchanges are basically operating as cartels in the cases discussed above. See R. Noll, "Comment," in *Regulatory Policy and the Social Sciences,* ed. R. Noll (Berkeley: University of California Press, 1985). I agree that they have manipulated price in the fashion of a cartel, and that the most powerful members of the cartel have the greatest influence on the organizations' actions and policies. But self-regulation is more than a cartel. Futures markets maintain efficient markets that are open to new members. Cartelized markets are neither efficient nor are they open. Futures exchanges have thick rule books and complex organizational structures that control the behavior of their members far beyond the purview of most cartels. They are a unique form of collective action.

23. See J. Lurie, *The Chicago Board of Trade 1859–1905: The Dynamics of Self-Regulation* (Urbana: University of Illinois Press, 1979); T. A. Hieronymus, *Economics of Future Trading* (New York: Commodity Research Bureau, 1971) for accounts of futures pits in the 19th century.

5. Homo Economicus Restrained

1. J. Brooks, *Once In Golconda: A True Drama of Wall Street* (New York: Harper and Row, 1969); R. Sobel, *NYSE: A History of the New York Stock Exchange 1935–1975* (New York: Weybright and Talley, 1975), p. 17; R. J. Teweles and E. S. Bradley, *The Stock Market,* 5th ed. (New York: Wiley, 1987), p. 300.

2. I had the fear, common to modern ethnographers, that perhaps I was being manipulated. Over time I became convinced of the sincerity of these claims based not only on the real changes that had come to the floor, but the adaptive reaction of specialists to the increase in regulation and their own loss of power. See the next chapter for a fuller explanation of this phenomenon.

3. This proposition is suggested by the recent work of Harrison White, *Identity and Control: A Structural Theory of Social Action* (Princeton: Princeton University Press, 1992).

4. H. Stoll, "Alternative Views of Market Making," in *Market Making and the Changing Structures of the Securities Industry,* eds. Y. Amihud, R. Schwartz, and T. S. Y. Yo (Lexington, Mass.: Lexington Books, 1985); New York Stock Exchange, *Annual Report 1988* (New York: NYSE, 1989).

5. Teweles and Bradley, *The Stock Market.*

6. Stoll, "Alternative Views."

7. D. A. Oesterle, D. A. Winslow, and S. C. Anderson, "The New York Stock Exchange and Its Outmoded Specialist System: Can the Exchange Innovate to Survive?" *The Journal of Corporation Law* 17 (Winter 1992), p. 240.

8. N. Wolfson and T. A. Russo, "The Stock Exchange Specialists: An Economic and Legal Analysis," *Duke Law Journal* (1970), pp. 707–746; J. Seligman, *The Transformation of Wall Street: A History of the Securities and Exchange Commission and Modern Corporate Finance* (Boston: Houghton Mifflin, 1982).

9. Wolfson and Russo, "The Stock Exchange Specialists," p. 721.

10. Quoted in Sobel, *NYSE: A History,* p. 34.

11. Ibid., p. 345.

12. Ibid., p. 345.

13. Seligman, *The Transformation of Wall Street,* p. 324.

14. Ibid, p. 339.

15. Sobel, *NYSE: A History,* pp. 255–256.

16. Kennedy threatened to boycott the companies that went along, to investigate for antitrust violations, and to initiate IRS probes. The steel companies backed down.

17. It should be noted that most of the time this is a profitable strategy because specialists are able to buy at or near the bottom of a trend and sell at or near the top. In trading this is called a "contrarian" strategy and is favored by many professionals.

18. Summarized from Wolfson and Russo, "The Stock Exchange Specialists."

19. The 1960s saw the return of an activist SEC. The NYSE's Batten Report notes that between 1968 and 1976 nine instances involving sanctions of a specialist took place without public notice. See Oesterle, et. al., "The New York Stock Exchange," p. 253.

20. Gonif is a Yiddish term for thief. It is interesting to note that the speaker in this case was of Irish descent. Yiddish terms were commonly used by specialists of varied ethnicities.

21. See Chapter 1 for a discussion of "institutional rules." When the rules are comprehensive and integrated, as they are among specialists, we may call them an ideology. Lofland lists these characteristics of ideology as important facilitators of both normal and deviant identities. See J. Lofland, *Deviance and Identity* (Englewood Cliffs, N.J.: Prentice-Hall, 1969).

22. After hours trading, as well as dealerized markets, are competitive threats to the specialist. Both suggest that current arrangements are not the only possible ones.

23. New York Stock Exchange, *Floor Official Manual* (New York: NYSE, 1990), p. 23.

24. U.S. Securities and Exchange Commission, *Institutional Investor Study Report*, 92nd Cong., 1st sess. (Washington, D.C.: GPO, 1971); New York Stock Exchange, *The Quality of the New York Stock Exchange Marketplace in 1979* (New York: NYSE, 1980).

6. Coping with the Threat of Extinction

1. "Big Board, at Age 200, Scrambles to Protect Grip on Stock Market," *Wall Street Journal*, 13 May 1992, p. 1.

2. "The Future of Wall Street," *Business Week* (5 November 1990); "Drifting and Dreaming," *Intermarket* (August 1989); "Who Needs the Stock Exchange?" *Fortune* (19 November 1990).

3. M. Scheler, *Ressentiment* (New York: Free Press, 1961). Note that the word "ressentiment" is more frequently associated with Nietzsche, but is used here in Scheler's more sociological sense of the term.

4. R. K. Merton, *Social Theory and Social Structure,* (New York: Free Press, 1968).

5. M. Hannan and J. Freeman, "The Population Ecology of Organizations," *American Journal of Sociology* 82 (March 1977), pp. 929–966.

6. For a critique of these views see M. Y. Abolafia and N. W. Biggart, "Competition and Markets: An Institutional Perspective," in *Socio-Economics: Toward a New Synthesis,* eds. A. Etzioni and P. Lawrence (Armonk, N.Y.: M. E. Sharpe, 1991).

7. Mr. Meehan suggested that his statements about the association could not be disguised, given his leadership position. I agree. His name is used with his permission.

7. Opportunism and Innovation

1. R. K. Merton, *Social Theory and Social Structure* (New York: Free Press, 1968), pp. 195–196.

2. The robber barons, and more recently, Michael Milken, are the subject of continuous revisionist battles. For some, the railroad industrialists were heroes. For others, they were robbers. Recently, Alfred Chandler has made the case that Jay Gould was the leading "system builder" of the railroad age. He writes, "no man had a greater impact on the strategy of American railroads than Jay Gould, the most formidable and best known of the late nineteenth-century speculators." See Alfred Chandler, *The Visible Hand: The Managerial Revolution in American Business* (Cambridge, Mass.: Belknap Press, 1977), p.

148. There is a mini-industry thriving on the competing interpretations of Michael Milken. See C. Bruck, *Predators Ball* (New York: Simon and Schuster, 1988); J. Stewart, *Den of Thieves* (New York: Simon and Schuster, 1991); and F. Bailey, *Fall from Grace* (New York: Birch Lane Press, 1992).

3. For an analysis of the fraud, see Mary Zey, *Banking on Fraud* (Hawthorne, N.Y.: Aldine de Gruyter, 1993).

4. Quoted in R. Alcaly, "The Golden Age of Junk," in *New York Review of Books*, 26 May 1994, p. 28.

5. Quoted in Bruck, *Predators Ball*, p. 271.

6. The social drama model is taken from the work of anthropologist Victor Turner. See V. Turner, *Dramas, Fields, and Metaphors* (Ithaca, N.Y.: Cornell University Press, 1974). For an earlier application of this model to financial affairs, see M. Y. Abolafia and Martin Kilduff, "The Social Destruction of Reality: Organizational Conflict as Social Drama," presented at the American Sociological Association Meeting, Chicago, Ill., August 1987.

7. Turner, *Dramas, Fields, and Metaphors*.

8. This story is told in Bruck, *Predators Ball*; Bailey, *Fall from Grace*; and Stewart, *Den of Thieves*.

9. Stewart, *Den of Thieves*, p. 45.

10. Bruck, *Predators Ball*, p. 29.

11. Stewart, *Den of Thieves*, p. 46.

12. Robert Sobel, *Dangerous Dreamers* (New York: John Wiley, 1993), p. 78.

13. Stewart, *Den of Thieves*, p. 48.

14. Bruck, *Predators Ball*, p. 48.

15. Ibid., p. 57.

16. It was during this period, in 1978, that Milken moved the junk bond department of Drexel to Beverly Hills. Some observers have suggested that this was an attempt to get out from under Drexel's control. This may be so, but it seems equally likely that, as Milken claimed, he simply wanted to go home to southern California. (He bought a house a few blocks from his parent's home in Encino.) He merely had no compunction about challenging the norm, which said that all significant investment banking is done in New York. It was part of his challenge to the establishment.

17. Turner, *Dramas, Fields, and Metaphors*, p. 38.

18. Sobel, *Dangerous Dreamers*, p. 128.

19. There are a number of books which make this argument. See T. Boone Pickens, *Boone* (Boston: Houghton Mifflin, 1987); Bailey, *Fall from Grace*; and Sobel, *Dangerous Dreamers*.

20. Sobel, *Dangerous Dreamers*, p. 143.

21. Turner, *Dramas, Fields, and Metaphors*, p. 41.

22. Sobel, *Dangerous Dreamers*, p. 148.

23. Bailey, *Fall from Grace*, p. 116.

24. Ibid., p. 117.

25. Ibid., p. 125.

26. Paul Hirsch notes that the normative framing of the junk bond raiders (Steinberg, Icahn, and Pickens) by their targets was more extreme than in contests among large corporate-status equals. See P. Hirsch, "From Ambushes to Golden Parachutes: Corporate Takeover as an Instance of Cultural Framing" *American Journal of Sociology* 91 (January 1986), p. 821.

27. All figures in this paragraph are from Alcaly, "The Golden Age of Junk," p. 29.

28. It is impossible to know with certainty what ended the wave of hostile takeovers because merger waves seem to always have a limited life span, but it is clear that the threat of legislation, inspired by an activist corporate elite, was a critical factor in the timing.

8. Cycles of Opportunism

1. Field notes, 33-year-old silver futures trader.

2. See P. L. Berger and T. Luckmann, *The Social Construction of Reality: A Treatise in the Sociology of Knowledge*, (New York: Anchor Books, 1966), p. 48.

3. For a fascinating account of the sting operation and the fraud and corruption it uncovered, see D. Greising and L. Morse, *Brokers, Bagmen and Moles: Fraud and Corruption in the Chicago Futures Market* (New York: Wiley, 1991). Although a significant percent of the prosecutions resulted in acquittal, much of this is attributed to the complexity of the cases and the incompetence of the government's prosecution. My own fieldwork suggests that the types of violations identified by the sting operation are part of floor culture. Most traders acknowledge that such things go on, and that they are most common in the financial futures pits where young, undercapitalized traders are most likely to trade.

4. A. Swidler, "Culture in Action: Symbols and Strategies," *American Sociological Review* 51 (1986), p. 284.

5. N. W. Biggart, "Explaining Asian Economic Organization: Toward a Weberian Institutional Perspective," *Theory and Society* 20 (1991), p. 224.

6. Field notes, a 36-year-old sugar futures trader.

7. Self-regulation can come very close to operating as a cartel, and on occasion the two forms seem indistinguishable. But, in most cases, antitrust law inhibits self-regulators from fixing prices. According to antitrust law, the restraint found in self-regulation is legitimate when it enhances the conditions for competition. This recognizes that competition cannot occur without some degree of restraint. Competition is enhanced when competitors agree to play on the same field, at the same time, completing their contracts, and limiting their deceptive practices.

8. For a recent exception see D. P. McCaffrey and S. Faerman, "Shared Regulation in the United States Securities Industry," *Administration and Society* 26 (August 1994).

9. The New York Stock Exchange is most notable in this regard, as it has been trying to advertise its regulatory advantage over NASDAC, the over-the-counter stock market. This, of course, correlated with the reality of increased enforcement discussed in Chapter 5.

10. The financial pages in many newspapers publicize the occasional large fine handed out by NYSE, usually to large brokerage firms for failure to supervise a particularly egregious violation which they have reported. The impact of self-regulation on market making is largely the affair of market insiders because it is between members of the Exchange and because it is relatively invisible.

11. Berger and Luckmann, *The Social Construction of Reality*, p. 75.

12. G. Kolko, *Railroads and Regulation 1877–1916* (New York: Norton, 1965); G. Stigler, *The Citizen and the State* (Chicago: University of Chicago Press, 1975).

13. U.S. Supreme Court, *Chicago Board of Trade v. United States* 246 U.S. Reports 231 (1918).

14. K. Polanyi, *The Great Transformation: The Political and Economic Origins of Our Time* (Boston: Beacon Press, 1944).

15. J. O'Connor, *The Fiscal Crisis of the State* (New York: St. Martin's Press, 1973); J. Habermas, *Legitimation Crisis* (Boston: Beacon Press, 1975); D. M. Gordon, R. Edwards, and M. Reich, *Segmented Work, Divided Workers* (Cambridge: Cambridge University Press, 1982).

16. An occasional trader is tempted to make the quick killing and retire, but most realize that there is far more money to be made from an extended career in the market than from a single killing.

17. Polanyi, *The Great Transformation*, p. 73.

18. "Economic liberalism made a supreme attempt to restore the self-regulation of the system by eliminating all interventionist policies which interfered with the freedom of markets for land, labor, and money . . . It became, in effect, the spearhead of a heroic attempt to restore world trade, remove all avoidable hindrances to the mobility of labor, and reconstruct stable exchanges." Ibid., p. 231.

19. At this writing the United States is still in a conservative political trend that has a relatively high tolerance for opportunism. A nearly continuous string of major trading losses began with Paul Mozer at Salomon (see the Introduction) and continued with Joseph Jett at Kidder Peabody, Victor Gomez at Chemical Bank, and the largest such loss in history, $1 billion, involving Nicholas Leeson at Barings. No one wants to be the one who kills the goose that lays golden eggs.

20. J. Seligman, *The Transformation of Wall Street: A History of the Securities and Exchange Commission and Modern Corporate Finance* (Boston: Houghton Mifflin, 1982), p. 335.

21. Ibid., pp. 487–489.

22. This argument is a direct response to the organizational economists who claim that organizational arrangements exist because they are the most efficient response to moral hazard, i.e. opportunism. This book has shown that organizational arrangements in markets emerge and change as a result of the self-interest of powerful actors and dominant coalitions. Conflicts among powerful coalitions are unpredictable and their outcomes even more so. Institutional arrangement, dependent on these outcomes, are social constructions susceptible to market politics.

23. This is because computer matching is only practical where there is a continuous stream of buyers and sellers. In markets with low liquidity, an intermediary, such as a dealer or other kind of market maker, is needed to maintain price continuity.

24. For studies of criminogenic factors in white- collar crime see H. A. Farberman, "A Criminogenic Market Structure: the Automobile Industry," *The Sociological Quarterly* 16 (Autumn 1975), pp. 438–457; N. K. Denzin, "Notes on the Criminogenic Hypothesis: A Case Study of the American Liquor Industry," *American Sociological Review* 42 (December 1977), pp. 905–920; N. Reichman, "Regulating Risky Business: Dilemmas in Security Regulation," *Law and Policy* 13 (October 1991), pp. 263–295.

25. P. Selznick, *The Moral Commonwealth: Social Theory and the Promise of Community* (Berkeley: University of California Press, 1992), p. 126.

26. This notion is an extension of Selznick's more general contention about delinquency in society. Ibid., p. 127.

27. See Burk for an informative discussion of how federal regulation shaped the moral order in the stock market. J. Burk, *Values in the Marketplace: The American Stock Market Under Federal Securities Laws* (Berlin: Walter de Gruyter, 1988).

28. This notion lies at the heart of communitarian thought. For an explication of these ideas, see A. Etzioni, *The Moral Dimension: Toward a New Economics* (New York: Free Press, 1994).

29. See M. Y. Abolafia, "Self-Regulation as Market Maintenance," in *Regulatory Policy and Social Sciences,* ed. R. Noll (Berkeley: University of California Press, 1985).

30. For a discussion of the limits of control by impersonal trust, see S. Shapiro, "The Social Control of Impersonal Trust," *American Journal of Sociology* 93 (November 1987), pp. 623–658.

31. M. Granovetter, "Economic Action and Social Structure: The Problem of Embeddedness," *American Journal of Sociology* 91 (November 1985), pp. 481–510.

32. In this study we saw the stable relationships among specialists and their customers as compared to the transitory relations in the bond market. For applications of the structural embeddedness approach, see the work of H. White, "Where Do Markets Come From?" *American Journal of Sociology* 87

211

(March 1981), pp. 517–547; R. Burt, *Corporate Profits and Cooptation* (New York: Academic Press, 1983); W. Baker, "The Social Structure of a National Securities Market," *American Journal of Sociology* 89 (January 1984), pp. 775–811.

33. In this study we focused on the different definitions of opportunism in three related markets. For discussions of cultural embeddedness, see Swidler, "Culture in Action"; and P. DiMaggio, "Cultural Aspects of Economic Action and Organization," in *Beyond the Marketplace*, eds. R. Friedland and A. F. Robertson (New York: Aldine de Gruyter, 1990).

INDEX
